YORK HAN

GENERAL EDITOR:
Professor A.N. Jeffares
(*University of Stirling*)

ENGLISH LITERATURE FROM THE THIRD WORLD

Trevor James

BA BD PH D (LONDON)
Senior Lecturer in English,
Darwin Institute of Technology

LONGMAN
YORK PRESS

Acknowledgements

Without the scholarship of many others this book would not have been possible. My thanks are due to many, but particularly to colleagues at the Centre for Research in the New English Literatures at Flinders University, Yasmine Gooneratne at Macquarie University, and to Edwin Thumboo and Kirpal Singh at the National University of Singapore.

YORK PRESS
Immeuble Esseily, Place Riad Solh, Beirut.

LONGMAN GROUP LIMITED
Longman House,
Burnt Mill,
Harlow,
Essex

©Librairie du Liban 1986

First published 1986

ISBN 0-582-79277-0

Produced by Longman Group (FE) Ltd
Printed in Hong Kong

Contents

Chapter 1

Introduction

Some definitions

'Third World' or 'Commonwealth'

It was only about the end of the Second World War that what is now commonly called 'Commonwealth' literature began to be recognised as not merely writing in English but as something separable from English literature, as had been the case with American literature. The term broadly covered the diverse phenomenon of Commonwealth writing in English and, while allowing for differences of individual talents and cultural and national contexts, acknowledged the common factors of colonial experience and the transplantation of English culture and traditions. Initially the most substantial examples were from those parts of the Commonwealth where a British society has been permanently established: in particular, Canada, Australia, New Zealand and South Africa. Any illusion of homogeneity vanished as the non-British nations of the Commonwealth in Asia, Africa, the Caribbean and the Pacific began from the nineteen-forties to assert a new sense of identity and increasingly to produce new national literatures in an English medium.

The term 'Third World' has been primarily coined by political and economic users. It denotes the developing non-aligned nations of the world: that is, those which belong to neither capitalist nor communist blocs. The non-European Commonwealth is included within this wide grouping, although much of the Third World does not use English and has never been part of the British colonial system. Common factors make this natural. First, whatever the colonial power, the colonial experience has shaped the consciousness of most Third World nations. Second, the common economic, social and political problems of the Third World form part of the context shared by writers in these nations. Within this are contained writers as diverse in experience, concern and style as, say, V.S. Naipaul (*b.* 1932)* or Wole Soyinka (*b.* 1934). The mixture of what is 'shared' points to the reality of this

---

* Personal dates of the authors under discussion are given on their first mention in this volume, and repeated if the author is discussed at some length later. It has, however, not been possible to obtain this information about every author mentioned.

grouping, just as the distinctions of the various national literatures and individual talents mark its limitations.

What is shared includes the experience of English traditions, culture and literature; historical parallels in the process of colonisation and decolonisation; and, often, the emergence of a local literature in English along with a new cultural awareness in which the writer may be torn between his creative aspirations and the needs of his society.

English: a shared language

As the Romans used Latin as the administrative language for their scattered and culturally diverse empire, so English provided a uniform medium for commerce, education and political power in the Commonwealth. It made two things possible: first, it gave access to the resources of westernisation, and, second, as a common language it helped to create a new national identity where previously differences had dominated. Although his remarks apply specifically to India, Nirad Chaudhuri's (b. 1897) comments are representative.

> In Delhi when an Indian from a particular region speaks to a fellow-Indian who does not know his language, he speaks in English. In the capital of India, as things stand, English is the only language for the pan-Indian mind. If modern Indians spoke their natural languages, all of which are highly developed, the regional groups would remain strangers to one another, not in language alone, but also in mind and outlook.*

In the new nations English, where adopted as a literary language, has also been transformed. In the process of literary appropriation at least two things have happened: first, the language has been adapted —as in 'pidgin' English in the Pacific; second, local languages, cultures and traditions have shaped its literary use. These have enriched and transformed it as writers have adopted myths, legends, folk-tales from local culture. Some examples of this are the works of Wilson Harris (b. 1921), R.K. Narayan (b. 1906) and Wole Soyinka. By reshaping English to reflect a specific cultural situation writers have been better able to communicate with their own society and still aim for an international readership. In *Morning Yet on Creation Day* the Nigerian writer Chinua Achebe (b. 1930) has expressed this linguistic challenge.

> [He] should aim to use English in a way which brings out his message without altering the language to the extent that its value will be lost.

* N. Chaudhuri, 'Asserting a Doxology', *Journal of Commonwealth Literature*, xiv: 2, August 1979, pp.134–5.

He should aim at fashioning out an English which is at once universal and able to carry his particular experience.*

From colonialism to nationalism: a shared experience

Strategic and economic purposes lie behind the colonial history of the Third World. In particular most of the empire in Africa, the Caribbean and Asia stemmed from two aspects of Britain's economy—the West and the East India trades. Through the introduction of missions, education, and forms of government, cultural elements were soon interwoven with the economic and political factors. The practical consequences were dramatic changes. As towns developed alongside a colonial administrative and economic order, so the indigenous social order changed as new 'classes' arose. Educated in the English language, these classes served the colonial regime. They acquired skills, entered professions and, later, assumed responsibilities. This new elite became the seed-bed for nationalism.

Institutions such as the Hindu College (1816) in India and the universities established after the Macaulay Minute (1835) in Bombay, Calcutta and Madras (1857) and Fourah Bay College in Sierra Leone (1876) fostered a new cultural and political awareness by providing a centre of learning from which future leaders were drawn. English was an important element in the process and although some of the educated westernised elite came from old ruling classes as in Uganda, Ceylon and northern Nigeria, many others represented a new urban society which enabled nationalism while at the same time sustaining a local colonial government. Likewise some slavishly imitated the language and customs of the colonial power while others, usually later, articulated their estrangement from British culture and the contemporary mix of old and new with its contradictions and tensions.

In the early stages of evolving a new identity, educated elites often formed associations or parties which consciously adopted elements from indigenous folk culture and thereby sought both to gain some popular acceptance and to give focus to their cultural and political aspirations. This is easily demonstrated in Asia, Africa and the Caribbean. For example the Indian National Congress was formed in 1885; the first Pan-African Congress met in Paris in 1919; while in the nineteen-twenties the Caribbean had such movements as the Trinidad Working Mens' Association and Marcus Garvey's (1887–1940) Universal Negro Improvement Association.

---

* Chinua Achebe, 'The African Writer and the English Language', *Morning Yet on Creation Day*, Heinemann Educational, London, 1975, p.61.

The shape of nationalism

While literature is not politics, sociology, or indeed anything other than itself, it is useful to have some understanding of the pattern of events that have led the Third World from colonialism to a new self-realisation. First there was the initial fracture of relationships and cultural identity under the impact of western influences. Second, following from this, was the growth of an educated, urbanised elite that inhabited a cultural and psychic void between the indigenous traditions and western culture. Third, to compress a complicated process, cultural and political associations formed a critical part of what was a complex task of mediation between old and new that at its end enabled nationalism to evolve. Behind this was an international spectrum of change, example and encouragement: the rise of Japan; the Pan-Islamic movement; the Harlem Renaissance and Negro Civil Rights movements; the Chinese nationalist movement. Fourth, the effects of the Second World War both weakened the basis of colonialism and gave servicemen and leaders from Asia, Africa and the Caribbean expectations of change. Hence the rapid spread of independence movements and assertive nationalisms that have led to the 'Third World' as a potent factor in contemporary affairs.

The writer and society

A general consequence of colonialism was the implication that European cultural standards were definitive. So, for example, while the imaginative content of colonial literature in New Zealand, Australia and South Africa suffered to begin with, because many writers tended to look over their shoulders at a London market and failed to affirm their own position and identity, for writers without racial and cultural ties with Europe, colonialism meant racial and cultural inferiority.

As a consequence of this, despite many examples of subservience to European culture, the primary tasks of writers in the Third World have involved the retrieval of cultural dignity and an imaginative mediation between old and new to reconstruct and affirm cultural values. A writer such as Kofi Awoonor (*b*. 1935) of Ghana sees this prophetic function clearly.

> An African writer must be a person who has some kind of perception of the society in which he is living and the way he wants the society to go.*

* Quoted in *The Writer in Modern Africa*, ed. Per Wästberg, Africana Publishing Corporation, New York, 1969, p. 31.

The writer as teacher

In 'The Novelist as Teacher' Chinua Achebe has offered an almost classic definition of the writer's responsibility in a new nation. Achebe emphasises social commitment. In his words: 'the writer cannot expect to be excused from the task of re-education and regeneration that must be done. In fact he should march right in front.' Achebe recognises that this process commits the writer to identifying and celebrating those particular activities of daily life which will enable his society both to recognise and be proud of itself.

I think it is part of my business as a writer to teach . . . that there is nothing disgraceful about the African weather, that the palm tree is a fit subject for poetry. Here then is an adequate revolution for me to espouse—to help my society regain belief in itself and put away the consequences of the years of denigration and self-abasement.*

Publishing

The options confronting a writer, whether to accept cultural exile from his society, be a propagandist for it or be a mediator, have been tied to the practical questions of publishing. Though less serious now, the difficulties that faced the first writers were immense. Of necessity their writing presupposed not traditional society but an English-speaking and -reading audience. To this extent they were bound to write for the dominant culture and be estranged from their own past. For example, Jomo Kenyatta's (c. 1900–78) *Facing Mount Kenya* (1961) was an explanation of Kikuyu customs that a European readership—rather than an African one—could appreciate.

Of course, writers have always had to identify a market. Market considerations determine the product: for example, the Onitsha literature of Nigeria, which Achebe identifies in Nigerian pidgin as 'how-for-do' writing, with its handbooks for those who are anxious to succeed in an urban environment. Such commercial restraints are one of the major reasons for the importance of the short story in the development of the new literatures. Here magazines and newspapers have been crucial. One of the great experiments in African literature was the magazine *Drum* where many able black South African writers first managed to have their work published on a commercial basis. In the same way individual poems could be published, but extended forms such as novels and collections of poetry only became common when a local readership developed.

* In *Morning Yet on Creation Day*, p.44.

Autobiography: an important phenomenon

The parallel between the writer and his society can be demonstrated by the popularity of autobiographies. As a writer established his own bearings and identity he represented the dilemma of his society. For example, one of the newest literatures, Oceania, has produced *Kiki: Ten Thousand Years In A Lifetime* (1968) which is the autobiography of Albert Maori Kiki who formed the first trade union in Papua–New Guinea. Compiled with the help of Ulli Beier, this articulates a process of rapid transition and adjustment. Examples from Africa include Soyinka's *Aké* (1981) and Ezekiel Mphahlele's (*b.* 1919) *Down Second Avenue* (1959). The latter, reprinted several times, details his early life in the slums of Pretoria's Second Avenue district and his response to racism and poverty as well as affectionate memories of the people he knew. The recurring autobiographical elements in Mphahlele's work— he does the same thing more obliquely in *The Wanderers* (1971)— demonstrate how quickly autobiography can metamorphose into fiction. In this later work he deals with the theme of exile and, while places and personal names are changed, the points of similarity with his life are obvious. Another variant of this is Achebe's first book *Things Fall Apart* (1958) of which he has remarked: 'although I did not set about it consciously in that solemn way, I now know that my first book, *Things Fall Apart* was an act of atonement with my past, a ritual return and homage of a prodigal son.' *

The evolution of a literature: some common elements

The shared experience of the new literatures extends to the general phases of literary development. Usually the first colonial writing was imitative of English literary models. In the nineteenth century William Wordsworth (1770–1850) and Robert Browning (1812–89) were assiduously copied. Soon these models were adapted to local conditions, while in newspapers and journals short stories began to express a new consciousness. One example in the late nineteenth century of the exchange between English literary models and local culture is the young Indian woman Toru Dutt (1856–77), who rendered traditional Indian ballads and legends into English verse. Later Gandhi (1869–1948) and Nehru (1889–1964) used English-medium journalism in their writing and pamphleteering while, in the thirties, Anand (*b.* 1935), Rao (*b.* 1909) and Narayan appropriated the novel for Indo-Anglian writing. In short, there is a common movement from imitation through to affirmation of identity which holds true, with minor variations, for

* In 'Named for Victoria, Queen of England', *Morning Yet on Creation Day*, p.70.

all the new English literatures. What may have taken English literature four hundred years, these accomplished in a few generations and in a cultural situation of enormous complexity.

For the new literatures cultural assurance has come very quickly. With independence achieved, writers have quickly turned to appraise their own traditions and the new social and political order with a critical eye. Achebe is a good example of this. *A Man of the People* is, on one level, a commentary on the limitations of both traditional African communal values and local nationalism. In an essay he remarked with typical candour:

> I had hardly begun to bask in the sunshine of reconciliation when a new cloud appeared, a new estrangement. Political independence had come. The nationalist leader of yesterday (with whom it had not been too difficult to make common cause) had become the not too attractive party boss.*

Again for Achebe the Biafran war was a critical post-colonial experience before which his own mythology of a tight village community and a secure ethnic identity began to disintegrate.

There are numerous examples of writers who have attempted to direct their society. For example the Sri Lankan writer Punyakante Wijenaike in *Giraya* (1971) criticises the elite upper classes of modern Sri Lankan society. Through appropriate literary devices she offers a muted but effective criticism of a misguided social order: a society closed in upon itself where even 'the family crest stamped on the face of the porch is covered with a fungus'.

Themes and concerns

Each literature adapts English to suit its cultural situation. Between language and context there is constant movement which shapes national and regional literatures in English. Whether a trick of speech, a mood, or a specific cultural reference, these are touchstones that test the writer's self and society. However, there are also general concerns and themes which are shared between the new literatures and which spring, however affected by local conditions, from the shared experience. These include: exile; the retrieval of history, whether personal or national; the quest for identity; the negative legacy of colonialism—particularly racism; the encounters between the old and the new; and, more generally, a range of concerns shaped by cultural complexity and political ideology.

---

* Chinua Achebe, 'Named for Victoria, Queen of England', *Morning Yet on Creation Day*, p.70.

Exile

The image of the writer as a cultural exile, a genius starving in a garret neglected by his society, is modern and, more particularly, western. In traditional societies the bond between writer and community is close and most art is conservative, expressive of a stable social order. The innovative artist can only express individual awareness in a conservative community at the risk of being an outcast, or, if not an outcast, he may feel that he has no-one to write for and that to find a readership he must go elsewhere—as, for example, is the case with the Caribbean writers of the nineteen fifties. The nuances of exile are almost endless. In Mongo Beti's (*b.* 1932) *Mission to Kala* (1957 (French); 1964 (English translation)) Jean-Marie is, by his education, estranged from traditional tribal life. On another level Achebe's self-conscious attempts to recover and celebrate the past mark a personal sense of estrangement which is, perhaps, a motivating force behind the numerous autobiographies of the new literatures. The return to a remembered childhood in which self was secure recurs in many ways: for example, Jean Rhys (1894–1979) wrote in Paris of her Caribbean homeland just as in England and America African writers have retrieved their own childhoods. In this recognition of exile and the return, if only in imagination, to the homeland, there is also a new beginning. Ngugi Wa Thiong'o (*b.* 1938) has recognised in George Lamming's (*b.* 1927) *In the Castle of My Skin* (1953) the sense of discovery latent in the recognition of exile.

> The novel ends with a double exile: of the villagers from their plots, their home, their 'customary' land, their old relationships, and of G. from the village, going to Trinidad. But . . . we are given hints that the moment of exile in urban industry in Trinidad, America, Britain, is also a moment of discovery of one's perspective in history and of identity of interests with one's people (or class).*

History

Achebe's *Things Fall Apart* with its retrieval of a forgotten tradition demonstrates an individual need for a history, while Narayan's novels set in the imaginary community of Malgudi evoke the tide of history and tradition. However emphasis is placed, the need for a history issues from the cultural and psychic displacement wrought by colonialism. Consequently two African writers, Ouologuem (*b.* 1940) in *Bound to Violence* and Ayi Kwei Armah (*b.* 1939) in *Two Thousand Seasons*,

---

* Ngugi Wa Thiong'o, 'George Lamming's *In the Castle of My Skin*', *Homecoming*, Heinemann Educational, London, 1972, p.126.

have attempted to provide an historical overview from a black African perspective. Ouologuem's work has been especially contentious: his critique of African history has been seen by many as a betrayal of negritude and black experience. Armah's work has been more idealistic: while in style it echoes African oral narrative, it projects a mythical past in which black experience is called 'the way' or 'our way'. Through this poetic and polemical assertion of a past, it secures black experience, values, culture, and, above all, dignity. In the rapid transition and uncertainty of the contemporary African situation this literary reassurance expresses the writer's social commitment. In English literature W.B. Yeats (1865–1939) did the same for Ireland.

Identity

Identity as a problem is implicit in the themes of history and the sense of exile, while the attempts to secure identity are many and various. In Africa and the Caribbean the doctrines of negritude or creolisation are one form: both affirm identity in ethnic terms. Both are strategically contentious. For example, some of the most pointed attacks on negritude have been made by Ezekiel Mphahlele:

> Let negritude make the theme of literature if people want to use it. But we must remember that literature springs from an individual's experience, and in his effort to take in the whole man, it also tries to see far ahead, to project a prophetic vision, such as the writer is capable of, based on contemporary experience . . .
> Literature and art are too big for negritude, and it had better be left as an historical phase.*

Mphahlele sees identity as a phase, a concern which belongs to the early development of a new literature. In the Caribbean, India and Africa the issue is almost finished, whereas in Papua–New Guinea and parts of the Pacific, where the colonial experience is still recent, individual and national identities are still being asserted. Kasaipwalova's *Reluctant Flame* was an early poetic expression of the attempt to establish a national identity in Papua which could be related to an international black identity. The problem was to secure an identity through images that had not been turned into stereotypes by the colonial mentality. In short, he had to define the culture through something other than betelstained teeth, traditional dances and art; which is why he uses the less accessible images of an internal river and an internal flame. The problem had been appreciated by Mphahlele.

* Ezekiel Mphahlele, 'Remarks on Negritude', *African Writing Today*, ed. Mphahlele, Penguin Books, Harmondsworth, 1967, pp.252–3.

Notice also that while negritude poetry evokes images of ritual, animals letting out blood for the sacrifice, naked feet and breasts, these are only outward trappings: the poet still does not, perhaps cannot as an uprooted person, penetrate the essence of tradition.*

The negative legacy of colonialism

Implicit in all these themes is an appraisal of the colonial experience itself. Many writers deal with colonialism quite directly. From Papua–New Guinea John Waiko's play *The Unexpected Hawk* † shows how colonialism has implied inferiority and been destructive. In this play the supposedly benevolent government burns a village in order to compel its people to move to an approved government centre. Waiko's technique is to interpret events from a standpoint which contradicts the official protestations of the colonial administrator. A further extraordinary, and fairly recent, example of this is V.S. Reid's (*b.* 1913) book *The Leopard* (1958) which interprets the Mau Mau revolution in Kenya from a viewpoint where the European is presented as a monster who must be destroyed.

Conflict between old and new

At another level writers can document the mutual mystification that confounds the relationship between the two cultures and, sometimes, mediate between them. At the most elementary level this is possible because the writer is, presumably, educated in the west while his ethnic and family ties belong to the local culture. Standing between the two worlds, for example, Waiko's play mentioned above, expresses the confusion of the local people and the incomprehension of the European officials. For the local community a matriarchal figure says:

> All the spirits know me—what harm can they do to me? But if you speak to them, tell them that we cannot understand what has happened today. That we cannot understand the thinking of these white men. We see their actions but they make no sense.**

By contrast the European official is shown as one who perhaps could never really understand. He exclaims: 'They don't want to be civilized. My God! And they *are* a primitive lot up here.' Again, there are many variations on this theme but they generally tend to reflect the pain of transition experienced by a traditional society in the throes of

* Ibid., p.251.
† Included in *Five New Guinea Plays*, ed. Ulli Beier, Jacaranda Press, Brisbane, 1971, pp.20–32.
** Ibid., p.30.

modernisation. Education is one aspect of this, as in Okot p'Bitek's (1931–82) long poem *Song of Lawino*. Lawino is a peasant woman deserted by her husband Ocol, who leaves her for the town and a mistress. The mistress, Clementine, is the perfect symbol of the new world: she distorts her figure, pads her breasts, reddens her lips, and even bleaches her skin. Against this parody of sophistication Lawino mourns the loss of authenticity:

> ...Only recently
> We would sit close together touching each other!
> Only recently I would play
> On my bow-harp
> Singing praises to my beloved.

Cultural and political aspects

Cultural complexity is an obvious theme of the new literatures. In part this reflects the way colonialism established arbitrary boundaries so that future nationhood had to be created rather than built upon an innate homogeneity. Ngugi Wa Thiong'o has remarked of Kenya: 'In Kenya then, there is really no concept of a nation. One is always a Kikuyu, a Luo, a Nandi, an Asian or a European. I think this diminishes our strength and creative power.'* The problem is particularly obvious where groups with a strong cultural identity such as Indian and Chinese stand out in, for example, a dominantly black or Polynesian environment. The problems of marriages across the cultural lines are one literary example of this subject while what has been called an 'indenture consciousness' has marked the development of fiction and poetry from Oceania's Indo-Fijian community. There, as in the Caribbean, the creation of plantations and the introduction of external labour created political instability and racial distrust. A sense of betrayal and loss echoes in the work of the Indo-Fijian poet Satendra Nandan:

> oh my father's fathers
> what forgiveness is there in me?
> oh my children's children
> listen to the voice of the *Syria*
> drowning the silence of the sea.†

For a society in the throes of change politics are of the essence and often the writer is a politician *manqué*. The forces that align a writer with the cause of nationalism can change, and new events make him

* 'Kenya: the Two Rifts', *Homecoming*, p.23.
† 'The Ghost', *Faces in a Village*, Deepak Seth, New Delhi, 1970, p. 22.

critical of the new order. For example, Achebe in his *A Man of the People* (1966) castigates post-independence Nigeria; another Nigerian writer, Wole Soyinka, in *Season of Anomy* (1973) shows the destruction of an idyllic village community to voice his horror for the consequences of the Nigerian civil war. The Indian writer Mulk Raj Anand (*b.* 1935) in *Untouchable* (1935), *Coolie* (1936) and *The Village* (1939) demonstrates a political alignment with profound social commitment. He is not prepared merely to summarise the failings of a colonial power but reveals the shortcomings of his own society, its entrenched privilege and servitude. So in *Coolie* Munoo suffers not just from the British but from his fellow Indians, rich and poor. In such works we can see writers in the new literatures accepting the role of social reformers through works which have a political cutting edge.

Chapter 2

The Caribbean

—I have no pride—no pride, no name, no face, no country. I don't belong anywhere.

This statement by the narrator in Jean Rhys's novel *Good Morning, Midnight* (1939) summarises the concerns that pervade West Indian writing. In turn this new literature, and the culture which has nurtured it, has been moulded by the forces of the physical environment and local history. In the Caribbean the overwhelming physical reality is that of small island nations often separated by considerable distances. Diminutive size, isolation, and a dense population have tended to produce an environment so compact that social or racial pressures are quickly and keenly felt. Attempts at a regional identity have therefore foundered upon local self-interest while within each island it has been easy for a closely knit and traditional communal life to discourage those imaginative individuals who wish to try to do something different. This is one reason why so many West Indian writers have chosen to live abroad.

In short, the physical environment of the West Indies has had political, economic and artistic consequences. This almost claustrophobic quality of life has found literary expression in the work of writers such as Roger Mais (1905–55), in, for example *The Hills Were Joyful Together* (1953), who have focused upon the urban barrack-yards where most of the poor have to live.

Historical factors and literary consequences

History has compounded the limitations imposed by the physical environment. First, there is the sense of an historical void: these islands lack indigenous, pre-European history. The known history is that of the colonisers, and colonisation and slavery are the two most influential historical factors in the literature. As colonisation created a transposed British culture in imitation of home, slavery expressed the economic aspect of colonialism. Slaves were the work force for the plantations that helped to sustain the British economy: they came from different parts of West Africa, often did not share a common language, and were regarded as chattels to be bought, sold, and mortgaged at will. When slavery was broken by the Emancipation Act (1833), labour was imported by indenture from the East Indies to compound the problems of the future.

The literary consequence of a transplanted culture was a body of secular writing, sentimental in style and diction and blatantly imitative of English literary modes. Of the plantations and slavery the imaginative consequences were more profound. This mix of European, Asian and African peoples in an environment where none had deep roots is the reason for the uncertainty of cultural identity that has been a dominant concern in West Indian writing. The descendants of planter, slave and labourer all inherited a history of exile and a sense of estrangement. When the population pressures forced many West Indians to seek employment in Canada and England during the nineteen-fifties and sixties, this created another exile and further questionings about identity, a theme which dominates Edward Braithwaite's (*b.* 1930) *Rites of Passage* (1967).

Moves toward identity

The most obvious attempt to overcome insularity and lack of a strong national identity was the British idea of a West Indies Federation. Although this appealed to the intellectual elite, the Federation lacked popular support and only lasted from 1958 to 1962. The idea of a regional identity appealed to some writers and one influential journal gave considerable support to the idea—this was the Guyanese journal *Kyk-Over-Al* (1945–61) edited by A.J. Seymour. Failure of this ambitious plan demonstrates that in a region of fragile identity local cultures are inevitably defensive, even introverted and suspicious of grand plans.

Political and cultural elements were involved in more successful attempts to find local nationhood and identity. For the first, the period when nationalism began to make the most progress was between the First and Second World War, particularly during the grim nineteen-thirties. Local associations were formed to advance indigenous political parties. These included, for example, the Representative Government Association formed by T.A. Marryshaw in Grenada in 1914; the Trinidad Working Men's Association led by Arthur Cipriani, and, of course, the attempt by Marcus Garvey to form a negro nationalist movement in Jamaica. For the second, largely as a result of contributions from West Indian intellectuals living abroad, local culture received an influx of ideas that encouraged further experimentation. In Jamaica as early as 1921, under the impetus given by Edna Manley, painting and sculpture turned with increasing confidence to the local scene, and it is from this period that the evolution of a modern West Indian literature in English took its course.

Black culture has provided another reference point for a national identity. Religious cults, music and language—the slaves evolved the creoles from their original languages and the language of the colonial powers—are reflections of an original African origin now incorporated into the rhythms of Caribbean life. Writers such as Claude McKay (1889–1948) and many other black West Indians contributed to the Harlem renaissance. Marcus Garvey gave political, religious and cultural identity to black culture through the Rastafarian sect which sees Africa as home and Jamaica and the west as types of a Babylonian exile. The evolution of the Rastafarians from about 1936 has been a story of continuous growth and their speech rhythms and mythology are a continuing and influential part of the Caribbean search for identity which has included the Black Power movement from the United States.

This search for cultural identity in racial terms is reflected in the literature. Edward Braithwaite has been the most influential exponent of 'creolisation'—for example, in his *Contradictory Omens* (1974). Against this the fear of the Indian community, who from the nineteen-forties had felt that nationalisation in racial terms meant a loss of individual ethnic identity, found expression in the views of V.S. Naipaul (*b.* 1932). With a background in the Trinidadian–East Indian community, and familiar with the racial stereotyping that has kept East Indians at the bottom of the social ladder and deprived of power in Trinidad and Guyana although the largest racial group, Naipaul registers the inadequacy of identity conceived in racial terms.

The development of West Indian writing: an outline

West Indian writing encompasses a number of small regional literatures that have many common features and interests. Small presses, periodicals and reviews have from the first helped writers to get into print; provided the opportunity for public debate; and, perhaps most important, helped to create a sense of cultural and even national identity. Through these journals writers helped to form the identity of the Caribbean. Every region tended to have its own journals, but the most influential were *The Beacon* in Trinidad, *Bim* in Barbados, *Kyk-Over-Al* in British Guyana and, in Jamaica, *Focus*. Although these journals had limited circulation, they helped to create a climate of opinion and literary awareness that was pervasive, while cultural awareness and regional consciousness were enhanced by the BBC's programme *Caribbean Voices* (1945–58).

The development of the literature can be briefly summarised. The colonial period was primarily imitative: while there are works from the eighteenth and nineteenth centuries for example, Francis Williams, the black Jamaican poet of the eighteenth century, English prosody and literary models were the norm. In the early twentieth century Claude McKay and H.G. de Lisser (1877–1944) voiced a new awareness of things Caribbean and initiated an appropriate literary diction and style. De Lisser's two most influential novels, *Jane's Career* (1914) and *Susan Proudleigh* (1915), use dialect, local experience, and present a sympathetic view of black and lower-class life. They pulse with the feel of the Caribbean and anticipate later themes of its literature, *Jane's Career* that of emigration, and *Susan Proudleigh* that of black consciousness. McKay is better known as a black American writer than as a Caribbean one, largely because of his novels *Home to Harlem* (1928) and *Banjo* (1929); but before he left Jamaica in frustration to become the first self-exiled West Indian writer he had written poems in which subject and dialect were clearly Jamaican. His short stories in *Gingertown* (1932) show the influence of the contemporary Pan-African consciousness, as does *Banjo* (1929) with its setting among the black communities of Marseilles. Of the novels only *Banana Bottom* (1933) has a Jamaican setting, while through Bita Plant, the pivotal character, McKay rejects western values and rediscovers those of black Jamaica.

Behind the social concerns following the depression in the nineteen-thirties and forties, the Russian revolution and the First World War were potent symbols of a new order. Middle-class writers divorced themselves from their own social position and identified with the poor, the people, and the 'barrack-yard' folk culture. The short story was the dominant genre, and experiments with local dialect and speech patterns increased. Writers such as Alfred Mendes (*b*. 1897) and C.L.R. James (*b*. 1901) established a tradition for later writing: they were the most adventurous, aimed at realism and used dialect. Poetry was less popular. It was harder to find a readership. However, in the forties Martin Carter (*b*. 1927) of Guyana provided innovative poetry which experimented with local speech rhythms, as in his 'Death of a Slave'.

The nineteen-fifties established a West Indian literature. In all the arts there was a demonstrable awareness of a West Indian identity founded upon the discoveries of the earlier writers and artists. At this time George Lamming made a breakthrough with his novel *In the Castle of My Skin* (1953) while other writers whose work flowered during these years include Edgar Mittelholzer (1910–65), Roger Mais, Andrew Salkey, V.S. Reid, V.S. Naipaul and Samuel Selvon (*b*. 1923). The human landscape was more thoroughly explored: in his novel *A Brighter Sun* (1952) Selvon looked at Trinidad's Indian community while Roger Mais in *The Hills were Joyful Together* used an urban setting and concentrated upon the Kingston yards, their stagnation and frustration.

Since the nineteen-fifties the dominant genre has remained fiction with poetry in second place and drama still lagging. The major recent fiction has been produced by Wilson Harris, and more recently by Michael Anthony (*b.* 1932) of Trinidad, Austin Clarke (*b.* 1932) of Barbados and Garth St Omer (*b.* 1931) of St Lucia. Of these Harris has the most firmly established reputation. Michael Anthony is precise and restricted in his work: he explores childhood experience, especially in *The Year in San Fernando* (1965) and *Green Days by the River* (1967). Austin Clarke in his Toronto triology (*The Meeting Point*, *Storm of Fortune*, *The Bigger Light*) explores the experience of the West Indian in exile and must be compared with Selvon and other Caribbean writers who have recorded the West Indian diaspora. He provides an able presentation of the black man in a white world. Garth St Omer is particularly concerned with the experience of alienation at home and his work is a demonstration of the way West Indian writing has moved beyond concern with colonialism and to an examination of the limitations of the present situation. This is demonstrated again in poets such as Derek Walcott (*b.* 1930) and Edward Braithwaite: Walcott has also made valuable contributions to drama with four plays in *Dream on Monkey Mountain and Other Plays* (1970), while Braithwaite has brought poetry into the centre of the debate by using it to express West Indian black experience. Braithwaite is a controversial poet and in the work of other poets such as Anthony McNeil, Mervin Morris and Denis Scott there is distrust of rhetoric about 'consciousness' and greater concern with alienation as a universal human condition.

Jean Rhys

A. Alvarez wrote of Jean Rhys in 1974, 'to my mind she is, quite simply, the best living English novelist'. Jean Rhys's writing career extended over a long period. She was born in Dominica of a Creole mother and an English father, but left for England in 1910 when she was sixteen. Born Gwen Williams, she changed her name to Rhys after her father's death later that year, when she had to earn her living as a chorus girl. After the First World War she moved to Paris and with the help of Ford Maddox Ford (1873–1939) had her first collection of short stories, *The Left Bank*, published in 1927. By 1939 she had written five novels. Little more was heard of Rhys until 1966 when *Wide Sargasso Sea* was published and her place in West Indian writing more fully appreciated.

Jean Rhys's experience of life made her vulnerable. The urban settings of her books often describe the seedy hotel rooms and characters of London or Paris. Her heroines are invariably sensitive, threatened by life. This gives her work its continuity: each story traces nuances of feminine suffering, exploitation and bondage. In short this crisis of identity links her European writings with the Caribbean setting of *Wide Sargasso Sea*.

The place of *Wide Sargasso Sea* in Caribbean writing is much debated. It is a work of imagination and memory, for Jean Rhys writes as a cultural outsider and exile. Emotionally drawn away from Dominica in her adolescence, in her old age she returns with a sense of curiosity, nostalgia and the need to devise a myth to comprehend her experience of estrangement. In this she makes a recognised contribution to the literature of the white West Indian creole society.

> It was a song about a white cockroach. That's me. That's what they call all of us who were here before their own people in Africa sold them to the slave traders. And I've heard English women call us white niggers. So between you I often wonder who I am and where is my country and where do I belong and why was I ever born at all.

The heroine, Antoinette, expresses the experience of the white creole who is denied a place in the old plantation world as well as in the new Caribbean society. This is a double exile. For this reason *Wide Sargasso Sea* has to be set alongside such books as Phyllis Shand Allfrey's *The Orchid House* (1955) and Geoffrey Drayton's *Christopher* (1959). More formally, in *The Wretched of the Earth* (French version 1961; English translation 1965) Frantz Fanon has analysed the problem of such minorities at the end of the colonial period who find themselves without status, power or sympathy in a new society. Rhys explores this concern with a sense of vital engagement.

Like Jean Rhys herself, Antoinette is rejected by the old plantation society of the nineteenth century. The novel traces events from the emancipation of slavery in 1838 with society in a state of transformation, estates decayed and a new social order evolved. Neither at home in black society nor accepted by polite white society, Antoinette turns to the England she has read about. Yet for her England is a place of dreams, not reality: there she retreats into her own imaginary world. Her suicide marks her inability to accept her experiences and her nostalgia for an irrecoverable past. At this level the story demonstrates the estrangement of the white creole. At another level the story states the problem of the exploited woman: Antoinette is also a victim of Rochester who progressively undermines her identity and so deepens and enforces her cultural alienation. In this way *Wide Sargasso Sea* brings together the themes that mark Jean Rhys's contribution to West Indian literature.

The Beacon Group

The Beacon was the most ambitious literary journal in the Caribbean. Published monthly in Trinidad (March 1931–November 1933) by Alfred M. Gomez, it covered both creative writing and regional and international politics. All influenced by the Russian revolution and the Indian nationalist movement, its contributors attempted to align their writing with a new political order. From this new 'realism', its sense of social responsibility and commitment, the short story emerged. The editors were concerned that creative writing should not imitate the west but accurately reflect the West Indian condition: the speech patterns, characters, conflicts and situations. This was theory with a purpose. The writers associated with the journal—Alfred Mendes (*b.* 1897), (*Pitch Lake*, 1934 and *Black Fauns*, 1935), C.L.R. James (*b.* 1901), (*Minty Alley*, 1936)—depicted in their novels the back yards of Trinidad's lower classes. They marked a rather self-conscious new beginning. Their choice of subject matter and, above all, their attempt to capture the dialect of the Caribbean, rejected the stigma attached to local speech and recognised that the experience of West Indian life required this sort of language. From these departures the tradition of West Indian literature was to grow.

Edgar Mittelholzer, V.S. Reid, Roger Mais

Edgar Mittelholzer (1910–65) was the first of the writers of the nineteen-fifties to establish the reputation of West Indian writing and to dedicate himself to a literary career. It was his second novel, *A Morning at the Office* (1950), which stimulated critical interest in the region and led the way for the writers who followed. Mittelholzer's writing reflects his unhappy personal life marked by hypochondria, guilt, and attempted suicide; and the characters of his novels reflect the divided consciousness imposed by his mixed racial origins. If his personal obsessions undermined his art, nonetheless he delineated the hierarchic structure of West Indian colonial society. His appalling suicide by fire symbolises the schizophrenia in Caribbean literature which Derek Walcott has identified as that 'contradiction of being white in mind and black in body'.

The Jamaican V.S. Reid (*b.* 1913) is an early exponent of local culture and the anti-colonialism of the nineteen-fifties. For example, in his researches into Jamaican history for *New Day* (1949), and during his investigation of the rebellion of 1865, he discovered a tradition of active resistance to colonial oppression. Yet he calls England a 'mother bird', an ambivalence which demonstrates the fragility of identity and the residue of thinking moulded by the colonial experience. His second novel, *The Leopard* (1958), goes beyond colonial Jamaica and, with little concern for historical accuracy, and depicting characters that are almost stereotypes, he turns to the multi-racial inheritance in Africa through the stories of three major characters in Kenya during the Mau Mau rebellion. The Gibsons represent the decadent white colonialism, Nebu an African freedom fighter, and Toto a mulatto who is the physically and spiritually crippled victim of his inheritance. Despite obvious deficiencies the book marks a new exploration of the association between Africa and the Caribbean, while at the same time it clarifies the common experience of colonialism and the crises of a multi-cultural society.

Roger Mais (1905–55) shared Reid's concern, but with an emphasis that reflected his experiences as detainee during the disturbances of 1937. Although Mais's concerns are many, he attempts to give social and political thrust to his writing while still exploring the emotional and intellectual qualities of his characters. The individual, however, is invariably subordinated to the group: in short, the group is the 'hero'. *The Hills Were Joyful Together* (1953) uses the framework of the Kingston yards for a symbol through which to interpret the experience of the poor, the dispossessed and the estranged. Here yards, and prison, stand for a stagnant social condition in which the whole community suffers without hope of change. Despite this constraint his characters enjoy a degree of freedom: adolescents seek meaning and move toward maturity; Ras pursues tranquillity, while Shag and Euphemia are thwarted by their own personalities.

Though shorter and presented in a more compact form, *Brother Man* (1954) uses the same realism and individuals are again subordinate to the group. The urban setting of the yards is still the framework through which Mais explores the forces that direct the lives of the poor. Again, character and setting, structure and action, speech and symbolism combine to point the direction of the reader's thoughts and to provide depth and substance. Here, however, the emphasis has shifted slightly from the group to the tension between the group and the gifted individual. Ras, a slight figure in *The Hills*, has now developed into a major force in the yards. Rastafarianism emerges here for the first time as a significant element in Caribbean writing: with obvious parallels between Power and Christ, the Rastafarian John Power survives the mob that adulates and yet tries to destroy him.

Mais's third novel *Black Lightning* (1955) uses a different setting, a small Jamaican village where there is more freedom of choice and an idyllic pace of life, to facilitate concentration upon a gifted individual and his relationship with the community. In Jake, the village blacksmith and sculptor, he shows a flawed consciousness which destroys the character when he attempts to be wholly independent in his life and his art. Again another crude parallel is drawn, this time with the biblical story of Samson—of whom Jake is making a sculpture— when Jake's own wife deserts him. The point of the story gains force with the realisation that the painful individual awareness of Jake was Mais's own as well. Where many other writers evaded imaginative constraints by voluntary exile, Mais remained. *Black Lightning* is a seminal exploration of the dilemma of West Indian artists and their relationship to the rather conservative and constrictive community from which most of them have come.

Samuel Selvon

Born in 1923, Selvon, while the least political of the literary exiles of the nineteen-fifties, demonstrates a consistent interest in recording social change. *A Brighter Sun* (1952) established his reputation as a writer and confirmed him in his decision to be one. Of Indian descent and domiciled in London since 1950, his novels explore West Indian themes whether in the Caribbean or in London.

Set in Trinidad, *A Brighter Sun* traces the fortunes of a young Indian family moving from the rural plantation to town. Racial tensions between Indian, creole and white communities are set against a wider background of international affairs—particularly the Second World War. With apparent ease the book succeeds in overcoming the problem that faced many West Indian writers—how to capture a local and an international readership. First, on the most obvious level, Selvon uses language which is accessible both to outsiders and to West Indians. The narrator who holds the threads of the work together uses standard English while the characters speak in the Trinidadian dialect. So, at the formal linguistic level, two worlds are held together. In its themes the book is similarly integrative. The transition between the rural population and the urban, the tension between creole and Indian, both are maintained and explored throughout the work and are shown to be parts of a larger whole. Incidents, objects and settings have a symbolic significance in achieving this synthesis, but it is the Indian man, Tiger, himself, whose maturing vision we are made to follow, who points the way toward an integrated self. While the implications of social change are traced, the way forward is shown without political polemic, and the theme enriched by knowledge of the ironies and contradictions.

An Island Is a World (1955) is more hurried, more consciously political, and contemporary plans for a West Indies Federation indicate its topical relevance. *The Lonely Londoners* (1956) explores the plight of the West Indian diaspora: their retention of the Caribbean culture and their experience of bewilderment, homelessness, and the search for jobs in a culture which did not really want them. Here the linguistic tension is between standard English and a modified West Indian dialect while the mellow, slightly satirical tone, produces the mood of the blues.

The shift between London and Trinidad is remarkable. *Turn Again Tiger* (1958) returns to Trinidad and Tiger and Urmilla, the family of *A Brighter Sun*. In this story Tiger returns to his family roots in the cane fields and Selvon explores the psychological deprivation wrought by colonialism. The over-dramatised theme of inter-racial sexual relationships recurs in his later works where, for example in *Moses Ascending* (1975), Selvon continues both to explore the experience of being black in London and to experiment with dialogue and dialect. With a vivid sense for what is contemporary—such as Black Panther militants and illegal Indian immigrants—Selvon uses the folk tradition of the Caribbean, the humorous iconoclastic techniques of the calypso, in order to declare his independence from the mainstream of English literature.

George Lamming

Born in Barbados in 1927, George Lamming is one of the writers of the nineteen-fifties whose creative period coincided with the flood of West Indian immigrants into Britain and stimulated an interest in Caribbean writing. Lamming, Mittelholzer and Selvon all had novels published within three years of their arrival in London. Lamming's *In the Castle of My Skin* (1953), his most autobiographical work, is probably the most widely read West Indian novel. In this first novel Lamming begins the process whereby exploration of a personal history and experience represents West Indian life in general. This approach holds true for the first four novels in which he traces the development of Caribbean society from the disintegration of an imitative colonial order, through the diaspora of the nineteen-fifties to the present time with the still incomplete quest for a viable community.

As for many of the literary emigrants, for Lamming self-imposed exile brought a rediscovery of roots. In England he defined himself as an artist and a West Indian. *In the Castle of My Skin* with its celebration of a West Indian childhood and a close-knit village community undergoing radical economic and social change, he provides the symbol of a new cultural identity.

The unity of Lamming's work is readily demonstrated. *The Emigrants* (1954) continues the themes of his first novel. Here episodes are constructed around the myth of England where the hopes and identity of the diaspora will disintegrate. Set in San Cristobal, *Of Age and Innocence* (1958) demonstrates the limitations of a self-conscious nationalism. In Isaac Shephard and his rebellion with Singh and Lee, Lamming provides a criticism of independence movements, indigenous political leadership, and the subtle fetters of colonialism. This is extended in *Season of Adventure* (1960) where an alternative is suggested: in the tension between the europeanised elite who govern the republic and the popular folk culture with its own traditions and basic values, he finds a hope for the future. Here Lamming finds values which he believes West Indian society needs to rediscover. This effectively completes the imaginative liberation from colonialism. In short, this is true independence. In *Natives of My Person* (1972), these themes are drawn together: four hundred years of West Indian history coalesce within a survey of slavery and the various forms of European colonialism. The metaphor of the journey holds this complex work together. It accommodates allegory and the co-existence of concrete and abstract elements. In *Water with Berries* (1971) this use of allegory is again important but the theme is primarily a return to the artistic implications of *The Emigrants*.

Underlying Lamming's work is an awareness of duality, of being torn between Caribbean and European culture. In an influential critical work, *The Pleasures of Exile* (1960), Lamming uses Shakespeare's *The Tempest* to explain his experience: the relationship between Caliban and Prospero is turned into an allegory of colonialism, of the relationship between slave and colonist. In this way Lamming eases the tension between the two cultures and his imaginative healing of this psychic rift is the act of mediation which the artist must perform for his society.

V.S. Naipaul

Experience, education at Oxford, and domicile in England since the age of eighteen have isolated Naipaul (*b.* 1932) from his fellow writers and indeed from almost any attachment to race, place, society or belief. In his novel *In a Free State* (1971) we find the remark 'I myself, I think of myself as a citizen of the world'—an assertion that could be Naipaul's own. Born in Trinidad in a Brahmin family, he was freed by education from the cultural strictures of orthodox Hinduism and a background which he disliked. His work expresses the subsequent displacement of self blended with social history and satiric comment.

Without other certitudes Naipaul seeks psychic order and identity through writing, but what he achieves is a disillusioned clarity. Running through his work is a sense of the insufficiency of any cultural or political order, whether Indian 'spirituality' as in *The Mystic Masseur* (1957) or Black Power and racism as in *The Guerillas* (1975), while the fact of social disintegration underlies *A House for Mr Biswas* (1961) and *Mr Stone and the Knight's Companion* (1963). Although Naipaul's experience of alienation includes Europe his understanding is shaped by the colonial experience of the Third World. He has written historical and travel works about the West Indies and India. He visited the latter with some hope of finding a personal cultural identity and the failure, he records, obliged him to become 'content to be a colonial, without a past, without ancestors'.

His first three works of fiction, *The Mystic Masseur* (1957), *The Suffrage of Elvira* (1958), and *Miguel Street* (1959), are set in the period from 1939 to about 1950. The last of these, a collection of short stories, was probably the first he wrote. From these sketches he graduated to longer works, but in all of them he delineates tight-knit communities where individuals—'poets', 'artists', solitaries—live a fringe existence. The prose style is economical and accomplished, the perfect vehicle for these comedies of manners which satirise the inconsistencies, confusion and hypocrisy of a society in flux. If *The Mystic Masseur* is almost wholly comic and Ganesh an image for the absurdity of island politics, there are darker tones, for the final metamorphosis from Ganesh into G. Ramsay Muir foreshadows Naipaul's later concern with identity. *The Suffrage of Elvira* brings the political theme into the foreground: the collapse of the old traditions is felt in a community where the contrast between theoretical democracy and electoral reality is black comedy. Elvira is a world without moral values, where money is the only good and corruption and brutality inevitable.

Naipaul's 'classic', *A House for Mr Biswas* (1961), condenses the earlier themes. Through Biswas, his house and the Tulsis family, Naipaul depicts an enclosed traditional East Indian community adapting to a new milieu. As in Selvon's *A Brighter Sun* there is a move from the plantations to the town and, beneath this, the absorption of the East Indian into the popular culture. The events of Biswas's life show the harshness of colonial experience: he dies unemployed and in debt, the jerry-built house, hopelessly mortgaged, his only claim to distinction in a stultifying community. Yet the realism of the narrative, Naipaul's acute use of detail to present a culture and its psychology, his ear for dialect and his instinct for cant, demonstrate a balanced, disillusioned and comprehensive vision.

The construction of this novel is instructive. Technically similar to its predecessors in the unobtrusive use of an omniscient narrator, it has greater density and seriousness: the honed simplicity of the narrative does not slacken or obscure the unfolding plot. Enforced by the recurring images of decay, darkness and death, the plot's episodic structure is so shaped that the failure of Biswas's struggle appears a foregone conclusion. This sense of inevitability is objectified and enforced on a formal level by the use of a prologue and epilogue to frame the action: as in *The Mystic Masseur* these summarise, anticipate and enclose Biswas's world.

The later works build upon what has gone before. *The Mimic Men*

(1967) returns to the illusion of *The Mystic Masseur*, but with little of the comic relief. The main character, Ralph Kirpal Singh, is representative of a generation and a society which mimics independence, where fantasy replaces reality and slogans and movements are substitutes for effective action. This lack of allegiance to any particular cause has alienated Naipaul from many West Indian and Indian readers, but few writers have been so unsparing and even-handed in their criticism of colonial and post-colonial societies. Structurally, *The Mimic Men* is sophisticated, the narrative being in the form of memories with incidents selected for narrative contrast, comment and extension. *In a Free State* is set in East Africa and *The Guerillas* on a West Indian island. Both works mirror a chaotic post-colonial world and the narrative is fragmentary so that style and dialogue suggest the inner alienation and corrosiveness. While each novel—perhaps especially *The Mimic Men* —marks Naipaul's attempt to define his identity and place in this world, each also remains autonomous with a life and substance of its own.

Naipaul has, as an editor for the BBC's *Caribbean Voices*, as a reviewer for the *New Statesman*, and—above all—as a writer, promoted West Indian writing. His isolation from other writers, while sad, involves a critical issue. George Lamming has written: 'His books can't move beyond a castrated satire.' *A House For Mr Biswas* made Lamming's criticism out of date and Naipaul's subsequent writing continues to demonstrate the value of his independence.

Wilson Harris

Born in 1921 in Guyana where he has worked as a land surveyor, Wilson Harris has used the setting of the interior for most of his novels, which have, ironically, been written during his stay in England at the end of the nineteen-fifties. His mixed ancestry—European, African and Amerindian—and the Guyanese landscape are reflected in his work, where landscape and history form a mythic and sacramental universe through which his characters journey to attain fulfilment. The difficulty with Harris's novels lies, in part, in his technique. On the one hand he attempts to break down the limits of time and place—because psychic life involves both past and present—while, on the other hand, the meaning of the stories is to be found neither in the characterisation nor in the overt plot. In short, and the wisdom of it is debatable, Harris's approach dispenses with intellectual clarity in favour of imagination and vision. 'Literature has a bearing on society', writes Harris, 'by questioning and evaluating all assumptions of character and conceptions of place or destiny.' By refusing to accept a fixed literary, topographical or chronological framework, Harris breaks new ground in

Caribbean writing and connects Caribbean aesthetic issues with wider contemporary experimentation in literary form.

Despite the difficulty of description, the four novels of the *Guiana Quartet* demonstrate Harris's interest in history and his construction of a mosaic of displaced images and symbols through which a new imaginative order is apprehended. Written in the nineteen-sixties, these novels provided a new way forward when the limits of realism had been realised and solipsist aesthetics seemed a suicidal option. *The Palace of the Peacock* (1960) returns to the early days of conquest and exploitation; *The Far Journey of Oudin* (1961) is concerned with the period of slavery and Indian indenture on the East Indian rice plantations between the savannas and the coast; *The Whole Armour* (1962) examines the advent of law in a frontier society—the location is the Pomeroon River and the narrow territory between bush and sea; finally, *The Secret Ladder* (1963) considers the establishment of a modern state and the conflict between the old and the new. In each of these novels the past intrudes into the present. There are spirits, the dead reappear and the fixed order of things is deliberately eroded so that identity is never consolidated but always in the process of formation.

Heartland (1964) links the *Guiana Quartet* and the later novels. It is set in the jungle, which symbolises an intermediate world poised between life and death; its central character, Stephenson, eventually disappears leaving behind him fragments of letters and poems. Stephenson's movement toward a void, with which *Heartland* concludes, underlies Harris's next four novels: *The Eye of the Scarecrow* (1965), *The Waiting Room* (1967), *Tumatumari* (1968) and *Ascent to Omai* (1970). All explore conditions of emptiness or loss. Whether loss of memory or of eyesight; nervous breakdown or the loss of a parent; the condition of loss, the experience of the void, becomes the occasion for the protagonist's regeneration.

Black Marsden (1972) is set in Scotland, and, more particularly, Edinburgh. When asked why he set the work outside Guyana, Harris replied: 'In the earlier novels a certain kind of development is occurring, and that development runs into this new novel.' An epigraph from James Hogg's *The Private Memoirs and Confessions of a Justified Sinner*, 'I have two souls . . . the one being all unconscious of what the other performs' suggests that in Scottish literature and history Harris found a psychic conflict useful to his own philosophy of history. *Black Marsden* is concerned with self-integration and with the movement of history in which cultures are eclipsed and, perhaps, synthesised.

Harris's style is confusing, his portrayal of 'reality' appears 'irrational' but his work deserves to be taken seriously. Like William Blake he realises that without contraries there can be no progression and, unlike Naipaul, he sees the cultural diversity of the West Indian experience to be an opportunity for growth and enrichment rather than despair. He stands aside from cultural, social and political clichés and, through his search for a new mode of awareness, a new imaginative order, offers a prophetic vision.

Derek Walcott

Best known as a poet, Derek Walcott (*b*. 1930) is a writer of the nineteen-fifties who chose to remain in, and write about, the West Indies. Place, religion and race inform his writing: for out of his isolation as an educated mulatto Protestant in the predominantly black peasant Catholic society of St Lucia he drew inspiration for his poetry. Although Walcott left St Lucia for Jamaica in 1950, the place of his childhood continues to inspire his verse. His symbols and themes demonstrate the pervasive influence of its history, rugged topography, and the sense of the racial and cultural divisions of which it first made him aware.

Technically Walcott developed his poetry by conscious study of English and American literary models, including Eliot, Pound, Dylan Thomas and Auden. Yet alongside of his mastery of standard English is his consistent use of dialect—sometimes fusing the two, and this openness to both cultural resources is characteristic of him. As he has said, 'you can't be a poet and believe in the division of man'.

More generally the development of his poetry demonstrates a widening of range. In his second volume, *Epitaph for the Young: XII Cantos* (1948) Walcott moves from the short lyric to the larger structure based on the twelve divisions of the epic form. The speaker of the poem voyages through life like a modern Ulysses, while the myth gives a unifying structure to the various cultural phenomena that impinge upon the author's inner life. In *Poems* (1952) his concerns expand to the racial, cultural and economic problems of the Caribbean: the contrasts between poor blacks and rich whites is obvious, as too are the witty puns and rhymed verse that Auden and the poets of the nineteen-forties had made fashionable. Walcott holds back from ideological stances and moves toward the common shared experiences, so in the nineteen-sixties poems such as 'A Far Cry from Africa' and 'Ruins of a Great House' demonstrate a sceptical attitude to history. Here violence, whoever inflicts it, is an expression of cruelty and the wish to dominate. 'All in compassion ends', he says, and from this proceeds his hope for a new cultural and racial identity for the Caribbean.

Latent in Walcott's thoughts are the ideals of the Federation period and the attempts to emphasise a West Indian identity to which his play *Henri Christophe* (1951) gave support, and which inspired him in the poems of *The Castaway* (1965). In this work Walcott puts forward his hope for the Caribbean world as a new beginning, and attacks Black Power intellectuals who attempt to recover a false folk-culture and history.

Finally, his long autobiographical poem, *Another Life* (1973), takes the form of a confession in which Walcott relives his childhood and through which, as with Wordsworth, we watch the growth of a poet's mind. In terms of West Indian culture this sort of autobiography shows, perhaps initiates, what might be the beginning of a new cultural awareness as he confronts the bondage of the old world's culture and his legacy of inferiority and, from that, strives toward a new beginning:

> . . . to shake off the cere cloths,
> to stride from the magnetic sphere of legends,
> from the gigantic myth . . .
> to make out of these foresters and fishermen
> heraldic men!

Edward Braithwaite

Poet and professional historian, Edward Braithwaite was born in 1930 in Barbados, educated at Cambridge, lectured in Ghana from 1955 to 1962, and since then has lectured in history at the University of the West Indies. Braithwaite's poetry is underpinned by a historian's grasp of the range of dispossession effected by colonialism. His life and work parallel that of the other West Indian intellectual from Martinique, Aimé Cesaire, who coined the word 'negritude' in 1947 in his long poem, *Cahier d'un retour au pays natal* (Notes on a Return to the Native Land), which summarised Cesaire's emotional and intellectual journey toward a new identity in a black history, tradition, and culture. Braithwaite's sense of alienation in Barbados and England, his discovery of an authentic cultural tradition in West Africa, and his attempts to transfer this modified awareness into the West Indies, mark—along with Cesaire's—a crucial stage in the affirmation of a cultural identity.

The trilogy *The Arrivants* (1973) was first published in three separate volumes: *Rites of Passage* (1967), *Masks* (1968) and *Islands* (1969). In these poems Braithwaite takes up his place in the evolution of West Indian writing which he sees as moving from a preoccupation with alienation toward a new 'wholeness'. *Rites of Passage* evokes the dispossession and rootlessness of West Indian history. The colonial past merges with the present whether in Barbados or London:

> What do they hope for
> what find there
> these New World mariners
> Columbus coursing kaffirs

Masks is based upon the sense of belonging which Braithwaite found in Ghana. Against the sterility of the preceding work he evokes the new-found serenity and sacredness which helped him to interpret the world in a new way. It is not a substitute for achieving an authentic identity but rather—as the word *Masks* implies—a means towards that end:

> So for my hacked
> heart, veins' mem-
> ories, I wear this
> past I borrowed;

The trilogy concludes with *Islands*, which marks the narrator's physical and spiritual return to the new world which, seen through the experience of Africa, is no longer a place of dispossession but rather of new opportunity. Here the personal and public voices of the poet are fused. Braithwaite speaks to his society as a poet by trying to find the essence of identity, the longed-for meaning behind the finite and concrete experience:

> The streets of my home have their own gods
> but we do not see them
> they walk in the dust

Where Naipaul is pessimistic and sees the colonial legacy as an impasse, Braithwaite, more optimistic, moves from the impasse toward a repossession of the islands and their history. *Mother Poem* (1977) continues this approach: he finds a tradition in the creole cultures and he uses dialect as a means of repossessing an identity in the new world. Here the creolisation of Caribbean society for which he has been spokesman is seen as a way out of the impasse of history and into a viable future.

Chapter 3

Africa

... it seemed to me that, ultimately, what linked the various African peoples on the continent was the nature and depth of colonial experience; and this was the final irony. Colonialism had not only delivered them unto themselves, but had delivered them unto each other, and provided them, so to speak, with a common language and an African consciousness; for out of rejection had come an affirmation.

These remarks from Lewis Nkosi's (*b.* 1938) *Home and Exile* (1965) define the situation from which African literature has emerged. Despite the efforts of critics such as Janheinz Jahn and Claude Wauthier to defend the idea of an African sensibility which spans all literatures written by those of African origin there is no evidence of African cultural coherence before contact with the West. While African literature in English has only developed since the nineteen-fifties, from cultural dispossession there has emerged a new identity and a new literature shaped by the colonial experience.

The Portuguese explorer Vasco da Gama initiated the contact between Africa and the West toward the end of the fifteenth century. By the eighteenth century, the legend of the Guinea Coast was established and slavery was central to the purposes of British trade. Some of the earliest African writing in English dates from this time: based on European models, poets such as Phillis Wheatley and George Horton produced a sentimental apprentice literature which began to voice a sense of exile. Likewise *The Interesting Narrative of the Life of Olaudah Equiano or Gustavus Vassa* (1789) is, despite its limited scope, one of the first works by an African to deal with the encounter between Europe and Africa.

Literary developments reflected political and ideological aspirations. For example, Edward Blyden, the nineteenth-century Afro-American essayist, anticipated both the romanticism of creating a mystique about black Africa and the dependence of African nationalism and Pan-Africanism upon the West. Then between 1900 and 1945, six conferences on Pan-Africanism were organised by Dr William DuBois and Marcus Garvey: these gave a focus for the growth of nationalism among African students who were studying abroad. About the same time West Indian and African intellectuals in Paris appropriated negritude as a literary movement. Since political leaders and writers tended to come from dispossessed elites, it was easy for literature to be harnessed to the purposes of political liberation. At the first Congress of Negro Writers in Paris in 1956, one of the delegates declared:

> To contribute to the revision of the whole series of representations upon which colonialism relies to justify itself, that seems to us, at the moment, to be the most urgent task of the negro writer.

Beginnings

African literature reflects two major influences: traditional culture and colonial experience. Whereas the former varies from region to region and can shape the character of a regional literature, the latter is the shared experience which spans the diversity of African cultures. From the interplay between these two forces it has become possible to divide African literature into three main 'traditions': South African, English-speaking African and French-speaking African. Each of these has themes and experiences which belong peculiarly to its literatures. So, for example, in South Africa the predominant theme has been race relations and *apartheid*; French-speaking writers have stressed their resistance to the French policy of assimilation; by contrast English-speaking writers have addressed themselves to the encounter between traditional African life and westernisation. At the same time, as African writing grows, the particular quality of a geographical region, a cultural unit, has begun to emerge. It is now possible to talk of Nigerian literature or East African writing: as identity has been secured, particular and local features have been expressed.

The Palm-wine Drinkard (1952) by Amos Tutuola (*b*. 1920) marks the start of contemporary African literature in English. In West Africa a combination of literary, educational, and political developments enabled Tutuola's novel to be followed by Chinua Achebe with *Things Fall Apart* (1958). Others soon followed. One of the most influential factors in the rapid literary developments of this time was the journal *Black Orpheus*, founded by Ulli Beier and Janheinz Jahn in September 1957. Based in Ibadan, it introduced the English-speaking elite to black literary achievement in French. While the first issues consisted mainly of translations of French poetry by African and West Indian authors, the journal soon came to be filled with original work in English. In 1961, Ulli Beier helped to establish the Mbari Club in Ibadan which aimed at publishing, staging plays and arranging exhibitions, but also created a climate in which literature could grow. Major writers such as Wole Soyinka, Christopher Okigbo (1932–67), John Pepper Clark (*b*. 1935) and Dennis Brutus (*b*. 1924) all made early appearances in the Mbari Club's publications.

Developments in South and East Africa were somewhat different. While East African writers found an outlet in *Black Orpheus* their own cultural climate was quite different. Initially the dominant influence was Uganda's Makerere College but after the coup that brought General Amin Dada to power in Uganda, and due also to Tanzania's official policy of encouraging literature in Swahili, Kenya came to dominate East African writing in English. In South Africa, despite the existence of a large number of young writers who wrote with ease in English in the nineteen-fifties and sixties, the repressions of apartheid in the nineteen-sixties and seventies forced many of the most able to live in exile.

The novel

That the novel dominates African literature in English demonstrates, among other things, the conditions of cultural crisis in which the best writers have had to work. The Ghanaian writer, Ama Ata Aidoo (*b.* 1942) has commented on this:

> I feel almost guilty myself writing the type of thing I write but my own sort of alibi for wanting to continue writing in English is that one gets the chance to communicate with other Africans outside Ghana. Even in Ghana alone, if you are writing in English, you are more able to carry yourself over, and if you have a message, to carry your message over to more people outside.*

The irony is, first, that, in order to recreate a culture, the writer is compelled to use the language inherited from the cultural power and even to accept a hybrid culture in which African and European elements meet through a common language. Second, since the novel form epitomises the European emphasis on individuality whereas traditional African values are communal rather than individual, this choice of genre maximises the writer's sense of cultural dislocation. Therefore questions of language, style and audience become critical. By contrast, poetry and drama are genres with indigenous equivalents and consequently represent less radical departures from traditional art forms.

Poetry and drama

In the tension between old and new, the oral literary traditions of Africa have been revalued by African writers, especially poets and dramatists. From the various cultures sacred songs, praise poems, religious chants, funeral dirges have influenced the poets writing in English who have mediated between inherited African modes and poetic

* Ama Ata Aidoo, Interview in *Cultural Events in Africa*, 35, October 1967, p.11.

techniques and the English language they have acquired. In some cases the poem has been written first in the indigenous language—as in p'Bitek's *Song of Lawino*. By contrast drama in English has been relatively slow to develop, perhaps because its indigenous forms have been so tied to social rituals: the seasons, birth, initiation, marriage and death. The problem has been how to make the shift from a traditional drama which speaks for the community as a whole to a drama for the educated elite, the new middle classes, to which African writers belong. This genre offers an especially apt instance of the problem of mediating between the old and the new, and exciting examples come from the two Nigerian playwrights Wole Soyinka and John Pepper Clark, whose dramas draw upon indigenous mythologies, religions and customs.

Negritude and commitment

Although the concept has been transcended, the debate about negritude has its place in history. Initially it offered a large number of would-be writers reassurance as black Africans with a vital cultural heritage; it promoted solidarity with other Africans and supported a literature which spoke to their needs. However, English-speaking writers were generally critical of negritude. Ezekiel Mphahlele, the South African writer and critic, saw negritude as another version of a racist ideology: in an essay called 'Writers and Commitment' he commented 'black pride need not blind us to our own weaknesses'. Although the ideological force of negritude is outdated the 'black consciousness' movement in South Africa suggests its presence, albeit in a modified form.

The issue of commitment is inescapable in a literature where freedom, social justice and racial equality are pervasive concerns. Mphahlele's criticism that negritude was excessively uncritical toward traditional African values raises the question of the relationship of the writer to his society: is he to affirm its values or reform them? For example: South African literature is dominated by the 'protest' theme; in Tanzania ideological emphasis upon literary production in Swahili has harnessed art to the political and cultural revolution. In his essay 'The Patriot as an Artist' Ali Mazrui (*b.* 1933) has traced the relationship between nationalism and literature, particularly in East Africa. Mazrui argues that disillusionment and criticism can be an artist's contribution to nationalism, quoting Soyinka:

> When the writer in his own society can no longer function as a conscience, he must recognise that his choice lies between denying himself totally or withdrawing to the position of chronicler and post-mortem surgeon.*

* Ali Mazrui, 'The Patriot as an Artist', in *African Writers on African Writing*, ed. G.D. Killam, Heinemann Educational, London, 1973, p.89.

West Africa

The pioneer role of West Africa in producing a literature in English reflects both its particular form of contact with the west and an advanced education system. These provided a foundation from which nationalism developed more quickly than, for example, in East Africa. Nationalism emerged from the new classes created during protracted cultural contact, while a long tradition of African prose writing in English reflects this cultural familiarity. For example, Lalage Brown has cited a nineteenth-century Ibo diarist, John Christopher Taylor, who accompanied Bishop Crowther on his voyages up the Niger. Taylor's allusions to the Onitsha people and their market demonstrates that in the nineteenth century there was already an established commercial network and the chapbooks of the Onitsha market symbolise the vitality of a new class whose rudimentary literary tastes later provided a readership for writers such as Cyprian Ekwensi (*b.* 1921).

From the tertiary institutions of West Africa came its writers and literary journals: both combined to meet new expectations. *The Horn,* a Nigerian student poetry magazine, reflected this:

> ... students in such small classes were very much aware that they belonged to a highly-selected group from which much was expected and from whom anything seemed possible. It was not felt shameful to belong to such an elite.*

As a result of this environment, by the mid-sixties Nigeria had reached a level of English literary achievement unsurpassed in Black Africa.

In part this reflected Nigeria's huge multi-national population: its two hundred different languages and dialects, and its three main ethnic groups, the Yorubas in the west, the Igbos in the east and the Hausas in the north. From each of these ethnic groups come the elements that enrich Nigerian culture. The Igbos are most firmly established in the literature written in English; the Hausas have been more conservative because of their Muslim culture, although they have retained their own traditional poetic forms and have begun to adopt western genres. More complex are the Yorubas who, with their adaptation of modern literary forms to their elaborate mythology and folklore, have had an immense impact upon Nigerian writing in English. In short, as Nigeria has become representative of the African experience, and its literary journals and educational institutions have formed a reference point for aspiring writers in English, so its influence has spread.

---

* Quoted in W.H. Stevenson, '*The Horn*: What It Was and What It Did', in *Critical Perspectives on Nigerian Literature*, ed. Bernth Lindfors, Heinemann Educational Books, London, 1979, p.209.

Amos Tutuola

Amos Tutuola (*b.* 1920) presents a paradox. In a literature where the writers belong to an educated elite and mediate between the old and the new, it is Tutuola's *The Palm-wine Drinkard* (1952) which has marked the beginning. A Yoruba, with elementary education and humble origins, Tutuola has been an outsider in Nigerian intellectual life and the target of severe criticism from fellow writers. Criticism usually focuses upon the supposed gaucheness of his 'imperfect' English, his adaptations from Yoruba oral literature and the image he presents of Nigeria. Certainly Tutuola is an unconscious cultural hybrid. He looks backwards toward the oral and folk culture of the Yoruba people, while his presentation of this communal heritage ignores ideology and realism to present an effect reminiscent of modernism and, more particularly, surrealism. The first review of *The Palm-wine Drinkard* was by Dylan Thomas who commented on 'this...brief, thronged, grisly and bewitching story, or series of stories'. What Thomas responded to and what many Nigerian intellectuals found embarrassing, was that this was not standard English. Tutuola's semi-literate English was the perfect expression of a collision between two languages, English and Yoruba, and their ways of viewing the world. His spoken and written English are identical: both present an immediate vision in which the material objects of traditional life and the flotsam and jetsam of modern society are brought into the dream world of the spirits. Set in a characteristic Yoruba milieu, his concerns are the archetypal issues of world literature.

It has often been pointed out that Tutuola is dependent upon traditional Yoruba mythology and that he demonstrates little creative originality. His works are generally, as he himself has stressed, composed rapidly from recollections of old people re-telling Yoruba legends. Although his plots may be a reworking of traditional material, it is the element of choice, of collation and confirmation which demonstrates the instinct of a fine story-teller. More than this, the unique language, and the choice of words drawn from Yoruba or English, are the mark of Tutuola's own unique style.

Although Tutuola attempted to 'improve' his command of English in his later work, the quest theme of traditional mythology remained dominant and he continued to rely heavily on traditional material. Works after *The Palm-wine Drinkard and his dead palm-wine tapster in the Deads' Town* include *My Life in the Bush of Ghosts* (1954), *Simbi and the Satyr of the Dark Jungle* (1955); *The Brave African Huntress* (1958); *Feather Woman of the Jungle* (1962); *Ajaiyi and His Inherited Poverty* (1967).

Cyprian Ekwensi

To Cyprian Ekwensi (*b*. 1921) belongs the credit of West Africa's first contemporary realistic novel published in English, *People of the City* (1954). An Ibo, Ekwensi started writing short stories during the mid-nineteen-forties. His first book, *Ikola the Wrestler and Other Ibo Tales* (1947) was based on traditional stories learned during childhood. He wrote stories for Radio Nigeria, and became a member of the Scribbler's Club in Lagos. During these early years Ekwensi began to write popular novellas such as *When Love Whispers* (1948) and *The Leopard's Claw* (1950) for the Onitsha market.

Ekwensi is a popular novelist. The literary taste of his readers is undiscriminating and he exploits cliché and sensationalism. Based on urban life, his plots are melodramatic and contrived, with a repetitive formula. His language is commonplace and his characters remain unconvincing stereotypes, whose arbitrary actions reflect the casual construction.

Despite the limitations of Ekwensi's works, his description of urban life captures the moral and cultural confusion of a new generation: those who moved to the cities and lost their bearings. So Samgo, driven by ambition, moves from one experience to another; and the brashness and cruelty of the city symbolises a new consciousness. Ekwensi's willingness to comment on any subject of topical interest is demonstrated by the way he includes incidents which reflect the clash between generations, between materialism and spiritual values, and touches on the independence movement of the period. He alludes to the Miners' Union and the violence which gave a focus to Nigerian nationalism: 'Samgo discovered that this shooting had become a cementing factor for the nation.'

The later works continue in the same sensational style. *Jagua Nana* (1961) tells the story of a Lagos prostitute and the violence of post-independence Nigerian politics. *Burning Grass* (1962), *Beautiful Feathers* (1963), *Iska* (1966) and *Survive the Peace* (1976) all go on exploring the themes introduced in *People of the City* but with adjustments to include matters of topical interest. *Survive the Peace*, for example, is about the Biafran war. With remarkable consistency Ekwensi has explored aspects of social disintegration in urban West African life, and identified and voiced the experiences and the aspirations of a massive readership. Later, more skilful writers have built upon the social realism he made popular.

Chinua Achebe

Written by probably the best-known black African writer today, Chinua Achebe's (*b*. 1930) first book, *Things Fall Apart* (1958) so builds upon the achievements of Tutuola and Ekwensi that its publication marked a watershed in the development of African literature in English. Here was a new mastery of the emotionally charged themes of cultural conflict which balanced commitment with objectivity. He utilised history but without false idealisation of the past: 'We have to admit that like other people's pasts ours had its good as well as its bad sides.' He also used language to maintain objectivity, achieving a delicate balance between the need to write for an international readership, and the desire to reflect and sustain the Nigerian context.

Things Fall Apart (1958)

The title comes from a poem of W.B. Yeats fraught with cultural anxiety, 'The Second Coming', and by this allusion Achebe's commitment to Nigeria is drawn within the wider scope of art and human experience. At the heart of the novel is not just the consequence of human pride but a study of the processes of history. Set in Iboland during the years 1850–1900 when European colonisation began, Achebe's novel presents the original Ibo society, the consequences of opposing change, and what happens in a traditional society when an individual opposes the collective mind of the village.

Central is the conflict between the old and the new. The hero is Okonkwo and through his story Achebe gives unity to the work. Three stages of development can be observed in the novel: Umuofia before the white men; then the story of Okonkwo's exile and, finally, the story of his suicide. The first section is a literary presentation of the old tribal structure, its dignity and its order. This is no slight achievement for Achebe—this order had passed by the time of his grandfather—moreover the account is kept free of sentimentality by a critical objectivity which ensures that cruelty and materialism are not passed over. When Achebe refers to Ibo customs it is with a literary rather than an anthropological intention. Okonkwo's ambition, which ultimately causes his downfall, is an extreme manifestation of the competitive materialism which Achebe shows to be ingrained in Ibo society. Land is presented as the basis of power, without which the symbol of success, yams, cannot be cultivated. Okonkwo's urge to possess land and titles reflects his society's values. The fertility of the land is safeguarded remorselessly: the Earth Goddess is 'ultimate judge of morality and conduct' and Okonkwo is exiled because he had inadvertently offended her. Okonkwo's friend, Obierika, tests the spiritual foundations of this traditional life.

> Obierika was a man who thought about things. When the will of the goddess had been done, he sat down in his *obi* and mourned his friend's calamity. Why should a man suffer so grievously for an offence he had committed inadvertently? But although he thought

for a long time he found no answer. He was merely led into greater
complexities. He remembered his wife's twin children, whom he had
thrown away. What crime had they committed? The Earth had
decreed that they were an offence on the land and must be destroyed.
And if the clan did not exact punishment for an offence against the
great goddess, her wrath was loosed on all the land and not just on
the offender. As the elders said, if one finger brought oil it soiled the
others.

Obierika's doubts remain as part of a complex of images and events
which present the reader with the difficulty of making a final judgement. If the traditional customs are inadequate—even brutal—in some
situations, they stem from a spirituality with a practical cohesive purpose.

The second and third parts narrow the concerns of the novel so that
the issues of change are seen through Okonkwo and his son Nwoye
who represent both cultural and generational conflicts. The focus upon
Okonkwo enhances his importance as a tragic hero, and Achebe's
method is to create the sense that, however Okonkwo rebuilds his life,
his aspirations are doomed. The statement by the omniscient narrator
brings this apprehension toward the surface: 'The saying of the elders
was not true—that if a man said yea his *chi* also affirmed. Here was a
man whose *chi* said nay despite his own affirmations.' Nwoye's con-
version to Christianity undermined Okonkwo's spiritual foundations
since the gains of the new religion have only, at this stage in the novel,
been to those who have no social position—the *efulefu* : 'Okonkwo felt
a cold shudder run through him at the terrible prospect, like the prospect of annihilation.' If the new faith has any appeal it is at those
points where the tradition is shown to have been weakest. Obierika's
doubts have raised this point earlier, and now Nwoye expresses his own
doubts: 'the question of the twins crying in the bush and the question
of Ikemefuna who was killed'. When Nwoye accepts Christianity his
decision marks a change from the old ways to a new era; a move from
his father and his society to a more individualised and very different
way of living.

When his 'exile' expires Okonkwo returns to Umuofia with the
hopes that he will both realise his old ambitions for influence in the village and oppose the missionaries. Yet the traditional village life is open
to the gains of trade and Okonkwo's efforts against the new order
bring humiliation. When he realises that the village will not go to war,
he hangs himself rather than await the consequence of killing a court
messenger. His death is a final irony: it excludes him from his own
people and the Europeans have to arrange for the removal and burial
of his body. From the European view there is further irony. While the
District Commissioner is arrogant, even absurd, his opinion that 'The

story of this man who had killed a messenger and hanged himself would make interesting reading' ironically emphasises European incomprehension.

No Longer at Ease (1960)

Set in Nigeria just before independence, this work is a sequel to *Things Fall Apart* with regard to characters, themes and method. Obi Okonkwo is a grandson of the earlier Okonkwo and is himself caught in the conflict between European and traditional culture. As the story opens with his public disgrace and retraces his moral, professional and social disintegration, so the emphasis has shifted from social conflict to the break-up of individual values in a society where traditional and modern values co-exist in a welter of contradictions and ambiguities. Obi's mental and emotional identity is fractured by the tension between what his western education has demanded and what his family expects. The irony of this is implied by his name: Obiajulu, his full name, means 'the mind at last is at rest', which contrasts with the title drawn from T.S. Eliot's poem 'Journey of the Magi'. Like the wise men of Eliot's poem, Obi is caught between the old ways and a new order which has still to be established.

Two incidents are revealing. The first is Obi's desire to marry Clara, which conflicts with tradition. She is an *osu*, a descendant of slaves who traditionally must be kept separate from the Ibo free-born. Tradition surfaces in the proverb 'If one finger brings oil it soils the others' which echoes Obierika's doubts in *Things Fall Apart* and enforces the links between the two works. The second incident is relatively minor and occurs during Obi's interview for a post in the Public Service. The Chairman of the interview is interested in literature and a brief discussion about the nature of tragedy takes place. Obi remarks that for real tragedy there cannot be an outlet such as suicide and that 'there is no release' and it 'takes place in a corner' where 'the rest of the world is unaware of it'. While this again recalls the earlier Okonkwo it also defines the wasteland of modern tragedy: its absence of heroic action and sense of futility.

Arrow of God (1964)

Though subsequent in composition to *No Longer At Ease*, *Arrow of God* is concerned with the earlier period, shortly after the First World War, when, under British protection, Nigerian society was transformed and a new class of African administrators created. The Obi Okonkwo of *Things Fall Apart* is the direct ancestor of these self-interested indigenous agents of change who were loyal only to a remote authority. At a time when the old religion and customs were cohesive forces, this new class of mission-educated bureaucrats gradually led Nigerian society away from the traditional ways into the new.

The fractured quality of life in this transitional period is presented at a number of levels. There is, for example, the conflict between Winterbottom, the District Commissioner, and the protagonist of the novel, Ezeulu the Chief Priest. Equally telling is Ezeulu's inner conflict as he balances individual and communal obligations. At yet another level is the obvious conflict between Ezeulu's supporters and those of Ezidemili. In brief, Ezeulu represents a society torn by changes he cannot control, his downfall as much the fault of his society as his own, so much has the social order been subverted by its materialism and western commerce.

Ezeulu's personal 'flaw' is his pride; he overestimates his powers of manipulation. When he sends his son to the missionaries he does so on the pretext of realistic acceptance, 'a man must dance the dance prevalent in his time', but his son is converted and Ezeulu's intentions and words rebound against him: '...the new religion was like a leper. Allow him a handshake and he wants an embrace.' His failure drives him into madness. His sacred power is concerned with deciding the times for harvesting and planting the yams, but he delays his announcement for two crucial months; partly out of a desire to punish his people, but mainly to restore some religious order in the traditional community. This is a final miscalculation. When disaster threatens the village the people abandon the god Ulu and turn to Christianity so that Ezeulu finds he has initiated what he most feared.

While Achebe has revised *Arrow of God*, the thrust of the novel remains intact. It shows, perhaps even more clearly than the other novels, Achebe's full creative and pragmatic intention. It traces the changes in material and spiritual life, and the role of British indirect rule in the process of social disintegration. Encompassing all, Ezeulu stands as a remarkable creation; doomed by the processes of history he evokes our pity and attains tragic stature.

A Man Of The People (1966)
In this novel Achebe turns to modern Nigeria. The changes in focus, the values of the new nation, are marked by a switch in narrative method; the omniscient narrator is supplanted by use of the first person. Instead of centering the novel on the hero whose fate is the combined result of historical circumstance and personal weakness, Achebe now satirises the new state, its innate brutality and lack of ethical sense. In *Morning Yet on Creation Day* Achebe has shown that the situation against which he wrote this work was a crisis: Nigeria was 'a cesspool of corruption and misrule. Public servants helped themselves freely to the nation's wealth.'

The narrator is Odili, a university graduate and secondary school teacher, whose idealism provides a moral centre to a novel which deals with corruption in public office. For the first half of the novel Odili is shown to be under the influence of Chief Nanga whose corrupt behaviour is the essence of the public corruption which Achebe attacks. When Nanga seduces Odili's girlfriend, Odili turns against him, not just for revenge but out of disgust. The second half of the novel is concerned with Odili's work in a rival political party and his personal stand against Nanga. Odili is not Achebe but he is the man Obi Okonkwo might have become; he attains something of heroic stature because, in spite of his human weakness, he is forced to rise above sheer self-interest as he attempts to work for the public good in a social climate where the pervading ethic of self-interest is expressed 'in language evermore suited to the times: "you chop, me self I chop, palaver finish"'. The recourse to pidgin marks the shift from Ibo proverbs. Here there is no traditional wisdom, no basis for cohesion, and pidgin is the only language appropriate to a society where values are brutalised and confused.

While the difference in tone, its urgency and polemicism, and the change in narrative method, set this novel apart, *A Man Of The People* marks the final stage in the tetralogy. In this sequence the changes in Nigerian national life have been traced from the first colonial encounters and Okonkwo's suicide, through to the post-independence disenchantement with Odili as its pessimistic spokesman.

Achebe's stature rests upon his achievement as a novelist but there are other works. *Girls At War* is a collection of short stories which reflect concerns similar to the novels. 'The Sacrificial Egg' shows the capacity of old superstitions and customs to influence even those young educated members of the society who denigrate tradition. If this concern dominates, and there are versions of it in stories such as 'The Madman' and 'Uncle Ben's Choice', the title-story reflects another concern, the Nigeria—Biafra war. This story mirrors the horror of that conflict and Achebe's anger and despair. It needs to be read in conjunction with Achebe's brief paper 'The African Writer and the Biafran Cause' in *Morning Yet on Creation Day*. These, combined with poems such as 'Refugee Mother and Child' which is part of the small collection of Achebe's verse *Beware, Soul Brother* (1971, revised edn 1972), are an impressive witness to his involvement in the issues that have formed modern Nigeria and, equally, to his instincts as a poet. The tragic quality of his heroes in the novels is reduced to small details of human tenderness in a holocaust:

No Madonna and Child could touch
that picture of a mother's tenderness
for a son she soon would have to forget.

('Refugee Mother and Child')

Wole Soyinka

Born in 1934 in a prominent Yoruba family, Soyinka was educated at Ibadan University College, where he met Achebe and Okigbo, and at Leeds where Wilson Knight's metaphysical interpretation of literature seems to have influenced him. This background and education colour all his work.

Soyinka stresses 'commitment': he spent two years in Nigerian prisons (1967–9) for alleged pro-Biafran activity and on his release said, 'Whatever it was I believed in before I was locked up, I came out a fanatic in those things'. *Season of Anomy* (1973) and *The Man Died* (1972) reflect his shock at the Nigerian civil war. While his recent long political poem *Ogun Abibiman* (1976) foresees the liberation of South Africa he has been critical of negritude, for example his famous remark, 'A tiger does not proclaim his tigritude, he pounces', yet he affirms the need to 'restate the authentic world of the African peoples and ensure its contemporary apprehension through appropriate structures'. The force of his concern for the reconciliation between old and new emerges through his fusion of literary commitment with ethnic origins by means of his use of Yoruba myth and cosmology: in particular the Yoruba god Ogun who with his combination of destructive and creative powers symbolises the role of the artist. Since bridges and roads are obvious emblems for Ogun's activities, Soyinka uses the Ogun myth to demonstrate how change or destruction can be harnessed to a creative or redemptive purpose. Invariably his use of language—it has been called 'Jonsonian'—is contentious: though rich and evocative, its density and contorted syntax can deter readers.

PLAYS:

Only twenty-three when his plays were first performed in London, Soyinka in his most serious works is preoccupied with African history. From the tragic, such as the metaphysically inclined *The Road* (1965), or *A Dance of the Forests* (1963) which was written for Nigerian Independence, even to the farcical false prophet in *The Trials of Brother Jero* (1967), African experience is central. Moral purpose connects these extremes, as for example in *Kongi's Harvest* (1967) with its attack on corruption in a hypothetical African state.

An early comedy, *The Lion and the Jewel* (1963), is a useful introduction to Soyinka's dramas. Apart from the language it has been alleged that the plot is drawn from Jonson's *Volpone*, but an African milieu dominates, both in the surprise conclusion where the 'old' defeats the 'new', and in the importance of dance, mime and proverb.

In the elderly Baroka's wooing of the village 'Jewel' Sidi, Soyinka's concern with tradition surfaces within a comic structure. Baroka's reliance on the old ways of wooing contrasts with the village school master, Lakunle, whose fumbling subverts the appeal of the new. Baroka's words, while they are not wholly Soyinka's view, suggest the new perspective and balance he seeks to find:

Yesterday's wine alone is strong and blooded, child,
And though the Christians' holy book denies
The truth of this, old wine thrives best
Within a new bottle. The coarseness
Is mellowed down, and the rugged wine
Acquires a full and rounded body...
Is this not so—my child?

The moral purpose that sustains Soyinka's works goes beyond the resolution of cultural conflict. Ultimately he is concerned with the need for redemption and, as the Ogun myth implies, he seems to require the artist to be a priestlike being whose suffering creates a new order. The idea echoes Percy Bysshe Shelley's (1792–1822) *Prometheus Unbound* (1819) and reverberates through Soyinka's plays and novels. *A Dance of the Forests*, with its heavy dependence upon Yoruba lore, especially the ancestor-worship ceremonies of the *Egungun* demonstrates this undefined but painful vocation.

My secret is my eternal burden—to pierce the encrustations of soul-deadening habit, and bare the mirror of original nakedness—knowing full well, it is all futility. Yet I must do this alone...

(A Dance of the Forests, p.88)

NOVELS:

The Interpreters (1965)
In this first novel, plot and characters demonstrate Soyinka's interest in the creative individual isolated in an unaccommodating society. Although the narrative creates an illusion of discontinuity the work is tightly wrought through the recurring images and flashbacks which compact past and present. The plot revolves round the experiences of a group of young, talented, and well-educated Nigerians and their response to dishonest bureaucracy and the claims of a tradition that is no longer convincing. From the 'chaos' they all feel, each creates an identity. Indeed the compulsion to integrate their pasts with the future they will create recalls Soyinka's interest in Ogun. Sekoni, a Muslim from the North, particularly embodies this concern: in defiance of tradition he marries a Christian girl, is disinherited by his family, and the bridge becomes his personal symbol. As a bridge may image the mediation between past and future, so in his person he reconciles various possibilities and conflicting traditions.

Alongside this interest Soyinka so continues to mock social and political hypocrisy that the novel becomes a comic prelude to *Season of Anomy* and a satiric perspective shapes both works. Soyinka uses laughter to destroy objects of contempt: the comic phantasy of the corrupt judge, naked in a wardrobe except for a brassiere—'For the medals young man'—demonstrates his skilful use of satire towards a deflatory end.

Season of Anomy (1973)

Here, despite a style which leans towards poetry, the plot is simple. Ofeyi, the principal protagonist, discovers an isolated community, Aiyero, and attempts to bring its traditional communal and spiritual values into line with the material values of a nation whose government is dominated by a cartel of corrupt business interests. These evangelical plans are brutally destroyed in scenes of violence so dehumanised that they surpass Ouologuem's *Bound to Violence*. Even when Ofeyi's mistress is successfully rescued (in a passage that calls to mind the Orpheus–Eurydice myth) the work closes with a barely qualified sense of waste. Density characterises Soyinka's style. European and African myths merge while narrative may work on different levels simultaneously: the literal, the allegorical and the fantastic. Here style images Soyinka's metaphysical bias: the novel is shaped by a tension between good and evil, the natural and its perversion. The oxymoron implicit in the title (whereas 'season' implies order, 'Anomy' implies the absence of order—lawlessness) demonstrates Soyinka's sense of a fundamental tension which can only be expressed through a metaphorical vocabulary. Aiyero is presented as good through association with seasonal rhythms and vegetative processes; by contrast the cartel is associated with a brutal and perverse natural imagery—'tentacles', 'spores' and a 'harvest' of blood and corpses. The perfect expression of the cartel is the leper-colony, prison and lunatic asylum of Temoko which has its counterpart in the Hades of European classical mythology.

Soyinka's concern with the proper use of tradition in the new African milieu colours the presentation of Aiyero. At the same time the Nigerian civil war has influenced the story and the political aspect of allegory should be considered. In particular Soyinka's absorption with death and his apparent post-war pessimism about peaceful change merge in his personification of the acceptable revolutionary as 'The Dentist' who removes carious teeth. In this style of writing characterisation tends to become superficial: allegory has replaced realism. Finally, the metaphysical order of the work implies the victory of the natural order: at the end of a journey through a wasteland there is the hope that remains in the natural cycles—'In the forest, life began to stir'.

POEMS:

Two collections (*Idanre* and *A Shuttle in the Crypt*) exemplify Soyinka's ability in this genre. Although his language and syntax can be obscure, the best of his poems have a spareness and a wide range of tone. 'Telephone Conversation' demonstrates both these talents put to withering satirical effect. 'Civilian and Soldier' shows that in poetry his themes remain the same as in his other works as he continues to focus upon the brutal void he senses in contemporary African society.

Beti, Ouologuem, Armah and Awoonor: writers and history

While Achebe and Soyinka use history to secure identity, Francophone writers such as Mongo Beti (*b*. 1932, Cameroon) and Yambo Ouologuem (*b*. 1940, Mali) are pessimistic. Beti's satirical novels—which include *The Poor Christ of Bomba* (1956) and *King Lazarus* (1958)—and Ouologuem's controversial *Bound to Violence* (1968) demonstrate scepticism about history as a source of cultural identity.

The novels of Ayi Kwei Armah (*b*. 1939, Ghana) move from disgust with present history, its political corruption, to a re-created and idealised history for the future. *The Beautyful Ones Are Not Yet Born* (1968) has been described as a modern fable with a Ghanaian context: an unnamed protagonist—'the man'—journeys within a corrupt society that is defined through excremental imagery. *Fragments* (1970) has a partly autobiographical, more defined protagonist in Baako the artist who goes insane. *Why Are We So Blest?* (1971) extends the concern with alienated artists through the characters of Modin and Solo: this western convention ends in an impasse in the divided societies Armah depicts. By contrast *Two Thousand Seasons* (1974) rewrites African history from an African standpoint in an inflated and idealised manner. Here the artists speak from within a secure communal identity and have a function. *The Healers* (1978) concentrates on the second Asante war of the late nineteenth century. The defeat of the Asante is explained but Armah also synthesises a model for the artist in a new society through Dofo, 'the healer' who combines isolation with cultural function.

Noted as a poet, Kofi Awoonor's (*b*. 1935, Ghana) first novel *This Earth, My Brother* (1971) provides another view of contemporary history as disillusionment. The hero, Amamu, journeys toward insanity and death: he mirrors a fragmented world in which colonialism has been replaced with a new bondage. With hope gone only madness remains. While the language is varied and rich, Awoonor uses a symbolic structure which suggests allegory. Although his poetry is distinctively contemporary, *Rediscovery* (1964), *Night of my Blood* (1971),

Ride Me, Memory (1973), blend linguistic forms and use African tradition.

Other West African writers: a summary

The variety of West African writing is striking. From Sierra Leone, William Conton's (*b.* 1925) *The African* (1960) was an early novel which told a simple story of an intellectual who falls in love with a white South African girl, is disappointed and eventually returns to his country to become a nationalist leader. In drama, the plays of Sarif Easmon (*b.* 1913) provide acute studies of familiar themes in the literature, notably conflict between generations (*Dear Parent and Ogre*, 1964); conflict between old and new (*The Burnt-out Marriage*, 1967) and humorous views on political morality (*The New Patriots*, 1965).

While writers such as Elechi Amadi (*b.* 1934), Nkem Nwanko (*b.* 1936) and Lenrie Peters (*b.* 1932) have made substantial contributions to the novel, and in the case of Peters to poetry as well, John Pepper Clark (*b.* 1935) merits special attention. Compared with Achebe's and Soyinka's fusion of expression with experience, Clark's African content can grate against the English idiom. A Professor of English, he describes himself as 'a cultural mulatto' and his plays, while echoing Greek drama, draw upon subjects from Ijaw tradition. *Three Plays: Song of a Goat, The Raft, The Masquerade* (1964) demonstrate this, as does *Ozidi* (1966) which is based upon an Ijaw saga, translated by Clark in a major scholarly work, *The Ozidi Saga* (1977). *The Raft*, despite its reflection of the culture of the Niger Delta, can also be read as an allegory of the Biafran war and this influence permeates the poems in *Casualties* (1970). While his themes and styles vary, his other poetry collections—*Poems* (1962), *A Reed in the Tide* (1965)—reflect his preoccupation with place and tradition: the much anthologised 'Night Rain' is a good example.

The work of Gabriel Okara (*b.* 1921) is characterised by a melancholy introspection which reflects his concern for the loss of traditional life and the tension of an imagination caught between cultures, for example in the poem 'Piano and Drums':

And I lost in the morning mist
of an age at a riverside keep
wandering in the mystic rhythm
of jungle drums and the concerto.

While the poems in *The Fisherman's Invocation* (1978) demonstrate Okara's poetic quest, *The Voice* (1964) is an almost allegorical novel in which realism is subordinated to Okara's moral purpose. It is a compact demonstration of both conflicts—old versus new, individual versus community—and the fusion of an English idiom with Ijaw imagery and rhythms.

After his death in the Biafran war, Christopher Okigbo (1932–67) remains an enigma. A philosophical and religious poet, he draws eclectically from African, classical and English contexts with unique assurance. *Heavensgate* (1962), *Limits* (1964) and *Labyrinths, with Path of Thunder* (1971) are all sustained by aspects of religious awareness while English literary echoes mingle with Ibo traditions.

From the sketchy novels of T.M. Aluko (*b*. 1918) to the new Ghanaian poets such as Kofi Anyidoho, West African writing has acquired further variety and substance. At the same time the work of an established writer—mainly in drama—such as Ama Ata Aidoo (*b*. 1942) is a skilful interpretation of experience from a woman's perspective: her short stories *No Sweetness here* (1970) exemplify this. Other women writers in West Africa include Buchi Emecheta (*b*. 1944), Flora Nwapa (*b*. 1931), who wrote *Efuru* (1966), *Idu* (1970) and *Never Again* (1975), and Mabel Segun.

East and Central Africa

History

Although the significance of East Africa's complex early history is gradually being appreciated along with the influences of Indian and Islamic cultures, the comparatively recent experience of British colonial policy has been decisive. Whereas in West Africa British influence had been exercised since the seventeenth century, in the East contact began largely in the eighteen-fifties, through attempts to end the Arab slave trade by pressure upon the Sultan of Zanzibar. One consequence of this chronological difference was that West African nationalism emerged gradually from the creation of new social classes whereas in the East it came rapidly, and was due to conflict with white settlers. Unlike the West, colonisation in the East reflected the strategic needs of the late nineteenth century (control of South Africa, the Indian Ocean and access to Suez) and the method was entirely different: while the West coast enjoyed a forbidding reputation as the 'white man's grave' the Eastern uplands attracted white settlers in large numbers. Another contrast with West Africa was the degree of colonial organisation: whereas in West Africa limited objectives were set, in East Africa policy was haphazard, circumstantial. For example, considerable powers were given to white settlers in Kenya and Rhodesia while in Tanzania the policy of 'indirect administration' ensured that it never experienced the intense colonial trauma of its neighbours.

East Africa's distinctive colonial experience is reflected in its literature: its tone and slower, uneven pace of development when compared with the West coast. There were regional variations in policy. Africans in Uganda and Tanzania were not alienated from their land as happened in Kenya, and their literature does not reflect the concern with the land that provoked the Mau Mau 'Emergency' (1952–60). At the same time, in comparing East and West, the very gradual colonisation of West Africa left traditions relatively untouched, which may explain why West Africans have tended to concentrate upon establishing a heroic past to secure cultural identity. In East Africa the impact of extensive European settlement entailed denigration of indigenous cultures and urban alienation on a large and rapid scale. So, for example, there is the relative absence of historical themes—the exception being the Mau Mau theme which is still recent—and a concentration upon 'economic' themes such as land, urban poverty, beggars and unemployment. Further qualifications are needed for Tanzania where rural themes have been encouraged for ideological reasons.

Literary development

From the early neo-European imitative writing produced in western educational institutions through to the short stories which grew progressively more experimental under the impact of West African writers, a common pattern can be discerned. Okot p'Bitek's *Song of Lawino* marked a stylistic breakthrough that encouraged imitators, and those who followed p'Bitek's example in satirical lyricism include fellow Ugandans Okello Oculi, Joseph Buruga and Cliff Lubwa p'Chong as well as Muthoni Likimani of Kenya. Quite different is the poetry of David Rubadiri (*b.* 1930), a poet and diplomat from Malawi, whose intuitive grasp of African life fuses with his linguistic sophistication in poems that mirror a delicate balance between cultures. Ngugi's novels form another landmark, a recreation of Kikuyu past and history from an African perspective. Intensely cerebral novels such as *Weep Not, Child* (1964) and *The River Between* (1965) encouraged other novelists to employ historical or political themes. These include Godwin Wachira, John Karoki, Stephan Ngubiah, Charity Waciuma, Lydia Mumbi Nguya, Leonard Kibera, Grace Ogot (*b.* 1930) and Kenneth Watene of Kenya; Peter Nazareth and Robert Serumaga (1939–80) of Uganda; Ismael Mbise and Gabriel Ruhumbika of Tanzania. To this evolving literature Taban lo Liyong (*b.* 1939, Uganda) has added critical flair, provocative comment and originality.

The trend toward popular writing with the spread of literature to a wide readership even beyond the cities is notable from the early nineteen-seventies. Charles Mangua with his novels *Son of Woman* (1971) and *A Tail in the Mouth* (1972) marks the popularity of light episodic narratives for writers which include Austin Bukenya, Samuel Kahiga, Mwangi Ruheni and Eneriko Seruma. David Maillu represents the extreme of pulp fiction, epitomised by *My Dear Bottle* (1973), yet the appeal of these works is not mere salacity but their presentation of characters who voice the aspirations of a new, largely urban, and often underprivileged class of East Africans.

While the universities and journals such as *East African Journal* and *Transition* helped to establish the new literature, the function of the urban press—magazines and newspapers—was critical. For example in Kenya *Joe*, *Weekly Review*, *Drum* and *Umma* were forums for writers prepared to cater to urban tastes. The East African Literature Bureau, established in 1948, set up competitions in schools, published journals such as *Buara*, *Dhana*, *Joliso*, *Maktaba*, *Mwazo* and *Umma* and did much to foster a new literature. At the same time the East African Publishing House was founded to produce the works when they emerged.

Drama developed erratically. School drama festivals, but in particular the travelling theatre groups associated with universities such as Makerere, brought live theatre to a wide and mainly rural audience. The role of Robert Serumaga has been especially important in developing an indigenous African theatre as his humour and sophistication also incorporate indigenous forms of music, dance and mime. Despite playwrights such as F. Imbuga, J.M. Kibwana and John Ruganda it is Ngugi wa Thiong'o's dramas that have been most influential. With *The Trial of Dedan Kimathi* and *I Will Marry When I Want* (first written in Kikuyu and acted before a rural audience) a new type of political and social drama can be noted.

Language and ideology

A brief colonial experience with an impact generally hostile to indigenous culture partially explains the East African style of English which lacks the enrichment from indigenous languages that can be noted on the West coast. In East Africa English has not been reshaped to become a fully identifiable regional dialect but is in the process of evolution as oral traditions and local languages become vehicles for contemporary literary expression.

Tanzania, with its relative insulation from colonial settlement and its commitment to socialism, has particularly encouraged the use of indigenous languages, especially Swahili which is the official language. Its literature reaches a mass readership and is often designed to promote a political programme. Hence urban themes have been discouraged because the economic and political programme requires the development of rural culture.

Okot p'Bitek

Ugandan-born Okot p'Bitek (1931–82) personifies the task of mediation between old and new. In his own words: 'The role of the creative artist . . . remains the same: to make man look at himself again and ask, "What is life all about?".' All p'Bitek's works demonstrate this concern. Whether in essays (*Africa's Cultural Revolution*, 1973), academic studies (*African Religions in Western Scholarship*, 1971; *Religion of the Central Luo*, 1971) or the poems and songs for which he is famous— especially *Song of Lawino: A Lament* (1966)—p'Bitek's focus upon the nature of the emergent East African society is consistent.

Although he had written other works in Acholi and this was also the original language for *Lawino*, the impact of *Song of Lawino* was felt only after it had been translated into English. The influence is most obvious in a writer like Joseph Buruga whose work *The Abandoned Hut* re-creates p'Bitek's perceptions.

Oral tradition and communal life form the background of *Song of Lawino* and at some points the Acholi idiom remains untranslatable; for example, the last chapter had to be omitted from the English version. Lawino's lament for her husband Ocol and his uncritical susceptibility to European values, expresses p'Bitek's realisation that just as there is no use postulating a primal African identity—the error of negritude—so adaptation to a new culture must not imply the loss of tradition, here denoted by 'the pumpkin' of domestic rural life:

> Let no one
> Uproot the Pumpkin.

Lawino embodies traditional values whereas Ocol mirrors the predicament of Africans who have been brought up in a European educational system—like the 'Been-to' of West African fiction. Lawino's lament sums up this conflict:

> Bile burns my inside!
> I feel like vomiting!
> For all our young men
> Were finished in the forest,
> Their manhood was finished
> In the class-rooms,
> Their testicles
> Were smashed
> With large books.

This example also indicates that while the poem reflects political and social developments it does not duplicate oral tradition: it lacks the rhythm for voice, drum or dance found in Acholi literature. Instead p'Bitek has suggested that the biblical love-poem *Song of Solomon* was an influence.

He has written other 'songs' with different themes, for example *Song of a Prisoner* (1971) with its adverse comment on 'uhuru' or politics in East Africa. At the same time his translations and adaptations of traditional oral literature, its poems and stories, in *The Horn of My Love*, and *Hare and Hornbill* have stimulated interest in East African oral literatures.

Okello Oculi

From northern Uganda, Okello Oculi has admitted his indebtedness to p'Bitek: 'the first nonsense I wrote was immediately after *Song of Lawino* . . . [it] touched exactly that nerve which we had been arguing.' Oculi's book-length poem *Orphan* (1968) was published in the same year as his novel *Prostitute*. The isolation implicit in each of these titles gives a clue to their common element: each explores, in a different setting—village and town—aspects of alienation.

It has been said that alienation is not a common theme in African literature and that it represents an importation from western thought in contrast to the African sense of social identity. However Oculi has argued that there are many people in contemporary Africa who are, metaphorically, orphans. At the very least this must include all those who have lost ties with land, tradition and identity. At the same time Oculi's poem attacks the new black bureaucracy and gives satirical expression to the conflict between old and new:

All of them in the Exclusive Club
Are allergic to my village simpicity,
To my crude pride in myself and my nativity.

In his novel *Prostitute* shock tactics expose a seedy urbanism and the simplicity of village life which itself is riddled with jealousy and hypocrisy. With no single character's integrity unchallenged, with the reek of putrefaction, the bed-bugs and derelict cars which symbolise the urban waste, the novel provokes disgust and despair. In short, desperate situations require desperate remedies.

With no clear plot the narrative is sustained through the prostitute's meditations. More than just a character, she stands for society and those occasions when individuals, classes and nations abandon their integrity. This sophisticated narrative technique and the style, often convoluted, mixing prose and poetry, reflect Oculi's determination to go beyond a simple realism and attempt to provoke his readers.

Ngugi Wa Thiong'o

A Kikuyu, born in 1938, the best-known of the Kenyan writers, Ngugi wa Thiong'o was first known as James Ngugi. Ngugi's change of name in the 1970s symbolised his commitment to restoring 'the African character to his history'.

A useful introduction to his work is Ngugi's collection of essays in *Homecoming* which indicate the integration of his ideas and the influence of other writers, such as George Lamming. The ideological rhetoric which clogs *Devil on the Cross* has its origins in these papers where neo-colonialism is always the enemy, while Ngugi attempts to create a new modern African identity and culture. The resources he draws upon include the Arusha Declaration (which launched Tanzania's cultural reforms by insisting upon a material socialist structure) and Ngugi's own pedagogical efforts on the staff of the University of Nairobi when he abolished the English department in favour of a new curriculum with African literature as its core. An increasing stridency and didacticism can be noted in his works together with an increasing use of indigenous languages—Kikuyu and Swahili—especially in his plays.

Before *Petals of Blood* Ngugi's novels show his indebtedness to Chinua Achebe: in these early works he recreates a history through which the present malaise can be interpreted. In these, and in the short stories, we find a cluster of themes which dominate East African writing: for example, master–servant relations, religious issues such as tribal circumcision and its prohibition by Christian missionaries, and, of course, the Mau Mau experience. Apart from *The River Between*, with its plot based on a love affair which is used to represent the conflict between modernism and tradition, the other early novels indicate how Ngugi's sense of history is overwhelmed by the closeness of the Mau Mau trauma. In particular this applies to *Weep not, Child* and *A Grain of Wheat*. Three representative works show the consistency of Ngugi's concerns: *A Grain of Wheat*, *Petals of Blood* and *Devil on the Cross*.

A Grain of Wheat (1967)

Set against the struggle for political independence in Kenya, *A Grain of Wheat* demonstrates Ngugi's pessimistic treatment of African history. There are no heroes. Instead, guilt and betrayal, the mental and physical scars of conflict, dominate a work where all—freedom fighters, white settlers and even whole villages—have participated in treachery of some kind or another. This experience of colonial history involves alienation from the remote past and, in the present, alienation from self and one another.

A popular freedom fighter, Mugo, dominates the work. It is ironic that he is really obsessed by his own guilt—the betrayal of another guerilla to the British troops who hanged him—and at the end of the work, in the independence celebrations, Mugo publicly confesses his responsibility. Structural devices enforce this pervasive anxiety. For example the time scheme, a present interpolated with flashbacks, stresses the connection between past events and the present fractured society and private despair.

Generally free of the strident tones and contrived character types that mar later works, the novel implies a need for national 'catharsis'; it suggests reasons for a present malaise and the way through the impasse. In the end the colonial trauma must be exorcised before past and future can be repossessed: Mumbi's words close the novel with the new attitude required for a new Kenya:

> People try to rub things out, but they cannot. Things are not so easy. What has passed between us is too much to be passed over in a sentence. We need to talk, to open our hearts to one another, examine them, and then together plan the future we want.
>
> (*A Grain of Wheat*, p.213)

Petals of Blood (1977)
This work anticipates the style and tone of *Devil on the Cross*; it demonstrates Ngugi's eclectic use of other writers' ideas, philosophies and works while foreshadowing his didactic stance. The title comes from Derek Walcott's poem 'The Swamp' and functions as a muted but effective cohesive device throughout the novel. Although the allusion recalls Ngugi's studies in Caribbean writing, numerous epigraphs from diverse sources, from Cabral, Blake, Whitman and the Bible, advance his radical political concerns.

Rhetoric dominates the story set in Kenya after Independence as the workers at the overseas-owned Theng'cta Brewery in Ilmorog, a new town close to the Trans-Africa Highway, plan a militant strike following the Brewery's decision against a pay increase. Hours later three Brewery directors are killed and three Ilmorog residents arrested: the headmaster of the primary school, a trade unionist and a shopkeeper. Each of the four main characters—Wanja, Munira, Karega and Abdullah (a former freedom-fighter)—are in some way victims of the new exploiters of Kenya and the local conflict of interests show Ilmorog as a microcosm of the nation: 'It was New Kenya. It was New Ilmorog. Nothing was free.'

Structure and plot amply demonstrate Ngugi's extreme position in the spectrum of 'committed' literature. The work envisages a popular uprising of 'the people' against the new masters in Kenya and, by implication, the book is intended as an instrument for generating political awareness. The novel closes with Karega, the imprisoned unionist, being told by a visiting woman seed-millet worker that the new resistance movement is active in Nairobi and the new underground leader has just

returned from Ethiopia 'to complete the war he and Kimathi started . . .
There are rumours about a return to the forests and the mountains . . . '
(p.344). In brief, the Mau Mau theme has now been incorporated into a
new and futuristic mythology and the battle for independence made the
preliminary of a deeper revolution.

Devil on the Cross (1982)
Ngugi's story about the writing of this novel is told in *Detained*. While
in prison for offence given to the Kenyan government by the drama *I
Will Marry When I Want*, he wrote *Devil on the Cross* on sheets of
toilet-paper that he concealed within the pages of a Bible kept in his
cell. Although the manuscript was discovered it was returned, and,
subsequently published in Kikuyu, became a best-seller in East Africa.
Ngugi's dedication reads 'To all Kenyans struggling against the neo-
colonial stage of imperialism'.

Few books so subordinate literary values to political interests. Here
plot is a vehicle for rhetoric. The female protagonist Wariinga represents the emergent classes in a new Kenya: she is a 'worker' and not an
object of economic or sexual exploitation. Wariinga never develops as
a character: she is a type that Ngugi hopes to create. Adept at judo and
karate, a member of the underground workers' movement, she represents an assertive and ruthless class struggle.

Ngugi's creed is supplied in his 'workers' catechism' which begins 'I
believe that we, the workers, are of one clan . . . '. From this concept of
national or class identity—rather than ethnic group—Ngugi develops
an egalitarian socialism. Since it is hard to think of any other serious
writer who has so strained the limits of literary 'commitment', the
value of the work lies in its demonstration of an extreme development.

Taban lo Liyong

In an interview with the American critic and scholar Bernth Lindfors in
1976, Liyong (*b.* 1939) almost identified the problem critics have
encountered when attempting to define his work.

> When I started writing my essays, each essay was different from the
> others. There was also a variety of styles for the short stories in
> *Fixions* and *The Uniformed Man*. All of them were different. I
> don't know whether readers have actually found that out: no story is
> told exactly as the previous one was. It was like saying, 'Okay, future
> East African writers, here are a variety of forms. Choose the one
> you like; choose the mode of writing you prefer.' That was the type
> of thing I was trying to do.*

---

* Bernth Lindfors, 'A Basic Anatomy of East African Literature', in *African Writing
Today, Pacific Moana Quarterly*, 6: 3/4, 1981, p.46.

Liyong's synthetic approach to writing has kept him aside from the ideological debates in East Africa. The mystique of negritude or black experience, the role of the writer in a political struggle, are not causes with which he has identified himself. Instead his first book, *The Last Word* (1969), was a collection of critical essays and autobiographical material which—apart from being the first book of literary criticism to be published in East Africa—embodied Liyong's idea of 'cultural synthesism'. In his own words, the necessity of Africans studying world literature comes from the 'need to know how our works stand in relation to other contemporary works throughout the world; we also need to compare our works with those by past societies'.

Liyong's short stories are a blend of old and new elements: a fusion of African traditions and the dilemma of the contemporary. His use of the fable form with Acoli characters such as Hare is not out of piety for tradition but because 'there are things you can teach through fable much better than through a poem or novel'. Likewise in *The Uniformed Man* he attacks authoritarianism and the forces that dehumanise and limit human freedom and dignity. In these stories it is possible to discern Liyong's sensitive response to a fragmented cultural situation and his attempt to answer the challenge he set in his essay 'Can We Correct Literary Barrenness in East Africa?'. Invariably Liyong's strategy is to closely reflect the world about him: as he says in the preface to *The Uniformed Man*, 'Nature and culture are broken; art which mirrors them can only correctly register broken images.'

Robert Serumaga

The dramatic elements of oral literature and restricted literacy account for the popularity of drama with those East African writers who have aspired to influence their society. For example, there are Ngugi's economic and political concerns in *The Trial of Dedan Kimathi* (1977) and *I Will Marry When I Want* (1980); John Ruganda's *Black Mamba* (1973) and Elvania Zirimu's *Family Spear* (1973) with its reconsideration of traditional social codes.

While Robert Serumaga's (1939–80) entrepreneurism brought his Ugandan theatre group, Theatre Limited, to London's Aldwych Theatre for the 1975 World Theatre Season, his capacity for taking the drama beyond the confines of the East African situation and endowing it with a universal appeal in style and subject are characteristic. Instead of allowing political and social issues to dominate he reduces them to the level of background and focuses on the plight of the gifted individual who, caught by his own awareness and the indifference of his society, is radically alienated. In this fusion of a particular context with a universal theme Serumaga manages to synthesise African and European perspectives.

Serumaga's preoccupation with alienated protagonists can also be traced in his only non-dramatic piece, the novel *Return to the Shadows* which he wrote while living in London. The hero, Joe Musizi, typifies Serumaga's isolated intellectual egoists. While his emotional and psychic development is recorded against a political background—a coup in 'Adnagu' (Uganda inverted)—(Serumaga was a loyalist and resented Obote's deposition of Sir Edward Mutessa the hereditary Kabak of Buganda) this background does not intrude.

PLAYS:

A Play (1968)
Conservative in construction and lacking in cohesion this first drama is dominated by a dream sequence in which Mutimukulu is troubled by an undefined sense of guilt on the anniversary of his wife's death. In the context of *Return to the Shadows* and the later plays it can be seen as an initial attempt to work out the dramatic representation of Serumaga's essential concerns.

The Elephants (1969)
In this work the character of David dominates; his affection for Maurice who, like him, has lost his family; Jenny, the white Peace Corps worker who plans to marry Maurice; these are the three characters whose lives are destroyed when their pretences and obsessions are exposed. The title is drawn from the play's central metaphor, the pygmy who kills the elephant by eating it from inside.

Majangwa: A Promise of Rains (1971)
The central figure of Majangwa is based on a real-life entertainer in Buganda whose reputation had become part of the folklore. Serumaga takes up the idea of the local artist, estranged by the duties and demands of his art, in order to consider what the task of the artist must be. Majangwa and his wife are shown to have sacrificed their own hopes of children in order to preserve the life of the community which resents them.

Renga Moi ('Red Warrior') (1972)
This play was first performed by Serumaga's own company, renamed the Abafumi Theatre Company. Based on the Acoli legend of a chief who defended his people at the expense of his children—who were then sacrificed by his own community—the work overtly takes up Serumaga's central theme, and social commitment appears delusive. In his own words 'We are posing a universal question about the choices an individual has to make, between himself and his social commitment.' Given the East African literary context it is not surprising that writers such as Peter Nazareth have regarded Serumaga as 'insensitive'.

Meja Mwangi

One of the few East African writers able to make a living from the royalties on his books and short stories, Meja Mwangi (*b.* 1948) has produced a considerable amount of work. His place in East African writing is founded on his skill in recording the experiences of new Kenya in a light and easy prose, and while the influence of Ngugi may be discerned in Mwangi's reflection on the Mau Mau theme in *Taste of Death* (1975) and *Carcase for Hounds* (1974), he is more detached. Mwangi shows no taste for fighting neo-colonialism in independent Kenya; he is more concerned with the contradictions in daily life, the social structures that simply do not work. These common urban themes of unemployment, loneliness, boredom and dissatisfaction are explored in his novels *Kill Me Quick* (1973), *Going Down River Road* (1976) and *The Cockroach Dance* (1979).

Kill Me Quick
Mwangi's social orientation is obvious in this first novel which won the 1974 Kenyatta prize for literature. The story follows the fortunes of two bright young men of good families who search for work in the city: their expectations are frustrated by the social realities of modern Kenya and, through no fault of their own, beggary and theft are the consequences.

It is noticeable that in this novel, as indeed in all Mwangi's works, the sense of the human spirit and the capacity for warmth and friendship despite appalling circumstances, holds firm. The two young men, Meja and Maina, retain their friendship. The same idea can be found in *Taste of Death* where, despite the death of the Mau Mau fighters, the capacity of the human spirit to resist and endure is clearly portrayed.

Further north: writers from Sudan, Somalia and Ethiopia

Here the cultural context is substantially different from East and Central Africa and the literatures reveal the influence of different religious and philosophical traditions: Islam, Sufism, and Coptic Christianity. Many of these writers have a well-established written literature behind them. For example, El Tayeb Salih (*b.* 1929) writes from an easy familiarity with writers of the Arabic Renaissance such as Taha Husayn, al-Tahtiwi and Muhammed Abduh.

From the northern Sudan, despite his European educational background and career as a Civil Servant, El Tayeb Salih mediates between Sudanese traditional life and western influences. For example, nearly all his fictions are set in Sudanese villages, and he uses their traditional Sufism in which the world is illusory, as a vehicle for his own concerns with reality and illusion. In the short story 'The Cypriote Man' (1972) narrative method, confused time scheme, and his interest in establishing a psychological connection between reality and illusion, show his capacity to fuse traditional settings, Arab literary techniques and a western psychological fiction. His works include *The Wedding of Zein* (1968) and *Season of Migration to the North* (1969).

Nuruddin Farah (*b.* 1945) comes from Baidoa, Somalia, and his novels show thematic variety and technical innovativeness. While *The Naked Needle* (1976) explores cross-cultural influences, *From A Crooked Rib* provides an acute portrayal of a woman's perceptions, and *Sweet and Sour Milk* belongs to the political-detective genre. At the centre of *The Naked Needle* is the burdened consciousness of the hero Koschin: he dominates the relationships between black men and white women in the novel, and his pessimism is a response to the corruption of Somalia's capital, Mogadiscio. Technically experimental, the book is overly dependent upon statement rather than demonstration.

An established writer in Amharic, Daniachew Worku (*b.* 1936) has already published a novel, plays, short stories and poetry in Ethiopia. His novel *The Thirteenth Sun* (1973) studies the tension between generations and the contradictions between old and new in Ethiopia. Goytom's pilgrimage with his aged father and his half-sister Woynitu is set against a harsh, beautiful landscape and a culture where ancient Christianity and local superstition exist side by side. Individual perspectives are held together by the symbolic structure which the background provides.

Conclusion

From the literary barrenness of the early nineteen-sixties East African writing has now become well established with new writers of considerable talent—such as the poets Jared Angira, Jack Mapanje and the novelist Legson Kayira—while the importance of indigenous languages, in particular Kiswahili, as a new literary medium for the region seems likely to increase.

In shaping this new literature two further writers deserve to be singled out, if only briefly: the Kenyan Grace Ogot and the Tanzanian Peter Palangyo. The work of both these writers demonstrates deep interest in the common themes of cultural displacement. Ogot's novel *The Promised Land* (1966) reflects the preoccupation with the land in Kenyan writing of that period while her collections of short stories tend to correlate traditional wisdom with modern situations—as in the story 'Elizabeth'. Her works include two collections of short stories *Land Without Thunder* (1968) and *The Other Woman* (1976). Peter

Palangyo's novel *Dying in the Sun* (1968) offers a close study of a traditional East African village. The protagonist Ntanya expresses the confusion and disillusion caused by the drift to the towns and the frustration he experiences when re-examining his village and family background. Ntanya's gradual apprehension of his identity amidst this society in flux is an accomplished study of the problem.

Southern Africa

The context

From Zimbabwe, through Botswana, Namibia to South Africa, including the states of Swaziland and Lesotho, no other region is so dominated by acute and long-standing racial conflict. Of all Africa, South Africa has been the region open to multi-cultural contact for the longest period; only there has a sizeable European population (over four million), with no ties elsewhere, become established; and only there has the racial and political policy of *Apartheid*, with all its injustice, become law. One result for readers of the literature is the need to be sensitive to the way *Apartheid* has penetrated cultural life: here nearly every stance is 'committed'—for or against the status quo.

The four racial groups of South Africa are dominated by the clash between black and white which began soon after European settlement at the Cape in the sixteen-fifties. The Europeans who settled at this time were of Dutch descent and they were soon joined, between 1688 and 1690, by the French Huguenots: the Afrikaner of today is a descendant of these settlers. The other European component was introduced in the early nineteenth century with the British settlement of Southern Africa and in 1899–1902 the South African War was fought between the Afrikaner Republics and the British Government. This rivalry between Afrikaner and British traditions in South African society still remains and forms one strand of the region's literature. The fact that the Afrikaners have their own national language and literature—Afrikaans—is one indication of the bond that exists between these people and the country they live in. The Coloured community denotes those of mixed race with two minor groups—the Griquas and Cape Malays—the latter group having been introduced by the Dutch East India Company from their Asian colonies. On the other hand the Asian community, predominantly from India, originates from the importation of indentured labour which the British government encouraged in response to the demands of Natal farmers for workers on the sugar plantations in the eighteen-sixties.

Racial relations have almost invariably been conducted in terms of conflict. The Afrikaners fought the British and both fought the blacks. In addition to white–black conflict there were internal hostilities between black tribes, and Shaka of the Zulus is still revered in African tradition and literature for his qualities of leadership along with other names, such as Mzilikazi, founder of the Matabele in Zimbabwe and Mantatisi, Queen of the Sotho.

Afrikaans literature

Literary developments in Southern Africa have a complexity to equal the cultural and political context. Afrikaans literature has astonishing vitality and many of its writers are turning to English in order to secure a wider audience. Its prose has been dominated by Etienne Leroux (*b.* 1922) and writers who have been openly critical of apartheid include André Brink (*b.* 1935), Uys Krige (*b.* 1910), Breyten Breytenbach (*b.* 1939). Other writers such as J.M. Coetzee are equally at home in English and have written all their major work in the English language although they are of Afrikaner descent. In this writing the trend has been to comment on South Africa's racial problems in terms that handle the sensitive material adroitly, to steer between the demands of political commitment and artistic objectivity. Brink in his novels *Looking on Darkness* (1974)—which was banned—and *A Chain of Voices* (1982) uses sexual relations between black and white as a touchstone. Both Brink, in *A Chain of Voices*, and Coetzee, in *In the Heart of the Country* (1977) and *Waiting for the Barbarians* (1980), resort to techniques which approximate myth in order to comment without polemic. The method was used much earlier in the prophetic political allegory by A. Keppel-Jones, *When Smuts Goes* (1947).

The writers who have dominated English writing with its distinguished tradition of liberalism in South Africa include Doris Lessing (*b.* 1919) of Zimbabwe, Nadine Gordimer (*b.* 1923) and Alan Paton (*b.* 1903). Gordimer writes penetratingly of the entombed white minority in novels such as *The Late Bourgeois World* (1966) while her short stories such as *Some Monday for Sure* (1976) define black frustrations. C.J. Driver expores the impasse of white South African revolutionaries in his novels: *Elegy for a Revolutionary* (1969), *Send War in Our Time, O Lord* (1970), *Death of Fathers* (1972), *A Messiah of the Last Days* (1974). A notable exponent of this liberalism is the playwright Athol Fugard (*b.* 1932) and the closing lines of *The Blood Knot* (1968) summarise the connection which links the various racial groups of Southern Africa despite an intransigent political situation:

... You see, we're tied together, ...
It's what they call the blood knot ...
the bond between brothers.

Black writing

The origins of a black national literature have been eagerly sought. Oral literature exists in abundance and much is now readily available through the work of scholars like Mazisi Kunene (*b.* 1930). For a written literature the earliest writing is claimed to be a hymn composed by Ntsikana (*b. circa* 1783) who has been described by the distinguished critic Albert Gérard as 'the first Christian Bard'.* The interest in Ntsikana is that his endeavour might offer the first *individual* composition by a black writer as well as link traditional oral techniques with a new cultural situation.

With the mission settlements the foundation for a new literature was established. John Ross's arrival at the Eastern Cape in 1823 with a Ruthven printing press began a trend and the Lovedale Institution and other presses initiated black writing in both vernaculars and English. Tiyo Soga (*b.* 1829) translated part of *Pilgrim's Progress* in 1867 while encouragement was also given to black journalism: for example John Tengo Jabavu (*b.* 1859) began by editing a mission-sponsored paper but soon established his own. The early generation of black writers in the vernaculars includes John Dube (*b.* 1870), who wrote the first novel in Zulu, *Insila kaShaka* (1930); while another early writer, S.E. Krune Mqhayi (*b.* 1875), apart from novels, poems, essays and biographies, is claimed to have written the first autobiography—a popular genre for later writers—*U-Mqhayi Wase Natabozuko* (1939). Pride of place is normally reserved for Sol T. Plaatje (*b.* 1876) whose *Mhudi: An Epic of South African Native Life a Hundred Years Ago* (1930) is the first novel written (though not published) in English and had the express purpose, as he put it, of interpreting 'to the reading public one phase of "the back of the native mind"'. Other writers whose claims vie with Plaatje's are the brothers R.R.R. Dhlomo (*b.* 1901) and H.I.E. Dhlomo (*b.* 1903). The former wrote the first published novel in English by a black—*An African Tragedy* (1928), while the younger brother was the author both of the first published play in English by a black South African, *The Girl Who Killed To Save: Nongqause the Liberator* (1936), and of the long poem *Valley of a Thousand Hills* (1941). Of the latter Gérard has commented that it is 'to be hailed as the first sustained attempt by a black South African at composing a serious long poem in the alien language of a dominant race'.†

The next generation of black writers in English followed the model of the Dhlomos in working both as authors and journalists. Most of

* Albert S. Gérard, Four African Literatures: *Xhosa, Sotho, Zulu, Amharic*, University of California Press, Berkeley, 1971, p.24.
† Gérard, *Four African Literatures*, p.237.

these writers were born in the nineteen-twenties and their educational background reflects urban life, particularly Sophiatown in Johannesburg (one of the black African townships which were later replaced by Soweto), with St Peter's School and Fort Hare as the centres of formal education. Sophiatown's dynamic urban environment nurtured the nascent literature and its talents; Nat Nakasa wrote that it was the 'only place I know where African writers and aspirant writers ever lived in close proximity, almost as a community'. The writers who belonged to this generation include Peter Abrahams (*b*. 1919), Ezekiel Mphahlele (*b*. 1919), Dennis Brutus (*b*. 1924), Alfred Hutchinson (*b*. 1924), Noni Jabavu (*b*. 1920), Alex La Guma (*b*. 1925), Bloke Modisane (*b*. 1923), Can Themba (*b*. 1924), Todd Matshikiza (*b*. 1924), James Matthews (*b*. 1929), Cosmo Pieterse (*b*. 1930), Mazisi Kunene (*b*. 1930), Richard Rive (*b*. 1931), Arthur Maimane (*b*. 1932) and, a little later, Lewis Nkosi (*b*. 1936) and Nat Nakasa (*b*. 1937).

In the journals which have helped establish black writing in South Africa, the magazine *Drum* has probably been the most formative. Most of the major writers in black South African literature of the nineteen-fifties and sixties figured in *Drum*'s pages, and Ezekiel Mphahlele was the Literary Editor in 1956. The language was an African English with a style which reflected the black American influence on urban black South Africans. In terms of literary development *Drum* provided an outlet for short stories—a genre which, along with autobiography, has dominated South African black writing.

If South African black writing has not yet produced novels to match those of West Africa, its pioneer work in *autobiography* is remarkable. In the nineteen-fifties and sixties autobiographies were produced by Peter Abrahams, *Return to Goli* (1953) and *Tell Freedom* (1954); Ezekiel Mphahlele, *Down Second Avenue* (1959); and Bloke Modisane, *Blame Me on History* (1963). There is a marked trend towards increasing fragmentation, and pressure toward exile, particularly in the later writers whose sectional autobiographies often deal with the decision for exile—as in Alfred Hutchinson's *Road to Ghana* (1960), and Todd Matshikiza's *Chocolates for My Wife* (1961)—or record despair, as in Can Themba's pieces 'The Bottom of the Bottle' and 'Requiem for Sophiatown'. Another version of the autobiography is *Familiarity is the Kingdom of the Lost* (1970) which, jointly produced by Dugmore Boetie (? – 1966) and the editor of the prominent South African magazine *The Classic*, is notable for its skilful witty narrative which features the adventures of a one-legged black ex-convict in a small country town.

Since the suppression of the nineteen-sixties, and the banning of many major black South African writers, the tendency has been for the best writing to be done outside the country—sometimes with tragic consequences, such as the suicide of the poet Arthur Nortje (1942–70) while studying at Cambridge. Of the writers who followed the most accomplished has probably been Bessie Head (*b.* 1937) who has written from Botswana since the mid-sixties. Botswana has provided a base for a circle of exiled black South African writers and artists, the Medu Ensemble. Based in Gaborone with writers such as M.W. Serote (*b.* 1944) and M. Tlali (*b. circa* 1930), the group has written plays—for example, *Shades of Change*—which have been favourably received abroad as well as in Botswana. At the same time a new generation of writers such as D.M. Zwelonkwe, E. Carim, Mtshali (*b.* 1940), A. Maimane, M. Matshoba, and D. Mattera have begun to find a new identity in a situation where political options seem limited to confrontation.

Perhaps the most noticeable contrast with other African writing is that black South African writers have very little interest in traditional life. One exception to this is Noni Jabavu (*b.* 1920), author of two autobiographical works *Drawn in Colour: African Contrasts* (1960) and *The Ochre People: Scenes from a South African Life* (1963); she, however, was brought up in an exclusive mission environment and left for England when she was fouteen. For the rest, the appalling political and racial facts, in conjunction with an established urban black culture now remote from traditional life, make reliance upon traditional culture inappropriate. What has been called the 'kola nut and masks' theme of West African writing simply has no corresponding basis in South Africa.

Regional distinctions

Free from apartheid, and without large urbanised, sophisticated black communities, other areas of the region have begun to develop literatures in English. Botswana with its agencies, the National Institute for Development and Cultural Research and The National Popular Theatre Workshop, and its fortunate history when 'British Protection' (which was aimed at securing the railway to the interior) kept it from absorption either by Rhodesia or South Africa, has begun to establish a literature. Lesotho, more quiescent, has had the early example of Thomas Mofolo (1876–1948) whose writings in Sesotho for the Morija mission included *Chaka* (1925), one of the first of many on this subject and an early classic; while in Swaziland recent writers include Xolile Guma and Chicks Nkosi; in Zambia the fiction of Dominic Mulaisho (*b.* 1933), whose lack of reverence for the past and determination to shape the future contrasts with other writers in the region.

In these regions, and in Zimbabwe, it has been possible to draw on the past and tradition: something not attempted by most South African writers. For example, the writers in Shona, the poets Wilson Chivaura

(1927–1968) and H.W. Chitepo whose *Soko Risina Musoro* ('The Tale without a Head') (1958) has become an early classic as the first epic poem in Shona, have tended to idealise a past golden age. Their peer, Solomon M. Mutswairo, has also written historical novels: *Mapondera: Soldier of Zimbabwe* (1978) and *Chaminuka: Prophet of Zimbabwe* (1978) which, with Chivaura's and Chitepo's works show how nostalgia can be used for lyrical but pungent political commentary. Other novelists, Stanlake Samkange (*b.* 1922) for example, have followed this use of history in English writing while others writing in Shona await translation. Of the latter T.K. Tzodzo is a good example, with *Pafunge*, a novel that was translated from Shona into English in 1975. Tzodzo is also the author of the first play in English by a MuShona, *The Talking Calabash* (1971).

1. FROM RHODESIA TO ZIMBABWE

Lessing and Style

Doris Lessing (*b.* 1919) is at home neither in Africa nor in Europe. Her left-wing alienated stance, her strongly feminist perceptions, and her prolific output have generated a critical industry, especially in the United States. *The Grass is Singing* (1950) reflects her origins in Rhodesia. Through its heroine, a town girl married to a farmer and uncertain how to conduct relationships with black servants, Doris Lessing provides a classic study in Africa's black–white relations which also echoes Olive Schreiner's (1855–1920) *Story of an African Farm* in its reflection of women's sensibilities in a man's world. Yet while Doris Lessing has been the international literary figure in Southern Africa, it is Colin Style's unobtrusive criticism and sponsorship of the arts, as well as his own steady work in poetry, that have encouraged the development of literature in Zimbabwe beyond the narrow type of colonial poetry which has abounded.

Samkange, Mungoshi and Marechera

To Stanlake Samkange (*b.* 1922) belongs the credit of the first novel by a black Zimbabwean, *On Trial for My Country* (1964). This work is of unusual interest because it echoes Olive Schreiner's *Trooper Peter Halkett of Mashonaland* (1897) which used the same device of a dream to comment, with equal force, on the same historical events. Professor Samkange reconstructs the events that led to the establishment of Rhodesia in the eighteen-nineties with a sense of detail that sometimes incorporates the actual words of Rhodes, Selous and Jameson. Rhodes's and Lobengula's motivations are satirically revealed through a dream in which both are on trial before their ancestors, and the futility of tradition is exposed: for example, Mzilikazi, interrogating Lobengula, asks, 'Was there no other way out of your dilemma?' and Lobengula replies, 'I did consider marrying the queen...'. If this work is compared with Samkange's *The Year of the Uprising* (1978), similarities will be noted. Again he reconstructs history, in this case the Mhondoro Cult which inspired a rebellion against white rule in 1896. Next, the effect is largely satirical: the comparison of two markedly different religious views provides opportunity for this—and Christianity does not fare very well. Samkange's foray into 'autobiography', *The Mourned One* (1975), is a heart-rending account of racial injustice which yearns for a pastoral golden age when Zimbabwe was uncolonised, and exposes the emotions which fuel his satirical vendettas.

The Coming of the Dry Season (1972), the first collection of short stories by Charles Mungoshi, was soon banned in Rhodesia, as was his first novel in English, *Waiting for the Rain* (1975). Mungoshi writes in both Shona and English, one of his Shona novels being *Ndiko Kupindana Kwama* ('The Passing Days'). While these works deal with the conflict between old and new, familiarity of theme does not detract from the perception and energy with which he writes. The resources of Shona itself, in which descriptions and names appear as metaphors, add richness to his translated style. Yet his protagonist, estranged from both old and new allegiances, is a highly developed individual character in a dilemma that resonates throughout the new literatures:

> ... to put roots on the fire with the same hand that makes the sign of the cross and mouth incantations to the ancestors with the same mouth that addresses the God of the Bible—that, he feels, is going a bit too far. It may be held against him as blasphemy. So he prays neither to his ancestors nor to the God of the Bible.

In Dambudzo Marechera's (*b.* 1955) works the sense of estrangement is taken to an extreme and a new direction in Zimbabwean writing can be identified. First the protagonists are estranged from Zimbabwe itself: a self-imposed exile has been chosen. Second, the protagonists are cut off from others by their mixture of guilt and despair. Third, the style of writing itself is sardonic and impressionistic; precisely adjusted to suggest a consciousness which has broken from reality; a mind driven into itself by an outside world where escape must be sought on whatever terms are possible—whether in exile, drink, madness or death.

The title of *House of Hunger* (1978) presents an image of Zimbabwe as a place where the past is irrelevant in an intolerable present. On the surface a collection of short stories, the work retains its unity through the pervasive sense of spiritual destitution in which education and sex, like nearly every other aspect of life, are versions of domination and usually a consequence of white domination. Here childhood and environment present a process of brutalisation in which feelings are eroded by the necessity to survive.

Black Sunlight (1980) advances both this technique and the alienated stance. The protagonist, Christian, is rootless. A photographer, he documents chaotic human experience:

> So this is humankind. Swinging. Backwards and forwards. Swinging through history. . . . You have no meaning. I have no meaning. The meaning is in the swinging. And that is ridiculous. Absurd.

Style has been pared to the subject and it echoes the disenchanted surreal perspectives which the fictions of Joyce, Beckett, Armah and Soyinka achieve. By comparison with the novels of a writer such as Wilson Katiyo (*b.* 1947)—*A Son of the Soil* (1976) and *Going to Heaven* (1979)—with their plots that concentrate upon black–white relations and unexceptional political comment—Marechera has pressed toward a stage where even political action is dubious.

Drama: a note

While drama has been relatively slow to develop, there is little doubt about the increasing popularity of this genre. This has been particularly the case in Botswana where plays such as B.L. Leshoai's *The Wake* have been welcomed as they convey not just the explosive racial issues of the region but an identity for the future.

2. WRITERS IN THE REPUBLIC OF SOUTH AFRICA

Peter Abrahams

For critics who expect certain themes and styles to dominate African literature, the works of Peter Abrahams (*b.* 1919) are an embarrassment. Abrahams began writing a decade before Achebe and although nearly all his works are dominated by South African themes, his characters tend to be contrived and, for contemporary taste, unconvincing. For example in one of his stories the protagonist is nursed by a prostitute who is emotionally innocent, 'I never gave myself to any of them', she says; a situation which anticipates Elzie Bezuidenhout of his later novel *Wild Conquest* who, despite her rape by Koos Jansen, remains emotionally unscarred and able to welcome her lover Paul van As. It is Abrahams's tendency to skim the surface rather than penetrate the depth of emotions, his inclination to amiable actions and optimism, which fail to ring true for many contemporary African writers.

His first four works show Abrahams's understanding of South Africa's racial situation and his own freedom as a 'Coloured' to move about within it. In the short stories of *Dark Testament* (1942) the themes of the later novels are anticipated while at the same time the literary artist, his self-consciousness and his use of a blend of feeling and technique, are vividly present. In brief, he provides a picture of a man who is set apart from the society he seeks to define: 'And with my pen and my burning heart I built canvas after canvas. The words became pictures. The pictures became stories. The stories became people.'

Building on *Dark Testament*, *Song of the City* (1945) is an ambitious mural of Johannesburg and South African society on the eve of the Second World War. Radicals (both black and white) reflect the tragic quality of a divided but enmeshed society. *Mine Boy* (1946) has a tighter focus with its concentration upon Xuma, a new arrival in Johannesburg. In the decrepit 'Daddy' Francis Ndabula, fouling himself on the floor of a Johannesburg shebeen, and in Xuma's Zulu girlfriend Eliza who claims, 'Inside I am not black and I do not want to be a black person', Abrahams sees the consequences of a society where hopes are raised but frustrated. In *The Path of Thunder* (1948) the focus is upon the issues of paternity and love across the colour line as Lanny Swartz eventually elopes with Sarie Villiers: although the novel closes on a note of violence the human relationships merge with the landscape itself to form an integrated work that is perhaps his most successful.

The next stage of Abrahams's writing is marked by more ambitious approaches. In *Wild Conquest* (1950) Boer and Zulu meet, both sides are shown, their strengths and weaknesses. Though much criticised, the work marks a new attempt to define a complex situation with something like objectivity, and in Paul van As, his willingness to learn from black Africans, the work closes with a token of hope for the future. Set in a fictitious African state, *A Wreath for Udomo* (1956) employs a similar objectivity in its study of a modern African political leader, his rise to power and his betrayal. This dispassionate (but not indifferent) stance recurs in both *A Night of Their Own* (1965) and *This Island Now* (1966) where the 'lump in my throat and the burning anger in my heart and mind' of the 'autobiography' *Return to Goli* (1953) are ever present. In the former there is the thriller formula of political subversion; set in South Africa it explores the web of friendships and relations that cross the colour line. In the latter, *This Island Now*, Moses Joshue, radical black leader turned tyrant, is the protagonist in a political allegory. Set in the Caribbean the story is not confined to the region and marks a new development in the political novel as a genre, at least in its application to African subjects. Simplicity and economy enable it to function as a parable: the island is a microcosm and Joshue's remarks indicate the scope of the work: 'Tell me how we can do a job, which I know you agree needs to be done, without soiling our hands?'

Alex La Guma

Although a defendant in South Africa's Treason Trial (1956) and one who has suffered greatly from *apartheid* since his exile, Alex La Guma's writing continues to reflect his devotion to his homeland. A 'Cape Coloured', born in Cape Town and a one-time member of the City Council, La Guma writes from his own knowledge and experience, and one incident from his early novella *A Walk in the Night* (1962), when the protagonist, Adonis, is being questioned by two white policemen, shows his marriage of technique and subject:

> You learned from experience to gaze at some spot on their uniforms, the button of a pocket, or the bright smoothness of their Sam Browne belts, but never into their eyes, for that would be taken as an affront by them. It was only the very brave, or the very stupid, who dared to look straight into the law's eyes, to challenge them or to question their authority.

This passage suggests a process of dehumanisation: its details of clothing suggest distance and non-communication across a colour line enforced by violence. La Guma similarly recreates his early life in South Africa, and the formative powers of the environment—in this case District Six, Cape Town's old equivalent of Harlem—and his characters, while static, mirror their society.

Although *A Walk in the Night* was banned in South Africa, La Guma continued with his descriptions of life in Cape Town where his second novel *And a Threefold Cord* (1964), written during a period of house arrest, was set in one of the outlying shanty towns. Here junk and dirt conjoin with the wet and dreary atmosphere of a Cape winter, and against these hostile elements he celebrates the power of a fringe community to hold together.

Descriptive powers and the ability to convey meaning by oblique means are less obvious in La Guma's later novels. *The Stone Country* (1967) concentrates on Georg Adams, a political prisoner in Cape Town whose character contrasts with the disgusting situation in which he has been placed. At the worst the story shows La Guma's own despair and his stylistic tendency towards statements of morality rather than the presentation he achieved in short stories such as 'A Glass of Wine' where the hopeless love of a white boy and a coloured girl could eloquently but silently state the evil of South Africa's Immorality Laws.

In *In the Fog of the Season's End* (1972) and *Time of the Butcher-bird* (1979) La Guma's political analysis of South Africa's affairs continues. The two main characters, Elias Tekwane and Beukas, are primarily means of defining alternative political responses. While Beukas echoes Adams of *The Stone Country* and Charlie Pauls in *And a Threefold Cord*, here character and detail have given way to a formula which, however 'committed', verges on cliché. The contrast with the short stories again is useful when *Time of the Butcherbird* is considered. Set in the karroo*, this novel offers a brutal but disorganised plot without the subtlety and perceptiveness of the short stories which contained their moral within a sufficiently substantial art form. If this is compared with say 'Blankets', the dangers of 'commitment' for the literary artist are demonstrated.

Dennis Brutus

Although he was born (in 1924) in Zimbabwe, Denis Brutus's parents were South Africans and all his literary and political activity reflects this. Educated at Fort Hare and Witwatersrand, in 1963 Brutus was arrested for his political activities and sentenced to eighteen months' hard labour on Robben Island, a grim penal institution near Cape Town. He left South Africa in 1966 and has been the most prominent black South African writer to continue political activities aimed at South Africa's international isolation: in particular he has worked for SANROC (South African Non-Racial Olympic Committee) and the International Defense and Aid Fund. His collections of verse include *Letters to Martha* (1968), *Sirens, Knuckles, Boots* (1963), *A Simple Lust* (1973), and *A Stubborn Hope* (1978).

Letters to Martha (1968) was written from prison in the form of supposed letters, when he was forbidden all other writing which might have been intended for publication. In these poems the essential features of Brutus's work are to be found: acute sensitivity shaped by the South African experience; responsiveness to human drama and beauty; anger that resonates with a sense of prophetic mission. These various strands are interwoven with fine spare poetry that despite its 'commitment' seldom lapses into polemic. Above all else Brutus is a disciplined writer who exacts a pattern from experience, as he says of Robben Island in ' "Letter" 10':

... The discipline does much to force
a shape and pattern on one's daily life...

While the poems never lack a deep concern for the human waste and misery of oppression and prison, they also demonstrate Brutus's use of images to secure identity: for example South Africa as a waste or a void. So, in his cell, he can say:

---

* A high pastoral tableland in South Africa.

but in the grey silence of the empty afternoons
it is not uncommon
to find oneself talking to God

('Letter 4')

In 'Letter 9' the idea is extended:

I send these fragments,
random pebbles I pick up
from the landscape of my own experience,
traversing the same arid wastes
in a montage of glimpses
I allow myself
or stumble across.

These elements are further extended when Brutus fuses prison life with
the weather, and Robben Island itself becomes a metaphor, as in the
poem 'On The Island':

Cement-grey floors and walls
cement-grey days
cement-grey time
and grey susurration
as of seas breaking
winds blowing
and rains drizzling

Anger is another strand in Brutus's poetry along with his political activities which have embarrassed South Africa in a variety of areas—particularly sport. 'Let me say it' both vents anger and provides catharsis
as he reverses roles and anticipates ultimate victory:

their great New Zealand rivals
the Olympic panoply and Wembley roar
for them these things are dead
are inaccessible
unattainable

waiting for the time of achievement
which will come if God wills
when I flog fresh lashes across these thieves.

Brutus's spare poetry—reflecting Chinese models, for example in
China Poems (1975)—expresses his fundamental concern with metaphysics. While poems such as 'Prayer' are set pieces in this type of writing, he is at his most speculative when addressing himself to the problem of evil in a poem such as 'Our aims our dreams our destinations'
where he questions the nature of God:

Is He the Infinite Hangman?
Executioner?
Torturer?

Must we be driven to the edge,
racked on the precipice of the world?

Here art has been hammered out of pain, and commitment has been maintained without degenerating into polemic, while these poems attempt both to 'find hope' and to establish confidence in a future 'transfigured humanity!'

Ezekiel Mphahlele

I must be buried in my country in my own homeland, my bones must replenish the black earth from whence it came, our bones must fertilize the ground on which we walk or else we shall never walk as men and women in the 21st century.*

These remarks summarise Ezekial Mphahlele's (b. 1919) reasons for his return to South Africa from a self-exile which had lasted from 1957 to 1977. He returned as a writer who had done more than almost any other African to establish modern African literature. Apart from numerous uncollected essays, poems, short stories and reviews his literary output has been substantial: three collections of short stories, *Man Must Live* (1947), *The Living and the Dead* (1961), *In Corner B* (1967); two volumes of critical essays, *The African Image* (1962), *Voices in the Whirlwind* (1972); a seminal autobiography, *Down Second Avenue* (1959); a novel, *The Wanderers* (1972); as well as two anthologies of African writing, *African Writing Today* (1967) and *Modern African Stories* (1964).

Like Peter Abrahams's, Mphahlele's response to the racial predicament in South Africa has been to affirm qualities held in common across the colour line. So his autobiography *Down Second Avenue* reflected not just racial tensions but domestic pressures within the Mphahlele household. In his short stories he concentrated upon 'people as people rather than political victims' and, consequently, 'their own ghetto life and their own little dramas and tragedies'. However, unlike Abrahams, Mphahlele is more adroit: political and social implications spring from his stories without the sense of contrivance and superficiality never quite absent from Abrahams's writing. For example, the story 'Dinner at Eight' offers an insight into the implications of a superficial white liberalism, and succeeds without any facile

* Sonia Sanchez, 'A letter to Ezekiel Mphahlele', *The American Poetry Review*, September/October 1977, p.30.

polarisation of values. As Miss Pringle, a social worker, has the African paralytic, Mzondi, to dinner, Mphahlele presents both liberal exhibitionism and the tragic consequences of a dehumanising condition.

In a situation of racial polarisation Mphahlele has refused to adopt a racial stance. As Secretary of the African National Congress he attended the First All-African Peoples' Conference held in Accra in December 1958 where he vigorously defended the notion of a multi-racial society in South Africa, and he has argued that negritude, despite its role in French Africa, has tended to falsify reality. He contrasts this concept with the South African attitude:

> We in South Africa have for the last 300 years of oppression been engaged in a bloody struggle against white supremacy—to assert our *human* and not African dignity. This latter we have always taken for granted. During these three centuries, we, the Africans have been creating an urban culture out of the very conditions of insecurity, exile and agony. We have done this by integrating Africa and the West.*

Although this vision of a mingling of traditions runs counter to the assertion of a specifically African identity, he has never abandoned it.

The Wanderers marks an adjustment in this view. While technically masterful in the reproduction of the varieties of African English it is essentially about exile and the penalty of rootlessness. Timi and Karabo leave South Africa for an indigent existence as writer and teacher; their son Felang eventually leaves 'home'—never having known one—and in the end is killed as a freedom-fighter trying to penetrate Zimbabwe. His death implies that a consequence of being 'disinherited' is the need to make some self-discovery. In this Mphahlele concedes the practical necessity of a black identity alongside a broader humanism—'even if I must reserve my humanism for those of my colour and fight power with the instruments of its own enthronement'.

If *The Wanderers* is compared with Mphahlele's recent novel *Chirundu* (1979) a sharper political awareness becomes obvious. Against South Africa's isolation in modern Africa, Mphahlele studies the human defects of power in independent Africa, its optimism and disillusionment, through the person of Chirundu himself who is symbolised by *nsato*, the python—an image which pervades the work. Again human and specifically African elements are the constant reference points in his writing.

* Ezekiel Mphahlele, 'Remarks on Negritude', *African Writing Today*, Penguin Books, Harmondsworth, 1967, p.247.

Mazisi Kunene

By contrast with Mphahlele's emphasis upon the human drama and its complexity, Mazisi Kunene's (*b.* 1930) particular response to the literary and human problems of South Africa has been to affirm both Zulu history and oral literature. Alongside this cultural stance he has taken an active part in the South Africa ANC and the Anti-Apartheid movement in Britain.

Emperor Shaka the Great (1979) is Kunene's reworking of Zulu oral history and has been a means of opening established theories of African poetry to new possibilities. Whereas many African poets—Soyinka and Okigbo for example—have consciously aligned themselves with universal modern trends, Kunene has followed the idiom of African oral poetry and retained the taut, coherent structure of it imagery, which achieves its effects by means of an accumulation of metaphors:

> The day stretched its horizons.
> The skies were adorned with red tails of dawn;
> The sun lashed down on the earth; it lashed on the stone.
> The dew vanished suddenly from the blades of grass.
> Such sweet scent of the wild plants would soon become drenched
>   with blood.

A reason for Kunene's commitmet to traditional forms is his perception that African 'elites' have been guilty of collaboration with Europeans by adopting western modes. As Lewis Nkosi has put it, at the extreme of this condition are those who are 'not only "educated" in the colonising power's sense but also who are so totally sterilised of their own culture that they are foreign in their own country'.

Creating the new

After the exiles of the nineteen-fifties with writers such as Bloke Modisane and Nat Nakasa leaving South Africa, a new generation of black South African writers began to emerge in the sixties and seventies which responded to the new urban situation and a changed political climate where Uhuru was the norm and South Africa an isolated exception. Responses varied: in Modikwe Dikobe's novel *The Marabi Dance* (1973) the marriage of Martha to Sephai mirrors the mutual incomprehension of urban and rural African life in South Africa; by contrast D.M. Zwelonkwe's *Robben Island* (1973) is written from personal experience and the narrator-protagonist tells the story of Bekimpi, a thug who becomes a political martyr. Unfortunately Bekimpi's motivations are vague, yet the novel asserts a vigorous individuality despite all that might dehumanise.

With the publication of *Sounds of a Cowhide Drum* (1971), Oswald Mbuyiseni Mtshali (*b*. 1950) took South Africa by storm: Nadine Gordimer announced, 'There is a new poet in Africa...'. Mtshali writes against the context of Soweto (South West Townships), the conglomeration of suburbs on the fringe of Johannesburg in which a new black South African consciousness is being affirmed. Violence and horror are set alongside beauty, and the note of protest is sustained by artistic dexterity. In poems such as 'This Kid is No Goat' and 'The Detribalized' the vision is satiric:

> Where have
> All the angry young men gone?
> Gone to the Island of Lament for Sharpeville.
> Gone overseas on scholarship,
> Gone up North to milk and honeyed uhuru.
> Gone to the dogs with the drink of despair.
>
> ('This Kid is No Goat')

> He knows
> he must carry a pass.
> He don't care for politics
> He don't go to church
> He knows Sobukwe
> He knows Mandela
> They're in Robben Island.
> 'So what? That's not my business!'
>
> ('The Detribalised')

At the same time Mtshali masterfully identifies those situations and emotions that shape life and form the substance of tragedy, as in 'Boy on a Swing', where to the movement of the swing:

> The four cardinal points
> meet in his head.
>   Mother!
> Where did I come from?
> When will I wear long trousers?
> Why was my father jailed?

This query of innocence is both a lacerating condemnation and the expression of a generous and perceptive imagination.

Keorapetse Kgositsile's (*b*. 1938) poetry with its black American idiom suggests Harlem rather than South Africa. At a relatively early age Kgositsile studied in America and absorbed the vehemence and invective of black radicals; his language deploys colloquialisms and scatological images, while polemic replaced a honed verse form, as, for example, in these lines from *My Name is Afrika* (1971):

Now
from the asshole of america
gutter smells rush
the blood like
a stampede to the head

(p.55)

Yet there is also a self-awareness which distinguishes his verse from the gimmicky material that it sometimes imitates. Kgositsile exhausts the language at his disposal against apartheid and his style echoes that fatigue, even as he considers the value of a literary response:

I have aspired to express, all these years,
elegant past the most eloquent word. But here now our
tongue dies into maggots . . .

Of 'Coloured' descent, Don Mattera has been subject to a banning order which was renewed in 1978 for a period of five years. He has been active in the Coloured Labour Party and the Black People's Convention. His literary predecessors include Bloke Modisane and Can Themba while his writing straddles the period from Sharpeville (notorious as the place where in 1960 police shot sixty-nine blacks demonstrating against South Africa's Pass Laws) to the new assertiveness of Soweto. *Gone with the Twilight* is an autobiography that evokes the richness of Sophiatown when races could still mingle, while his poems deal with both the depersonalisation effected by apartheid and the guilt of a white community that tolerates its continuance. Yet there is no hatred, only love for his country—as the poem 'God Bless Africa' demonstrates. An often quoted example of his capacity for isolating the truly significant detail and singling out the appalling irony is the poem which makes its play upon that revealing South African word, 'Baas':

Each morning
    corner of Pritchard and Joubert
    leaning on a dusty crutch
    near a pavement dust-bin
    an old man begs
    not expecting much

His spectacles are cracked and dirty
and does not see my black hand
drop a cent into his scurvey palm
but instinctively he mutters:
        Thank you my Baas!
Strange, that for a cent
a man can call his brother, Baas.

Mongane Wally Serote (*b*. 1944) is another poet who has interpreted the awareness of a new generation of black South African writers with exceptional lyrical accomplishment. The reason for the abundance of black poets—rather than novelists—in recent years has been explained by Mtshali in these terms:

> ... the urgency of the situation does not allow time to sit down and pen a lengthy piece on writing as demanded by a novel. Another factor against a novel is that poetry, music and drama can be shared with many other people at the same time. But a novel can only be read alone.*

Two collections of verse and one lengthy poem—*Yakhal'inkomo* (1972), *Tsetlo* (1974), and *No Baby Must Weep* (1975) respectively—stand to Serote's credit as well as short stories such as 'When Rebecca Fell'. While he can be delicate and sensuous in poems such as 'Night-Time' it is his assertiveness which marks the new stage of literary development.

> White people are white people
> They must learn to listen.
> Black people are black people
> They must learn to talk.

Writers who have attempted lengthier forms of fiction—as well as some poetry—include M.B. Mzamane with his short stories *My Cousin Comes to Jo'burg* and the novel based on the Soweto uprising in June 1976, *The Children of Soweto* (1981), as well as Lauretta Ngcobo, whose first novel was *Cross of Gold* (1981). Others are Sipho Sepamla (*b*. 1932), whose *The Root is One* (1979) covers six days in a township —'Johnstown'—where local opposition to a forced movement of the inhabitants provokes violence. The story concerns the tragedy of Juda Baloyi: the results of the move are betrayal of friends, the loss of his girlfriend and, ultimately, his own suicide. A concluding observation summarises the tragic dimension: 'Each had been harassed by the moment and, in a desperate bid for survival, had dug his own grave.' In Enver Carim's novels *Golden City* (1970) and *A Dream Deferred* (1973) a new black urban and political consciousness emerges. *Golden City* is a vivid celebration of life in Johannesburg while *A Dream Deferred*, with its extravagant lyricism, imagines an outbreak of urban guerilla warfare. The latter work offers some acute insights into aspects of black–white relations, particularly the violence done to white perception by the role of oppressor.

---

* C. Heywood (ed.), *Aspects of South African Literature*, Heinemann Educational, London, 1976, p.127.

Two women writers: Miriam Tlali and Bessie Head

Miriam Tlali's (*b. circa* 1930) first novel *Muriel at Metropolitan* (1979), is a collection of thinly veiled autobiographical sketches with sharp perceptions of a social situation and its ironies. On the other hand Bessie Head (*b.* 1937) has progressively assumed a dominant position in African letters as a woman writer. Of mixed race, she always writes from the outside, from the perspective of the oppressed minority: as a woman; a 'Coloured' who is received by neither blacks nor whites; as an 'exile' in Botswana where all her stories are set. Her works include: *When Rain Clouds Gather* (1968), *Maru* (1971), *A Question of Power* (1974), *Serowe: Village of the Rain-Wind* (1981) and *The Collector of Treasures* (1977)—this last being a collection of short stories.

When Rain Clouds Gather is a simple narrative in which Makhaya escapes South Africa to find sanctuary in Botswana. Bessie Head explores the complex tensions within the protagonist and the process of adjustment to a new life. In *Maru* the experience of being a racial outsider in Botswana is given substance while in *A Question of Power* alienation is pushed to a new extreme as the central character, a Coloured South African exile in Botswana, has a total mental breakdown. In this the insanity of a private world and that of a society divided by apartheid come together in terrifying hallucinations. In *The Collector of Treasures* another strand of Bessie Head's concerns is demonstrated: all these stories address aspects of women's experience and trace the forms of oppression. (In the story which provides the title to the whole Dikeledi finally castrates her brutal husband.) In brief, there is a coherence and continuity within these themes which reflect evils personally endured.

Chapter 4
The Indian sub-continent

THE INDIAN SUB-CONTINENT is a vast area of physical and human geo-graphy and its landmass is home to a complex variety of languages and religions. Political factors have further divided this mix—the partition of India, Pakistan's fragmentation and Sri Lanka's autonomy—and while each of these regions has an identifiable literature of its own, India itself, in size and literature, dominates the entire sub-continent. English has long been the mother tongue of one of India's recognised communities, the Eurasians, and, for practical reasons, it has neces-sarily been the language through which India communicates with the international community and, indeed, through which Indians from different language groups communicate with each other.

Since the Indian constitution recognises thirteen official languages which have both regional interests and distinctive literatures, it is not surprising that the identity of Indian literature is contentious. Indo-Anglian literature is the oldest of the 'new' literatures in English, and while Indian writing has not produced a Tutuola to refashion Indian English, some writers have adapted English to the Indian experience: for example in *Kanthapura* Raja Rao (*b*. 1909) adjusts sentence struc-ture to suggest a South Indian peasant version of English from Kan-nada; on a different tack Narayan resorts to the tone of the bazaar story-teller, although his idiom generally remains standard English.

Another factor is the effect of English and its literary forms, espe-cially prose, upon the indigenous literatures: for example Arunacala's attempts at blending written and spoken forms of Tamil tradition into a new prose style; or Malayalam writers such as Asan, Ullor and Valla-thol who experimented with the novel in the eighteen-eighties, as did Vetarayakam Pillai and Rajan Aiyar in Kannada. In the twentieth cen-tury writers in the vernacular languages abound and reflect the diversity of the sub-continent. Despite variety enforced by racial characteristics, there is a surprising unity which contrasts with the fragmentation of, for example, Africa. This unity within diversity registers the dominance and pervasiveness of Aryan Hindu culture which has proven to be remarkably accommodating to regional and credal differences.

The beginnings

In some ways India is a state of mind as well as a place: its diversity of cultures and its contrasts have greatly appealed to Europeans, and a substantial literature testifies to the fascination of the 'East'. For English society it was the colonial officials, the orientalists and the army officers, who took back home legends of opulence and violence, and fostered romance about the Raj. In this Anglo-Indian writers such as Rudyard Kipling (1865–1936) with his short stories and, in particular, his novel *Kim* (1901), established a literature which perpetuated and gave coherence to popular romance. With Edwin Arnold (1832–1904), Kipling and E.M. Forster (1879–1970) a literature began which was to provide both entertainment and exploration of racial and political tensions continued today by writers such as John Masters (*b*. 1914).

The first phase (1800–1920)

For Indo-Anglian writing the beginnings are symbolised by the founding of Fort William College in Calcutta in 1800. Between 1813 and 1923 dictionaries, grammars and English-language newspapers implemented a process of anglicisation, while William Carey's (1761–1834) Baptist press, set up outside Calcutta in 1823, both accelerated this process and stimulated awareness of regional cultures. Already, with a touch of irony, English became the medium for the assertion of India's identity and its cultures. The vernaculars were studied and taught to colonials while the increased awareness among Indians of indigenous regional culture stimulated demand for access to the instruments of western education.

During his term of office in India, as member of the supreme council, the British statesman and historian Thomas Macaulay (1800–59) produced what was to become known as 'Macaulay's Minute' (1835). The aim of Macaulay's Minute was simple: 'to form a class who may be interpreters between us and the millions whom we govern; a class of persons, Indian in blood and colour, but English in taste, in opinions, in morals, and in intellect'. This set the stamp of anglicisation upon the educated classes and Indians learned to memorise more of Chaucer, Shakespeare and Milton than many Englishmen. At the same time technology accelerated the change, demanding mastery of English which was both a 'door' to the new learning and a 'bridge' between cultures.

One of the earliest advocates of English as a 'bridge' was the Bengali scholar and linguist Raja Rammohan Roy (1774–1833) who sought to reform Hindu culture through western thought. Contemporary with

Roy were other writers for whom Indian subjects were paramount: Indian themes, landscape and history were all detailed in the language of Wordsworth (1770–1850), Byron (1788–1824) and Keats (1795–1821); for example the Eurasian writer Henry Louis Vivian Derozio (1809–1831) with his long narrative poem *The Fakir of Jhungheera*. Poets such as Michael Madhusudan Dutt (1824–1873) with his *The Captive Lady* (1849) mark the beginning of Indo-Anglian romanticism that culminated in Sri Aurobindo (1872–1950), Manmohan Ghose (1869–1924) and Rabindranath Tagore (1861–1941). During the height of Indo-Anglian romanticism came Toru Dutt (1856–77) who, apart from the later examples of Aurobindo and Tagore, was the most successful Indian poet in the English medium: she travelled in both France and England and her two novels, one in French and one in English, and poems—*Ancient Ballads and Legends of Hindustan* (1882)—were published posthumously. With the First World War this romanticism ended, as in English literature, and the first stage of Indo-Anglian literature closed. The outstanding writers of this phase are Aurobindo, Ghose, Tagore and Sir Muhammed Iqbal (1876–1938) whose poetry in Urdu, Persian and English made him the spiritual founder of Pakistan. From now on the emphasis was to change from poetry, and its romantic preoccupations, to prose.

The second phase

Prose was the natural medium for the writers who reacted against the models of 'renaissance' leaders such as Tagore while the examples of Ezra Pound (1885–1927) and T.S. Eliot (1888–1965) in English literature encouraged post-war experimentation in surrealism and symbolism. Social realism and the reform movement generated by liberal humanist ideals began to gather force and assumed a national and 'militant' form between 1920 and 1940 under the leadership of Mahatma Gandhi (1869–1948). Novels such as S.K. Venkataraman's *Kandan the Patriot* (1932) and *Murugan the Tiller* (1927) promoted the ideals of *satyagraha* (Gandhi's programme of non-violence) and summoned Indians to work for national regeneration and political freedom. While later disillusionment turned many writers to a more radical social commitment, often in a Marxist form (as in the case of Premchand), the novels of the thirties by Mulk Raj Anand and Raja Rao echo Venkataraman's themes. Yet both these writers are indebted to American and European models: introspection, political and psychological analysis, colloquial style and experimentation dominate. In particular Anand's blend of ideology and social realism prevailed and ensured that prose would be the medium for the definition of a new India and its aspirations.

From the thirties to the forties

R.K. Narayan's famous town, Malgudi, appeared in his first novel in 1935 and his ironic but sympathetic studies of this imaginary South Indian community have firmly established him in world literature. Narayan spans the traumas of the Second World War and partition while R. Prawer Jhabvala's (*b.* 1937) fiction focuses upon Indian family life. However for other writers with strong instincts for narrative, notably Manohar Malgonkar (*b.* 1914) and Kushwant Singh (*b.* 1915), partition and the war were more influential themes, while Kamala Markandaya (*b.* 1924) and Anita Desai (*b.* 1937) concentrated upon complex novel forms marked by nuances of alienation, self-analysis and personal problems. Although these elements are given an Indian context, the influence of Europe—through James Joyce (1882–1941), Franz Kafka (1883–1924), André Gide (1869–1951) and Albert Camus (1913–60)—is obvious. Other major fiction writers include G.V. Desani (*b.* 1909), Nirad Chaudhuri, Sudin N. Ghose (*b.* 1899), Bhabani Bhattacharya (*b.* 1906) and Arun Joshi.

Poetry and drama

By comparison with the vernacular languages where they have flourished, for Indo-Anglian literature these two genres have been minor modes of expression: epic range and the definition of society have been left to the novelists. Astringent criticism has, however, come from poets who have consciously sought to find a new role for Indian poetry in English, and leaders in this have been Nissim Ezekiel (*b.* 1924), P. Lal (*b.* 1929), Kamala Das (*b.* 1934), and Dom Moraes (*b.* 1938). Likewise notable in contemporary verse are A.K. Ramanujan (*b.* 1929), Pritish Nandy (*b.* 1947), R. Parthasarathy (*b.* 1934) and Adil Jussawalla (*b.* 1940). On the other hand drama, despite its early beginnings in 1832 (*The Persecuted* by K.M. Banerji), has not yet overcome problems of realistic dramatic discourse. Poetic drama has attempted to breach the impasse but the number of writers in this medium is very small—Gieve Patel and Nissim Ezekiel being the most notable.

Although there are exceptions to such an oversimplification, the evolution of Indo-Anglian writing is generally from poetry to prose, from romanticism to social realism. The initial dominance of poetry is probably a reflection of the substantial poetic tradition in the Indian vernaculars where the epics had been translated from the Sanskrit and, at the same time, the importance of poetry in English culture at the time of Derozio and those who came after him. The switch to prose reflected the changed political and cultural circumstances which required a more sustained form.

Other literary forms

There has been a long and well-established tradition in Indo-Anglian writing of journalism and political speech-making which includes Ved Mehta (*b*. 1934), Mahatma Gandhi, Jawaharlal Nehru (1889–1964), M.N. Roy and Jayaprakash Narayan. Nirad Chaudhuri (*b*. 1897) has produced the classic autobiography of this literature, *Autobiography of an Unknown Indian* (1951) while his *The Continent of Circe* (1966) is a remarkable assessment of Hindu life and culture. Nehru wrote superbly of Indian history and his *The Discovery of India* (1946) has, along with Gandhi's *My Experiments with Truth* (2 vols, 1927, 1929), assumed the status of a classic.

Mulk Raj Anand

The product of an author prolific in output and attuned to both European culture and the reality of India's situation in the twentieth century, Mulk Raj Anand's (*b*. 1935) novels, their style, period and themes, have made him generally recognised as the 'father' of the contemporary Indo-Anglian novel. Despite the wide range of his literary activity—apart from fiction he has written autobiography, works on art, cookery, criticism and philosophy—there is a unity to all his work. Always his focus has a human centre. The novels identify with the outcasts, the oppressed, while he attempts to provide an affirmation of true values and a sense of moral order.

Anand has remarked that his books are 'a miscellany which emerged from the compulsion to say my say about various moral problems about the year 1952 when I first went to England'. The influence of Europe in giving form to this moral focus is substantial. With literary activity came political involvement: Anand studied philosophy and attended reading parties in Marxist political theory and observed the class struggle in England. During this period of intellectual formation his thoughts turned back to India and his reminiscences of experiences, scenes and characters formed a two-thousand page writer's source-book which was to supply him with material for his later novels and was itself to be published as part of an autobiography—*Seven Summers: The Story of an Indian Childhood* (1951). Like many other Commonwealth writers have, Anand while 'exiled' in England rediscovered his own country, and his political morality meshed ever more closely with his assessment of India's needs.

Invariably Anand is described as a 'committed' writer. What needs to be appreciated is that he made the break from the literary image of a passive and contemplative India to a literature in keeping with the new national awareness. He represented a new order and critically examined the traditions of Indian culture. So, for example, toward the end of *Untouchable* the poet Iqbal Nath Sarshar tries to articulate the 'truth' about India, that 'We have throughout our long history, been realists, believing in the stuff of this world in the here and now, in the flesh and the blood.' A view is encapsulated here, which, while the speaker cannot be wholly identified with Anand, demonstrates his social and political realism. Despite the tension between mere propaganda and a proper literary realism, balance is maintained. This holds true despite the didactic formulae through which his characters are defined: the protagonists—who are usually victims; the oppressors, who resist change; the virtuous, social workers and enlightened politicians, who will help to create a just economic and social order. By these means Anand brought India into the international class struggle and out of the literature of romance.

For some Anand's emphasis upon the most shocking aspects of poverty and tradition seems contrived and facile: the reduction of human misery to an economic and social equation appears superficial. Yet, set in the context of the nineteen-thirties and forties it is far from that. Anand identifies with the sufferers about whom he writes. He seems to be at one with the spirit of his time. In 1919, in Amritsar, he was caned for breaking the curfew during the appalling Jallianwala Bagh massacre; when he wrote *Untouchable* in the early thirties he stayed with Gandhi in the Sabramati Ashram, and indeed Gandhi appeared in this novel and in *The Sword and the Sickle*. If there is some truth in Bonamy Dobrée's accusation that Anand substituted 'emotions for criticism', this is so when Anand allows moral pain to dominate the texture of a work. In *Untouchable*, *Coolie*, the trilogy *The Village*, *Across the Black Waters*, and *The Sword and the Sickle* and *The Private Life of an Indian Prince*, the difficult marriage between artist and reformer is Anand's highest achievement.

Untouchable (1935)

The story clearly demonstrates Anand's determination to demolish the colonial myth of 'romantic' India, and its subject is chosen to shock. In technique it has a classical simplicity: all the events occur in a single day in the life of the protagonist who is, typically, one of India's 'toiling masses'. However this is not simple Marxism: the problem Anand tackles is particularly Indian, the question of 'caste' and its appalling human consequences.

Anand's solution is materialistic. The protagonist is Bakha, an eighteen-year-old street sweeper whose task is to clean latrines and who is, therefore, 'unclean' as far as orthodox Hindus are concerned. Touching a Brahmin by chance makes Bakha aware of this for the first time. Shocked, he is offered hope in three forms. A Salvation Army Colonel says that in Christ there is no outcast and no high caste but contempt from the Colonel's 'Christian' wife causes Bakha to go elsewhere. Gandhi makes his appearance and comforts him with the teaching that sweepers are *Harijan*—God's people—because they purify Hindu life. Finally, Gandhi's ideology is given material reinforcement by the poet who says that Indian culture is really materialist and that when technology and a pure Vedic common sense prevail, bringing flush toilets to eliminate the sweeper's work, all will be well.

The strengths of this novel are obvious. Structure is clear and uncluttered, the element of satire is remorseless. The shams of traditional Indian life are exposed, particularly the notion about what is 'clean': for example the sadhu who chases Bakha out of a temple was earlier trying to seduce his sister. Other targets for satire include the pretensions of europeanised Indian intellectuals and Christianity. If the technological miracle at the end fails to convince perhaps it is because we have the advantage of hindsight!

Coolie (1936)

This work is far more savage than *Untouchable*, and its structure is more ambitious. At the centre is the innocent Munoo who leaves his village in the hills to work as a houshold servant in a lower-middle-class Indian family. Here Anand satirises Indians imitating English society and the consequences this has for those further down the social ladder. Munoo leaves to work in a factory but, when his protector is brutally beaten by the police, moves to Bombay and a cotton mill where the Indian and British exploitation of multitudes of passive workers is satirised in terms that echo Charles Dickens's (1812–70) *Hard Times* (1854). Ironies abound: a Union-organised strike becomes, absurdly, a Muslim–Hindu riot and Munoo, appalled, flees again, only to be knocked over by a Eurasian lady, Mrs Mainwaring, who keeps him as her gigolo while herself trying to pass as a white *mem-sahib*. Munoo pulls her rickshaw, and—so Anand implies—with his degradation complete, and his innocence lost, he dies.

While the economic and class elements are obvious, the novel transcends them. The story of rural innocence corrupted by urban life is an ancient one and, at the same time, the cruelty and vices portrayed are human rather than material. Munoo grows in maturity but, despite his capacity for affection and knowledge, finds neither a stable relationship nor, in an absurd situation, anything to understand. He dies, victim of a brutal society.

Two Leaves and a Bud (1937)

If this novel, which concentrates upon the plight of coolies caught in an unjust colonial economic system, is compared with *Coolie*, it becomes obvious how easily Anand's style can come to grief. In *Two Leaves and a Bud* the Europeans are caricatures whereas the coolies are unbelievably virtuous. In short propaganda dominates and the work fails to satisfy at all. By contrast *Coolie* remains a passionate but carefully poised treatment of a difficult subject.

The Village (1939), Across the Black Waters (1940), The Sword and the Sickle (1942) (a trilogy)
As the previous three works form a trilogy united by their proletarian victim-heroes, these novels are a natural trilogy built about the life of a young Sikh, Lalu Singh, and they trace his life (in a span that matches Anand's own) from boyhood before the First World War to the nationalism and socialism of the nineteen-twenties. Lalu Singh provides a parable for a new India, since, although he is exploited like Munoo and Gangu, he is successful in achieving independence and self-esteem.

Most notable in this trilogy is the change of focus. Here social realism is successfully achieved in the evocation of the lives of the expoited but independent Sikh and Muslim tenant farmers in the Punjab, and political satire recedes as Anand concentrates upon the circumstances of poverty and character which direct Lalu's life, from home to war and then to political struggle.

Raja Rao

Like Narayan, Raja Rao (*b.* 1909) is from South India but his literary output is much smaller than that of the other two who form with him the triumvirate of eminence in modern Indo-Anglian fiction—Narayan and Anand. With the humanist emphasis of Anand but without his materialism, Rao mediates between the mysticism and philosophy of India, with all that entails—risking the hazards of identifying with the old 'romantic' India of Tagore—and the specifically contemporary issues of nationalism and change. At the heart of this is Rao's Hindu belief and, stemming from that, his cautious, tolerant approach.

The introductory note to his first novel *Kanthapura* comments upon his literary diction and style in terms which show that these too are used in a cautious, tolerant fashion as instruments that mediate between the emotional tenor of Indian experience and its expression in intellectual terms.

> The telling has not been easy. One has to convey in a language that is not one's own the spirit that is one's own. One has to convey the various shades and omissions of a certain thought-movement that looks maltreated in an alien language . . . We can write only as Indians. We have grown to look at the large world as part of us. Our method of expression therefore has to be a dialect which will some

day prove to be as distinctive and colourful as the Irish or the American. Time alone will justify it.

The narrative method of the tale demonstrates the style of a village story-teller: the garrulity, the use of direct address to audience and reader, the diction with its repetition and lengthy description. Even the opening phrases of the novel evoke this:

> Our village—I don't think you have ever heard about it—Kanthapura is its name, and it is in the provice of Kara.

> High on the Ghats is it, high up the steep mountains that face the cool Arabian seas, up the Malabar coast is it, up Mangalore and Puttur and many a centre of cardamon, rice and sugarcane . . .

Kanthapura (1938)

The subject of this first novel is similar to Anand's *Two Leaves and a Bud*. In terms that recall a Hindu epic Rao describes an archetypal South Indian village inspired by Gandhi's Satyagraha and crushed by the army. Although the Seffington Coffee estate epitomises British oppression the social-realistic mode is superficial, and the work evolves from its symbolic framework as Rao constructs a tale that not only recalls Hindu epic but interprets experience in forms of Hindu thought: events are illusory; life is symbolic; the struggle of the people of Kanthapura is part of the continuing *Ramayana* of the Gods; Gandhi is an *avatara* sent to rescue Sita (India) from Ravana (the British). In brief, the old and the new are synthesised. Non-violence (*ahimsa*) and *Satyagraha* have been integrated with the ancient, violent tradition of Indian epic.

Through the garrulous narrative of the story-teller, his chaotic paratactic sentences, Rao evokes the 'idea' of India that appealed to Europe without, however, evading a realistic stance. Ancient history, religion, landscape and the life of this single village community which subordinates individual character to its own corporate being, all these provide a perspective which subsumes nationalism. Even while Rao appears to discuss politics he is really exploring more complex and fundamental philosophical questions. Gandhi's ethics, Moorthy's 'Marxism', the mythology of the *Harikatha* man all offer interpretations of the place of nationalism and good and evil in India's life. No one view is allowed to dominate. Kanthapura symbolises India, its capacity to absorb influences yet remain essentially unchanged.

The Cow of the Barricades and Other Stories (1947)

The short story lends itself to symbols and compression. In the title story of this collection the theme of Kanthapura, a village revolt against the British, is reiterated, when, as confrontation is about to lead to battle, the village cow, Gauri, mounts the barricades. Although a British officer shoots the cow the issue of morality versus force remains unresolved.

Not all the stories deal with rural India but all explore the Indian psyche. Myth and realism are Rao's dominant modes of approach but, beyond that, tone, depth and texture vary. Stories such as 'The True Story of Kanakapala, Protector of the Gold' are in the mythological mode while 'The Little Gram Shop', which recalls Maupassant's pitiless objectivity, is more realistic, even harrowing.

The Serpent and the Rope (1960)
One of the most influential in Indian fiction, this novel is clearly linked with *Kanthapura*. Using a post-independence setting, the writer is free to ignore politics, apart from a few references. Now metaphysics takes first place. The hero, Rama, quotes Gandhi:

> My freedom is not when the British leave India, for that is inevitable and will be soon, but when we become true satyagrahis—when we seek the Truth, humbly, fervently, and with non-violence in our hearts.

Rama comments, 'That for me is India, not a country . . . but a hypostatic presence.' Later in the novel Ramaswamy says, 'India is not a country . . . India is an idea, a metaphysic': the completion of freedom is the truth of Advaita Vedanta, the release from illusion. Rama's personality suggests the mental and spiritual quest which sustains his identity, his groping from the particular to the universal, from the imperfect to the pure; from illusion to reality.

In the title of the work is embedded its real subject: the metaphysical quest. In a conversation with his French wife Madeline, Rama observes:

> 'The world is either unreal or real—the serpent or the rope. There is no in-between-the-two—and all that's in between is poetry, is sainthood. You might go on saying all the time "No, no, it's the rope", and stand in the serpent. And looking at the rope from the serpent is to see paradise, saints, avataras, gods, heroes, universes. For wheresoever you go, you see only with the serpent's eyes . . . But in true fact, with whatever eyes you see there is no serpent, there never was a serpent . . . One—the Guru—brings you the lantern . . . "It's only the rope." He shows it to you.'

One of a series of protracted dialogues, journal entries and monologues, this conversation reflects a spiritual Odyssey in which the mental traits of India and Europe, in Rama and Madeline respectively, fail to mesh. Through metaphysical debate and philosophical conflict their marriage disintegrates and after a long 'exile' Rama returns to India and the faith of his ancestors.

In this lengthy philosophical novel Rao avoids the worst pitfalls of philosophy disguised as art. This is no mean feat, since the work has no plot, less action or obvious structure, merely varying forms of reflection. What makes all this credible is that Rao is careful to remind us that the narrator is a tubercular intellectual from an ancient Brahmin tradition: Rama's stream-of-consciousness, his fraught dialogues, reflect his illness and the morbid introspection it produces. While Catholicism, Buddhism, Hinduism and Marxism are all explored, Madeline's progress toward Buddhism—and this personal dualism—conflicts with Rama's belief in the truth of Advaita Vedanta, an impersonal monism, which finally keeps them apart. Ramaswamy is convinced that only in attainment of this final unity, the oneness of everything, will India's true freedom be found.

The Cat and Shakespeare (1965)
The protagonist of this novel, the ailing Ramakrishna Pai, recalls Rama of *The Serpent and the Rope*. Indeed there are similarities in both works. Ramakrishna Pai has to return to his Brahmin faith, and symbols and philosophy form the centre of the work. However, unlike Rama, Ramakrishna Pai remains a more shadowy figure and the work as a whole is surreal in its effect; the poetic language and flashbacks imply the unreality of phenomena and, as a consequence, the truth of *Brahman Atman*.

By the title Rao provides something of a moral fable. In a dream-like sequence the cat allows Ramakrishna to see reality as it is but at the same time it recalls the debate in Hindu theology over the dependence of the soul upon God. Whereas the northern (Vadagalai) school insisted that the soul was like a monkey clinging to its mother (God), the southern (Tengalia) school conceived the relationship to be like a cat (God) with its kittens. In this latter tradition the utter dependence of man is stressed, for his relation to God is as that of a kitten to the cat which, regardless of the kitten's wishes, picks it up and acts as she pleases. In this complex symbolic tale it is noteworthy how embedded in Indian thought Rao's work is, and how far in style his work is from the realistic vein of fiction which otherwise characterises Indo-Anglian writing.

R.K. Narayan

Born in Madras in 1906, Rasipuram Krishnaswami Narayan writes fiction which is quite distinctive: where Anand is a reformer and Rao a metaphysician, Narayan is a moral analyst. For his eleven novels he has created a particular geographical identity, the imaginary town of Malgudi, representative of South Indian provincialism and culture. Perhaps reminiscent of Mysore or Bangalore, it contains a rich sample of India life: its river is a place of sanctity, tragedy and recreation, while in the Mempi hills its people hunt or live as religious recluses in the cave-temples which are the setting for much of *The Guide*. Malgudi's blend of Hindu and British India is a perfect foil for the human drama of India as the old and new collide and change; its fixed setting allows Narayan to analyse and balance the complex elements of modern Indian society.

While Narayan considers subjects which belong to the common concerns of the new literatures—nationalism, modernisation, the impact of education, the attraction of 'overseas', the rebellion of the young against the old—Malgudi itself shapes the gentle humour and irony which sets him apart from Anand or Rao. Its 'Indianness', its solidity, permit his balanced humorous approach: for, while comedy is not a major genre in Indo-Anglian fiction, Malgudi provides a locale where humour is possible. Graham Greene recognised this: 'Comedy needs a strong framework of social convention with which the author sympathises. But the life of Malgudi—never ruffled by politics—proceeds in exactly the same way as it has done for centuries, and the juxtaposition of the age-old conventions and the modern character provides much of the comedy.' *

Narayan recreates the texture of life in a South Indian Tamil community through a vivid lucid language with only the delicate suggestion of 'Indian English'. Even in this respect he remains quite apart from the 'committed' stance of writers like Anand as his prose is, by comparison, an impeccable standard English.

SHORT STORIES:

Although Narayan's Malgudi novels are his highest achievement, his collections of short stories, in particular *An Astrologer's Day* (1964) and *A Horse and Two Goats* (1970), demonstrate his style and the subtle perception beneath the easy surface of his prose. Most noticeable is the way the stories feature a balance of perspectives and an emblematic quality reminiscent of this: first, the steam-roller which the narrator has won is grotesque, troublesome, hilarious; second, it symbolises the nonsense and instability of human desires. In short the technique provides a balance of perspectives whereby Narayan both celebrates and analyses the human condition.

1935–45 NOVELS:

Together with *The Bachelor of Arts*, *The Dark Room*, and *The English Teacher*, *Swami and Friends* belongs to the first cluster of Narayan's

---

* Graham Greene, Introduction to R.K. Narayan, *The Financial Expert*, Indian Thought Publications, Madras, 1958, p.vii.

novels which appeared in the years 1935–45, and which all deal with various aspects of the maturing of a young Indian from child to adult. Their mood darkens as innocence becomes experience and *The English Teacher* is a tragic tale compared with the racy episodic style of *Swami and Friends*.

In this first novel Narayan draws heavily upon his own experience in a mission-school. A simple style brilliantly evokes the stereotyped schoolboy adventures of Swaminathan: the pull of family relationships; the rich life of friends—Mani and Rajam—on the river-bank; the conflicts of school-life and the importance of the game of cricket. In this vital but troubled world, while there is disappointment there is always hope. Swami's viewpoint is still an innocent one, his relationship with Malgudi superficial, not yet touched by complex relationships and bitter disillusionments.

There is also satire here: Narayan's tolerance exploits the contradictions of Christian bigotry, Hindu legend, and Swami himself. While the Albert Mission and the exasperating Christian zeal of Ebenezer are mildly amusing, it is the game of cricket which most powerfully satirises the contradictions of modern India. Here Swami's impossible hopes image the human quest which, in one form or another, runs through Narayan's work. On the waste lots of Malgudi the local team parodies its English namesake, the MCC, and Swami's absorption in what is ultimately no more than a game implies the melancholy and absurdity of human ambitions.

The Bachelor of Arts (1937)

With the publication of this work, introduced by Graham Greene, Narayan's standing as a writer could not be ignored. The connection with Swami is obvious, since the process of maturation, here experienced by another hero, advances another notch. After gaining his degree the protagonist, Chandran, wanders for eight troubled months as a *sanyasi* (a holy beggar), held back from marriage by unfavourable horoscopes. Although the thwarted love affair between Chandran and Marathi mirrors the conflict between old and new, the novel's construction transcends facile categories. In the first part Chandran struggles for his BA, teeters between subservience to British academic officialdom and allegiance to a militant student body; in the second he falls in love but his dreams of love are destroyed; and in the third, after contemplating the options of debauchery or suicide, Chandran becomes a sanyasin only to find, when he subjects 'his soul to a remorseless vivisection', that he is a social parasite, a sham. This revelation concludes with his return home and marriage to a girl whose horoscope is favourable.

The quest here is obvious. Chandran pursues both western and Indian ideals, but finds both inappropriate. While learning, mysticism and romantic love may all be good, they appear self-centred in his case. Here even modest fulfilment has to be achieved within a social context while adherence to the traditional ways imposes a limit on ambition. Narayan's style clearly and dispassionately presents the shams of Indian experience: bribery, corruption, the tyranny of family life, the dangers of bogus religiosity. Characters complement the style and, whether the disreputable Kailas or the despicable Professor Ragavachar, foreshadow major creations in the later novels. Although through them Chandran attains 'a life freed from distracting illusions and hysterics', like the stages in the structure of the novel, the characters mark stages in Chandran's development, and the humour brings also moral insight as, despite disillusion, there emerges a gracious acceptance of life.

The Dark Room (1938)
The comedy is darker in this novel which centres on the philanderer husband Ramani and his much abused wife Savitri. The plot revolves about Ramani's affair with an employee in the Malgudi branch of the progressive Englandia Insurance Company, Savitri's flight, attempted suicide, and return to an essentially unchanged husband and family. The context for this unhappy story is the impact of modernisation on Malgudi and the consequent fracturing of social relationships, facilitated in Ramani and Savitri's case by an enlightened employment policy. The advent of the 'talkies', the films to whch Ramani takes his family when Savitri has left, is a token of the relentless process that remakes the town:

> Malgudi in 1935 suddenly came into line with the modern age by building a well-equipped theatre—the Palace Talkies—which simply brushed aside the old corrugated-sheet-roofed variety hall, which from time immemorial had entertained the citizens of Malgudi with tattered silent films.

In the collision of old with new Narayan shows the inevitable victor to be change, but, as Savitri and the lost variety hall demonstrate, he records the sadness of loss in human as well as architectural terms.

The fable-like character of the story operates on a number of levels. When Savitri attempts to drown herself in Malgudi's river she is rescued by a thief and taken to his village where she becomes the servant of the temple priest. Denied death she immerses herself in the traditional religious life. However, when her feelings for her children compel her to return, she is reclaimed by the real world of modern Malgudi; its middle-class mixture of India in the west. Again the quest for self is obvious and, as in *The Bachelor of Arts*, it is traditional peasant communal life which enables self-discovery.

The English Teacher (1945)
Here the focus is domestic: Krishnan, a lecturer in English literature, loses his wife, and the story follows his recovery from this loss. Eventually he moves from grief to service for others; a moral commitment which may reflect Gandhi's influence. While Krishnan seeks union with his wife through spiritualism it is only when he has a 'vision' of her spirit always being with him that he is able to move beyond self and know the unity of everything. If there is any irony in this very Hindu concept being experienced by an English teacher, it is muted but deliberate and entirely appropriate in the world of Malgudi.

By 1945 Narayan had completed the first 'sequence' of his Malgudi novels. These had been traumatic years for India. While allusions to the contemporary abound and map the course of social change, Narayan's use of Malgudi as a type of social laboratory in which he can present what endures in the midst of change, is commanding. In short, Malgudi is India, absorbing change yet unchanged in essence, and the stories are a 'committed' fiction where lessons are concealed within a subtle entertaining art form.

THE POST-INDEPENDENCE NOVELS:

All the novels published from 1949 onwards fall into this category. A common background is the triumph of the period, the misery of a bloody partition, and the tragic irony of Gandhi's assassination at the hands of a Hindu nationalist. The social texture of Malgudi changes with independence: Narayan shows it as partially industrialised and more corrupt, Congress politicians are wryly alluded to, new street names confuse postmen and locals, and foundation stones are laid for buildings that never materialise. Yet nationalism and independence remain subordinate to an investigation of personal life, character and motivation—perhaps as a consequence of Gandhi's death. Whether or not Narayan's emphasis proceeds from disillusion or distaste, humour is used adroitly as a controlling mechanism. All these novels achieve order only after Malgudi has experienced a comic disorder or madness introduced from outside. That social changes are shown in a comic and grotesque form does not undermine their seriousness; reminiscent of Jonathan Swift's (1667–1745) satire, the humour is used as a stylistic and psychic device which enables social analysis without alienation.

Mr Sampath (1949)
Sampath is the eccentric outsider who embodies the forces of change (or madness) in Malgudi. In a bizarre combination of ancient and ultra-modern his favourite project is a film of a famous episode in Hindu mythology, Siva's burning of Kama the god of love. Sampath

also promises to print the work of a local writer, Srinivas, who has to learn that his idealism is impractical, that Sampath is a confidence trickster and that the old ways of Malgudi and India will endure. Here tragedy is restricted to disillusionment. Although innocence has to give way to experience, there is regret at its loss.

The tension between illusion and reality is central. Sampath represents a new India. The humorous incident, where he makes love to the delectable Shanti and is interrupted by the love-sick Ravi, subverts the superficial world of the film-makers. Sampath escapes into the forest with Shanti until, tired of her, he returns—a chastened man. Srinivas, shaken by the incident, contemplates Malgudi and its past, and he too is emotionally restored, as Ravi will be also. Progressively illusion gives place to reality and, by implication, the perennial wisdom of India is shown to be able to accommodate what is new.

The Financial Expert (1952)
Compared with Sampath, the pornographer Dr Pal is irredeemable. In this work the hero is an old-fashioned Hindu money-lender, Margayya, whom Dr Pal makes prosperous through pornography after Margayya switches from the worship of Saraswati (goddess of learning) to Lakshmi (goddess of luck and wealth). With wealth Margayya embraces modernisation and big business, only to find that, having gained so much, he has become estranged from his family, and that his son Balu, perverted by Dr Pal, now covets his father's wealth, and has destroyed his credit by lies.

Like Mephistopheles, Dr Pal has to be seen as more than a human being; rather a force in man, an embodiment of the potential for evil. Posing as a benefactor he is revealed as a monster with Balu his perverted victim. Apart from this loss Margayya remains relatively untouched: he abandons everything and returns to the village banyan tree with his tin box, his hold on traditional values intact.

Waiting for the Mahatma (1955)
Here again illusion and reality are central concerns. Gandhi's incursion into the Malgudi community jars because his charisma contrasts with the mediocrity of Malgudi. This is intentional. Sriram, a youthful *satyagrahi*, has to recognise his own preference for violence, his superficial interpretation of Gandhi's teachings and his stereotyping of the British. His moral confusion is a perversion and he has to be restored to the reality epitomised by Gandhi's non-violence. It is Gandhi's death which most clearly demonstrates the foolishness of violence and the necessity of *ahimsa*.

The Guide (1958)
In this work Narayan returns to the bogus *sanyasi* theme introduced in *The Bachelor of Arts* and echoed in *Waiting for the Mahatma* in

Sriram's imperfection as a *satyagrahi*. Raju begins life as a tourist guide and through his infatuation with the selfish Rosie is utterly ruined and ends up in prison. Rosie and Marco are the ominous 'outsiders' who destroy Raju's life, but after coming out of prison he accidentally becomes a *sanyasi* in the eyes of some simple villagers for whom he fasts till death and the rains come. From innocence and corruption to redemption; the value of the old ways against the pretences of the new; these recurrent themes are tightly and sparely intertwined.

The Man Eater of Malgudi (1962)

Much of the power of this novel's bizarre humour stems from the sheer contrast between the monstrous Vasu who arrives in Malgudi, and the timorous, pretentious Nataraj on whom Vasu imposes himself as a lodger. Vasu images the plans for India's modernisation with his own proposals to hunt game, stuff and export them, while his American-English emphasises the crudity of the new era. The modernisation scheme is perceived in terms of traditional Hindu epic. A former strong man with enormous physical and sexual powers, Vasu resembles the demons of Hindu mythology while his end, through swatting a mosquito on his head, parodies the death of the legendary monster, Bismasura. Briefly, while Vasu and Nataraj respectively manifest tensions between epic violence and the power of *ahimsa*, Vasu is clearly defined as a real character with a story to tell, and stands for the deeper problem of evil which unless controlled will destroy those who are governed by it.

The Vendor of Sweets (1967)

The relationship between Jagan and his westernised son, Mali, recalls that of Margayya and Balu in *The Financial Expert*. Jagan keeps to the traditional way of life while his son epitomises the disturbing outside influences. This relationship combines the generation conflict and problems of modernisation. Jagan is a contradiction: a former *satyagrahi* (who went to prison for his ideals) he is a successful businessman who now practises *minor* asceticisms. Like Chandran in *The Bachelor of Arts* he deceives himself and his final decision to become a hermit suggests evasion. This novel clearly demonstrates Narayan's ability to explore a few themes and offer a consistent philosophy with tolerance and grace.

The Painter of Signs (1976)

It is ingenious but not surprising that Narayan creates comedy out of India's concern with birth control. In *The Painter of Signs* the outside influence is present in the outspoken Daisy, a representative of the new type of Indian woman. Ironically, she takes Raman, the painter of signs, about the countryside choosing sites for painting family planning slogans. Thoroughly westernised and casteless, Daisy is a contradiction of all that Raman, a rather provincial Brahmin, stands for, and when she is about to prove her love for him by coming to live with him, she leaves and advises him to marry a more conventional woman. Their relationship retells the old legend of King Santhanu and his goddess wife who kills her own children. Through this oblique and ironic use of traditional Indian mythology Narayan hints that Indian philosophy and religion have lasting value.

Kushwant Singh and Manohar Malgonkar

By contrast with the three major writers of Indo-Anglian fiction discussed above, both Kushwant Singh's and Manohar Malgonkar's works combine graphic excellence with a dominant interest in heroism, martial prowess and the military tradition of India rather than Gandhi's *satyagraha* and *ahimsa*. Both sacrifice depth of characterisation for brisk action in an optimistic, superficial milieu where courage and loyalty are crucial.

Kushwant Singh's (*b*. 1915) *Train to Pakistan* (1956) is directly inspired by partition. As with Narayan and Rao, his technique for handling this highly charged subject is to create a representative community: the village of Mano Majra, set on the Indo-Pakistan border, is a microcosm of India which stands alongside Rao's Kanthapura and Narayan's Malgudi. Its Sikh, Muslim and Hindu communities live in peace, apart from occasional dacoit raids, and the railway is the centre of village life. Partition and its horrors intrude to destroy the traditional community. Only 'outsiders' resist the horror: Juggut the bandit, a Sikh in love with a Muslim girl; Iqbal Singh, an ineffectual Communist; Hukum Chand, the corrupt magistrate, amiable and perverse. These last two also represent different aspects of India: Hukum Chand, the traditional sensuous and corrupt India of fiction, Iqbal, the intellectual radicalism of modern India. Yet both these men are powerless and it is the instinctive, active Juggut who sacrifices himself to rescue a train-load of Muslims.

The style is adept if not penetrating. First, Singh belongs to the realist tradition: the opening scenes with Juggut's love-making are graphic though not salacious. Where details—such as the horror of the massacres—might clog the text, he is reticent: it is only through Hukkum Chand's nightmares and memories that the horror is described in detail. Second, the style is employed for a purpose: Iqbal's facile ideology grates, as it is meant to, since his 'superiority' defines his absurdity. For example, there is his surprise at the acuteness of the villagers when they question the value of independence:

> Iqbal did not know how to answer simple questions like these. Independence meant little or nothing to these people. They did not even

realise that it was a step forward and that all they needed to do was to take the next step and turn the make-believe political freedom into a real economic one.

(Train to Pakistan, p.47)

Kushwant Singh's short stories in *The Mark of Vishnu* (1950), with their mixture of satire, violence and the bizarre, echo his novels. The novel *I Shall Not Hear the Nightingale* (1959) employs the style and themes of Singh's earlier works: a tendency to melodrama and a concern for the truly heroic. This novel is set in pre-independence India, particularly in the war years 1942–3: with the Japanese at the border, the Indian nationalists are ready for a revolution on which Singh focuses through the family of a Sikh magistrate Buta Singh, his son Sher Singh and the mother Sabhrai Singh. In this family the parallels with *Train to Pakistan* are inescapable: by trying to befriend Indian nationalists and British alike, Buta Singh is morally compromised, like Hukkum Chand. Sher Singh is a variant of Iqbal, an indulged young radical with doubts about his masculinity, who attempts revolution and is imprisoned only to be released by a friendly British officer. Sabhrai Singh, a pious uneducated Sikh woman, urges her son to die rather than abandon his friends and she herself dies before independence—an event which explains the title of the book.

Unlike Narayan, Kushwant Singh does not offer a profound social analysis, being too prone to melodrama; compared with R.P. Jhabvala, his satire is brutal and caustic; unlike Raja Rao, his view of religion is merely sociological. A work which illuminates his view of his Sikh religion and traditions is his two-volume *A History of the Sikhs* (1963–66). His literary achievement lies in his bold, optimistic celebration of heroic virtues in contemporary India.

Manohar Malgonkar's (*b.* 1914) highly readable novels celebrate heroic, military and aristocratic virtues. *The Princes* (1963) purports to be the reminiscences of a former ruler and centres on the relationship between the narrator and his father, the maharajah. Along with aristocratic failings, Malgonkar presents virtues of enduring value: while brutal and sensuous, his protagonists are also passionate and honest. The departure of this aristocratic order brings a sense of loss which qualifies an Indian nationalism where the principal political characters are motivated by hatred and self-interest.

G.V. Desani

Govind Desani's (*b.* 1909) name is remembered in Indo-Anglian fiction for one work only, *All About H. Hatterr* (1948), which in its mixture of subject, style and language remains almost unclassifiable. Written while Desani was in England, the work reflects formalist European fiction and a post-war situation in which literature was increasingly autonomous, avoiding contemporary references and creating an exuberant surreal world that is almost self-contained. Hatterr himself is a cultural alien: the son of a European merchant seaman and a Malay lady from Penang.

Sustained comic inventiveness is the essence of this amiable parody of Indian life and customs: T.S. Eliot remarked of it, 'It is amazing that anyone should be able to sustain a piece of work in this style and tempo at such length'.* For its models a reader has to turn to the great Spanish novelist Miguel de Cervantes (1547–1616) and to the influential twentieth-century Irish novelist James Joyce (1882–1941). Indeed Hatterr has much of Quixote about him, his Sancho Panza being his admiring friend Banerrji who involves him in seven adventures—the seven sections of the book. This sevenfold structure marks the careful craftsmanship. Each section marks one of Hatterr's seven consultations with seven sages from seven different oriental cities.

As the spirit of the work requires, Hatterr's quest for the truth is never completed. Here farce and satire are underpinned by the moral realism which belongs to the mock-heroic of, for example, Alexander Pope's (1688–1744) satirical poem *The Dunciad* (1782)—though without its venom. In his quest Hatterr is continually stripped, as are the religious experts he consults. The comedy is in the exposure which deflates pretension. By implication, reality will only be attained when illusions have been dispelled.

This, however, is almost too high a claim. Hatterr's seriousness is saved from didacticism by Desani's combination of slapstick situations that recall the surrealistic humour of the early twentieth-century American film comedians, the Marx brothers, with a verbal texture which almost rivals the British humorous novelist P.G. Wodehouse (1881–1975). In the stream-of-consciousness narrative we hear Hatterr's voice blending elegant and literary expressions with colloquialisms, the sources of which include Indian 'babuisms', commercial and civil service jargon, and colloquial 'sahib-English'. For example the account of Hatterr's humiliation at his club:

She went to my club.
Damme, to a feller's club!
The Secretary tried to disperse her; and failed.

Alongside Hatterr's narrative is heard Banerrji's impeccable literary English mixed with his own cultural affectations. This is how he comforts Hatterr:

* See C.N. Srinath, *The Literary Criterion*, winter 1970, pp.40–1.

Excuse me, but my heart bleeds for you! May I, therefore, make a present to you of this parcel of an all-in-one-pantie-vest? It has just come from Bond Street of dear England. It is delightfully snug, made in Huddersfield, forming no wrinkles . . .

Here the style *is* the work. Desani is no Indian Tutuola but he has made English *work* for him and his linguistic agility is as remarkable as his political independence and imaginative innovativeness. Though strangely ignored after its first enthusiastic reception, his creation was a breakthrough, prophetic of the psychic independence that was to come after political independence had been gained.

Ruth Prawer Jhabvala

Born in Cologne in 1927, British by naturalisation, educated in England, Ruth Prawer Jhabvala takes care not to idealise India but, alongside social satire, shows India as a place in which European expatriates —including, one suspects, Jhabvala herself—come to a new measure of self-knowledge. In *Heat and Dust* (1975) her narrator refers to Major Minnies's work 'on the influence of India on the European consciousness and character':

India, always, he said, finds out the weak spot and presses on it. Both Dr. Saunders and Major Minnies spoke of the weak spot. But whereas for Dr. Saunders it is something, or someone, rotten, for the Major this weak spot is to be found in the most sensitive, often the finest people—and moreover, in their finest feelings. It is there that India seeks them out and pulls them over into what the Major called the other dimension. He also referred to it as another element, one in which the European is not accustomed to live, so that by immersion in it he becomes debilitated or even (like Olivia) destroyed.

(Heat and Dust, pp.170−1)

Heat and Dust (for which she won the Booker Prize in 1976) epitomises those western female characters in Ruth Prawer Jhabvala's fictions —for example, the women in *A Backward Place* (1965), Lee in *A New Dominion* (1972), or Katie in *How I Became A Holy Mother* (1976)— who go to India on a quest or else find it to be in some way a crucible for their experience.

Objectivity, questioning and the search for a pattern which will enable wider comment without distortion are particularly obvious in the construction of *Heat and Dust*. The technique reflects Ruth Prawer Jhabvala's experience in writing scripts for film-makers: it is one of cutting and splicing—a variation of the literary flashback. Parallels and contrasts between two periods of time are made possible through having Ms Rivers, in India in the nineteen-seventies, read her great-aunt Olivia's letters written from India about 1923. This enables more than a concentration upon character: it is a flexible device through which major interests, in particular the consequences of cultural dislocation and the impact of India upon western sensibility, can be explored. At the same time the setting—its heat and dust, the passions and mortality these elements suggest—is part of its rich texture.

However, Ruth Prawer Jhabvala generally concentrates upon post-independence India and her focus is domestic, personal and social rather than practical. *The Nature of Passion* (1956) and *Get Ready for Battle* (1962) use modern Indian businessmen and a family business—a typically Indian institution—as the background for a study in intrigue and conflicts together with some sharp satire on europeanised alienated Indians with intellectual pretensions. *To Whom She Will* (1955) studies the conflict between notions of romantic love and the tradition of arranged marriages—the novelist ironically notes the convenience of conformity to tradition—while *The Householder* (1960) is set amidst the conflicts of extended family relationships. These settings are suited to Ruth Prawer Jhabvala's style, to her cultivation of detachment. Characteristic of this is her tendency to understate, to present an ironic satirical perspective through contradiction and incongruity. Bitterness is reserved for brutality and exploitation while her central characters, who remain substantial, fallible beings, gain disillusioned sympathy. Jahbvala's style and concerns combine the detachment of Desani and the subtle probing of later writers such as Anita Desai and Kamala Markandaya.

Kamala Markandaya and Anita Desai

'Of the writers who have but lately come into the limelight, Kamala Markandaya is perhaps the most outstanding' was the verdict of the influential critic K.R. Srinivasa Iyengar in 1962*. Subsequent events have only substantiated this judgement and, as early as 1969, Shiv K. Kumar was to assert simply that 'Of all the contemporary Indian novelists writing in English, Kamala Markandaya is the most accomplished'.† Change is the axis about which Kamala Markandaya's (b. 1924) fictional cosmos revolves as she traces nuances of this central theme in her novels. *Nectar in a Sieve* (1954) is about peasant poverty brought about by hostile nature and indifferent industrialisation. These elements recur with some consistency: *Some Inner Fury* (1955) maps the destruction of romantic love by nationalist violence, while *A*

---

* In his *Indian Writing in English*, Asia Publishing House, New York, 1962, p.331.
† In *Books Abroad*, Autumn, 1969, p.508.

Silence of Desire (1960) contrasts modern technological 'truth' with traditional faith. *A Handful of Rice* (1966) deals with the impossible decisions forced upon the urban proletariat whereas *Possession* (1963) explores the distortions of Indian identity under British patronage. *The Coffer Dams* (1966) deals with the impact of British industrial interests upon the tenor of Indian life, a theme explored more subtly in *Pleasure City* (1982) while *The Nowhere Man* (1973) concentrates upon the problems of alienation and racial antagonism experienced by an elderly Hindu immigrant in South London and his relationship with a somewhat older English gentlewoman.

Since Kamala Markandaya writes from a London base, and belongs to a class educated in England, her ability adequately to appreciate the depths and nuances of Indian traditional life, its thought and speech rhythms, has been questioned. However *Nectar in a Sieve* demonstrates her capacity to suggest the feeling of Indian peasants' speech without resort to Anglo-Indianisms. Here she has expressed the necessary inward sensibility in a subtle and elegant English, just as in *Some Inner Fury* she traces Mira's emergence from awkward adolescence into passionate maturity. If the familiar characters of a popular image of India are all present in her fiction—holy men, urban poor, passive villagers —it is because they cannot be wholly avoided in the marriage of art with reality. If change has to be interpreted, images and metaphors must be used in that task. Symbolic characters and situations set out the theme and the works variously suggest the presentation of moral truth in a fable. The consequences of the collapse of traditional life and the drift to the towns are expressed with a peculiarly Indian resonance, particularly in Mira's sense of inevitable loss under the pressure of impersonal forces.

> It is all one, I said to myself. In a hundred years it is all one; and still my heart wept, tearless, desolate, silently to itself. But what matter to the universe, I said to myself, if now and then a world is born or a star should die; or what matter to the world, if here and there a man should fall, or a head or a heart should break.
>
> (*Some Inner Fury*, pp.285–6)

Pleasure City faintly recalls Ruth Prawer Jhabvala's cut-and-splice technique since Kamala Markandaya makes Tully, the representative of AIDCORPS, a construction company about to build a tourist complex by a South Indian fishing village, the grandson of a former Consul of India; moreover one who had presided 'when the beloved ward, India, had at last turned on them all' (p.29). Contrasts and parallels develop and the themes that dominate are all aspects of change: the dream of India in the British psyche; the trauma of change in traditional life; the subtle shifts in values as a new Indian society is created; aspects of 'Third World' development, its contradictions and absurdity. A novel with a complex plot, it recalls *The Coffer Dams*, while Rikki the fisher-boy brings to mind Valmiki in *Possession*. Such echoes indicate that Kamala Markandaya is working over familiar ground while discovering fresh nuances in the overworked East–West theme.

Her restrained focus on the human face of tragedy marks the way later Indo-Anglian writers have sought alternatives to the larger political, metaphysical, and satirical themes initiated by Mulk Raj Anand, Raja Rao and R.K. Narayan. Anita Desai (*b.* 1937) follows Kamala Markandaya in this, and her first novel *Cry, The Peacock* (1963) is a despairing portrayal of Maya, an oversensitive young woman who is torn by conflicts within her family and between her and Gautama, her husband. Except for the last few pages the whole story is told by the heroine in a stream-of-consciousness narrative, and its poetic, emotive and metaphorical diction so wholly conveys her neurotic character that, while it enables us to follow her mental collapse, it prevents a balanced view. The reader is reminded of Maya in Anita Desai's second novel, *Voices in the City* (1965), where again a stream-of-consciousness narrative by the principal female character, Monisha, depicts the spiritual quest for self-realisation and fulfilment by a brother, Nirode, and his two sisters, Monisha herself and Amla. Their tragic search takes place against the townscape of Calcutta which symbolises perfectly the existential despair of the protagonists who, lost in this urban wasteland of modern India, seek to find their way without the familiar guides of family, customs, religion and tradition.

Other writers

The links in Indo-Anglian fiction demonstrate an evolving tradition in which certain themes allow the appearance of continuity free of a literary strait-jacket. Bhabani Bhattacharya (*b.* 1906) reflects the interests of the earlier writers, S.N. Ghose, Raja Rao and Desani. Both *So Many Hungers* (1947) and *He Who Rides a Tiger* (1954) use the Bengal famine during the Second World War as the background for social satire. In a domestic setting, *Music for Mohini* (1952) canvasses the possibilities of conflict within Indian life by the vying interests of traditionalism and modernisation while *A Goddess Named Gold* (1960) and *Shadow from Ladakh* (1966) press the dangers of modernisation more closely with warnings against profiteering and the misery of poverty. Unfortunately, Bhattacharya's style and characterisation tend to cliché and moralisation.

A more restrained writer is Balchandra Rajan (*b.* 1920) whose *The Dark Dancer* (1959) follows the difficulties of East–West, old and new relationships through the westernised Krishman's marriage to a conventional Indian girl, Kamala. Subtlety and irony characterise Rajan's style, and his second work *Too Long in the West* (1961) follows on the theme of his first, but spices tragedy and irony with sophisticated comedy as the western-educated heroine, Nolini, is reduced to choosing a husband through newspaper advertisements.

Indo-Anglian poetry

Indo-Anglian poets may also write in an indigenous language and so their poetry in English issues from contending cultural impulses and a literary context shaped by English romanticism and the Indian mythopoetic tradition. This context, with the influences of Tagore and Aurobindo, is something which 'The New Poetry', as Adil Jussawalla calls it, has reacted against—although the virile romanticism of P. Lal's poetry indicates that it still exercises a strong influence.

The 'New Poetry' developed during the nineteen-fifties and sixties as the post-war, post-independence situation fostered a fresh, abrasive, and disillusioned response to the politics, propaganda and nationalism of modern India. P. Lal (*b.* 1929), a professor in Calcutta College, founded the 'Writers' Workshop' and gathered about him a group of young writers and critics which, with the notable exception of Dom Moraes, included most of the 'New' poets: Nissim Ezekiel, Kamala Das, Pritish Nandy, Shiv K. Kumar (*b.* 1921) among them. The poetic influences are the leaders of European modernism and surrealism; T.S. Eliot, Ezra Pound, W.B. Yeats (1865–1939), W.H. Auden (1907–73), Wallace Stevens (1879–1955) and Dylan Thomas (1914–53). Of all influences, Eliot's has dominated: poetry has focused on the discrepancy between ideal and reality in terms that echo *The Wasteland*.

Dom Moraes

Born in Bombay in 1938, Dom Moraes was educated at Oxford and now lives in London. English is his first language, and he has made the most outstanding contribution to modern Indo-Anglian poetry. While his poetry is in the surrealist and symbolist mode, he favours metrical forms such as the sonnet and *terza rima* and, like Eliot and Thomas before him, draws upon mythological sources—usually Christian or Jewish—to give form to experience, and express the violence and terror beneath the everyday surface. Myth in these terms is a metaphoric device which defines personal experience, patterns chaos, and places the particular in a universal perspective. So, for example, in 'French Lesson' Moraes provides an illusion of tranquillity where 'horrible fears lie hidden beneath it, like rocks under sand'. Again 'Hawk Song' places suffering in a cosmic perspective and allows Moraes to be a diagnostician and fix, reminiscent of Eliot, a 'surgeon's eye on pain'. These perspectives, however, seem only masks, ploys which allow the poet to give greater autonomy to his emotional life.

One reason why Moraes has been too often excluded from anthologies of Indo-Anglian poetry has been his fluency which, when not toughened with irony or wit, has tended to glibness and the dangerous attractions of romanticism and dreaminess which have been so hard for Indian poets to resist. At his best his fluency has the gift of lyrical flight, for example:

After the sleepy throats of the first birds
Had creaked a madrigal into the sky,
A thin sun rose to separate the curds
Of sea, but my drab visitor stayed by
My bedside, and assailed me with the words
That had flailed sleep from me. Though I still fought,
Attempting flights to day, or back to sleep,
The cobwebs in his eyes, and on my coat
Moored all my life to him, till in the deep
Trenches of his dark language I was caught.

Nissim Ezekiel

By comparison with Dom Moraes's death-haunted poetry of the soul, Nissim Ezekiel (b. 1924)—like such poets as Arun Kolatkar (b. 1932), Parthasarathy and Ramanujan (b. 1929)—attains objectivity through tough, witty, ironic and cerebral verse. Ezekiel's poetry is more obviously Indian than that of Moraes. In some respects his subject matter is also simpler, since he turns to obvious conflicts such as old versus new, town against country. His poetry comes out of his reactions to his environment, his bemused response to the dilemmas of modern India. 'In India' captures this confusion:

Always, in the suns's eye,
Here among the beggars,
Hawkers, pavement sleepers,
Hutment dwellers, slums,
Dead souls of men and gods,
Burnt-out mothers, frightened
Virgins, wasted child
And tortured animal,
All in noisy silence
Suffering the place and time,
I ride my elephant of thought,
A Cézanne slung around my neck.

Set against the vivid scene the reference to Cézanne is an uncertain touch which implies not just irony but a doubt about the place of the poet in this environment. The poet remains an outsider. By contrast 'Night of the Scorpion' juxtaposes old and new by setting peasant superstitions against modern scepticism, another familiar theme but treated with perception, while the mother's comment at the end 'Thank God the scorpion picked on me/and spared my children' gives it emotional substance.

One feature of Ezekiel's work is a pervasive sense of balance. The oxymoron 'noisy silence' hints at this and suggests a mode of perception where vision and fact are juxtaposed. So in 'What Frightens Me' he says:

> I have seen the mask
> And the secret behind the mask

This approach links Ezekiel's early formalist writing and later less rigid prayer poems like 'Hymns in Darkness', and 'Distance' which offers a moment of self-discovery in which the poet is 'enhanced and also small'. The technique telescopes inward and outward dimensions of experience and, through self-directed irony, objectifies perception.

Ezekiel has also contributed to contemporary Indo-Anglian drama and shown considerable skill in handling the vexed issue of dramatic dialogue. *Nalini* is a satirical three-act comedy which combines realistic and symbolic modes to expose the supposed spiritual emptiness of sophisticated urban middle-class Indians. *Marriage Poems* is a tragicomedy on the subject of marriage, while *The Sleepwalkers* experiments with techniques from 'Absurd' theatre (twentieth-century drama which draws on existentialist philosophy to present human existence as meaningless and essentially absurd). Working over American-Indian relations the play's satire verges on caricature and the characters remain little more than shadows for wit.

Other poets

Although there are examples of 'commitment'—such as Adil Jussawalla's (*b.* 1940) *Missing Person* (1976)—this is not a dominant theme in the poetry. Among the new poets Kamala Das (*b.* 1934) published her first collection *Summer in Calcutta* (1965) to immediate acclaim. Her grammatical and stylistic errors mark a struggle for expression which seems to proceed from her intensity and compulsion to experiment rather than linguistic weakness. Das writes with a distinct awareness of women's experiences in Indian society and she rebels against masculine roles. Her poems are dominated by aspects of sexual love and lust and, at their limits, have a compulsive, neurotic, brutal energy:

I walked on streets where the night-girls with sham
Obtrusive breasts sauntered
And under yellow lamps, up-and-down wandered
Beaming their sickly smiles
At men ...

The poetry of A.K. Ramanujan(*b*. 1929) is in sharp contrst to that of Kamala Das. By profession a Dravidian philologist Ramanujan uses language with precision but also with a pliancy which conveys Hindu feeling. His verse forms, moreover, may also be indebted to his study of Kannada and Tamil poetry: in particular his translation of the vacanas (Kannadian religious lyrics), *Speaking of Siva*. Economic, even spare, Ramanujan's verses can be (at this point like those of Kamala Das) brutally erotic—but remain intellectually controlled with a compressed, almost epigrammatic style. Despite his 'Indianness', Ramanujan also echoes the wry irony and composed self-recognition of European imagists—as in 'Self Portrait':

I resemble everyone
but myself, and sometimes see
in shop-windows
        despite the well-known laws
        of optics,
the portrait of a stranger
date unknown,
often signed in a corner
by my father.

Here the language has a cool glass-like quality, it has precision and is simultaneously detached: in brief, language has become an artefact.

Another Writers' Workshop poet is Shiv K. Kumar whose personal lyrics like those of Kamala Das concentrate upon sexual love. 'The Indian Mango Vendor' is an example of his eroticism and brevity of style. We can see through 'the slits of her patched blouse'

two white moons [which]
pull all horses
off the track.

against this is set:

old man's leery eyes—
idle birds
pecking at the mango-nipples ...

While many of his poems are erudite, this poem suggests a disillusioned romantic, the bitterness of age and the likelihood of betrayal.

Arun Kolatkar (*b*. 1932) has written extensively in both Marathi and English. Breaking with romanticism, Kolatkar looked to a Maharashtrian poetic tradition of the poet saints, but with a modern sensibility. In his poetry, as in Ramanujan's and Ezekiel's, old Indian forms meshed with European poetic influences and verse emerged from a unified sensibility. The first phase of his work is heavily influenced by surrealism and 'Three Cups of Tea' (which uses an American tough-guy idiom to translate an original which was in pidgin underworld Marathi, 'Bombay Hindi') has a touch of surrealism about it.

Kolatkar's latter work, marked by the influence of Marathi holy poetry, is epitomised in *Jejuri* (1974). Here he handles a distinctively regional subject. Jejuri is a little village which contains the shrine of Kandoba—a minor deity with appeal to the humble. Yet pilgrimage is a very Indian theme and a sacramental aura hovers over all the activities he observes while his search is more one of self-discovery marked by his acerbic tone and modest irony. Belief and disbelief alike are suspended and, if the poet has not concluded his quest, the poem marks a stage in his awareness:

> What is god
> and what is stone
> the dividing line
> if it exists
> is very thin
> at jejuri
> and every other stone
> is god or his cousin.

Pakistan

The independence achieved in 1947, after all the difficulties of partition from India, established Pakistan as a political entity which was divided by India into East and West Pakistan. Despite the common cultural factor of Islam this Pakistan was in cultural and economic aspects two separate nations and after a tragic war (1971) in which India aided East Pakistan against an All Pakistan army, Bangladesh was created. Language differences again epitomise national identity. In Bangladesh Bengali was the indigenous language for the whole population and the medium for a flourishing national literature with Tagore as its great exponent. Here literature in English found little to encourage it. In the West, Pakistan had a dominant language (Urdu) which had to contest with a variety of regional languages: Sindhi, Pushto, Baloch, Punjabi, as well as English preferred by the Gujurati community. In this multilingual community prose in English has had to struggle to survive, with few major achievements, apart from the novels of Zulfikar Ghose (*b.* 1935) and Ahmed Ali (*b.* 1910). Although Iqbal (1873–1938), Jinnah (1876–1948) and the generation of these leaders of the Pakistan movement used English, it was far removed from the daily life and cultural tradition of most Muslims.

Poetry in English has proved possible: Taufiq Rafat (*b.* 1927) and Adrian Husain (*b.* 1942) have helped to evolve a Pakistani idiom in poetry in English, as with a limited reading public, poetry has developed where prose tended to be written in the regional languages. Since educational curricula have adopted an Islamic slant, the position of English as a controlling language has effectively been destroyed.

Although weakened, the influence of English as a literary medium remains. The development of an English voice in Pakistan began amongst Urdu writers with *Angarey* ('The Blazing Cinders') (1932), an early Urdu anthology* that was English in structure and stance. One of the writers in this progressive volume was Ahmed Ali who soon emerged as a major figure in a new Muslim literary movement with stories that have become classics of Urdu prose fiction and which foreshadowed his first novel in English, *Twilight in Delhi*, which laid the foundation of a modest literary tradition in English.

Although Ali's career as a diplomat allowed him little time for writing, he had showed the way to new writers in English; few novelists, however, matched his skill. Perhaps the best of the novels in English was Nisar Farooqi's *Faces of Love and Death*; others include S.M. Ayub's *Shall We Meet Again?* and *Love in Ruins* by Zahir Faruqu. Ali's short stories had also provided a potent example and new journals such as *Vision*, *The Pakistan Review* and *The Orient Literary Magazine* supported experiments in short stories and poetry. Writers such as Junus Said, the founder and editor of *Vision*, Anwar Enayatulloh and Iqbal Ahmed (*b.* 1921) began to define a new cultural situation: their stories reflect the importance of Karachi as the new urban centre of a new Pakistan and the experiences of an intellectual urban middle class under the pressure of radical change. At the centre is the cohesive power of Islamic tradition. Iqbal Ahmed vacillates between the power of the contemporary and the appeal of tradition: 'Time to Go' portrays young Karachi intellectuals in a coffee shop debate with a hopeless tragic undertone. In contrast, 'The Grandmother' affirms the human capacity to survive and create meaning: in the void of a new Pakistan he uses character and setting to indicate points of continuity and tradition which can secure identity. Junus Said's approach is ironic rather than tragic: 'Fidgety' is a fable in which, through the fortunes of a young Pole living in Karachi and dominated by his love of a woman

---

* Ahmed Ali *et al.*, *Angarey*, privately printed, Lucknow, 1932.

and an automobile, he shows the human condition of degeneration from hope to despair and death. Anwar Enayatulloh provides a romanticised and more hopeful interpretation of events in marked contrast to Iqbal Ahmed's tragic realism and Junus Said's cool irony. His stories display his interest in circumstances in which the limits of the human experience, especially evil, are transcended. So 'The Heart Had Its Reasons' with the background of post-partition riots, shows the young lovers separated and then reunited with a final heightened consciousness of the nature of human fulfillment.

No other Pakistani writer in English, however, has attained the achievement of Ahmed Ali in *Twilight in Delhi*, and the use of English as a literary medium has continued to decrease as educational curricula conform to nationalist and Islamic requirements. Some critics, such as Syed Ali Ashraf in his remarks in the journal *Venture* in 1969, have sought to find comfort in the decline of English as a literary medium. For those writers who continue to use English, he claims, 'it will be easier to know who they are, what sort of intelligence they have, what standards are evoked by them and how to please them.'* Among these writers one notes the continuing interest in the short story by Junus Said and M.A. Seljouk, while Bapsi Sidhwa—virtually the only established woman writer in the region—has provided several novels.

Ahmed Ali

Of Ahmed Ali's (*b*. 1910) two major novels *Twilight in Delhi* (1941) and *Ocean of Night* (which appeared in English in 1964), it is the former which has become a classic on the sub-continent. The microcosm of this novel forms also the background of his short story 'The Lane' which features the old Delhi and the Muslim community about the Jama Masjid, the Great Mosque of Delhi. In that early tale of Mirza the milk vendor who mourns his son killed in the clashes that accompanied the Non-Cooperation Movement, we can trace Ahmed Ali's sense of tragedy and the need for structures or wisdom which will survive.

Twilight in Delhi is a study in tragedy and what endures it. The city and the protagonist Mir Nihal are the centre of the work while the idea of transience is expressed through the cluster of metaphors associated with twilight. At the outset Mir Nihal is shown at the peak of his powers and fulfilment, then, through a series of misfortunes he loses mistress, sons, wife and health and has only death to look forward to. In short his life is reduced to 'twilight' while the city itself is similarly oppressed: the old Delhi is largely destroyed in preparation for the coronation of George V as King-Emperor in 1911 and behind this

* Syed Ali Ashraf, Foreword, *Venture*, VI, December 1969, p.3.

destruction is the memory of what Delhi has suffered in various forms over the centuries. What endures is not the city itself, neither individuals nor landmarks, but neighbourhoods and traditions such as the cry of the muezzin and the street vendors. This sample of Ahmed Ali's writing demonstrates how these concerns have been presented and a particular cultural situation defined in universal terms:

> It was with a heavy heart that Mir Nihal went home full of a sense of the futility and transience of the world. But great are the ravages of time, and no one can do anything against its indomitable might. Kings die and dynasties fall. Centuries and aeons pass.But never a smile lights up on the inscrutable face of time. Life goes on with a heartless continuity, trampling ideals and worlds under its ruthless feet, always in search of the new, destroying, building and demolishing once again with the meaningless petulance of a child who builds a house of sand only to raze it to the ground.

Zulfikar Ghose

Zulfikar Ghose's (*b.* 1935) poetry so concisely conveys his sensibility with its mixture of estrangement and delight in language that it is an appropriate starting point to his novels and other writings. Here are two stanzas from the poem 'One Chooses a Language':

II
The English alphabet dangled its A
for Apple when I was eight in Bombay.
I stuttered and chewed almonds for a cure.
My tongue, rejecting a vernacular
for a new language, resisted utterance.
Alone, I imitated the accents
of English soldiers, their pitch and tone.
They were mouths to my tongue's microphone.

IV
Back on the ferry, connecting two shores,
on the stateless sea among anecdotes
and duty-free liquor, I've nothing to say
who said little between Dunkirk and Marseilles.
There's England, my dictionary my ignorance
brings me back to. I give poetry readings
where people ask at the end (just to show
their interest) how many Indian languages I know.

Most noticeable is Ghose's linguistic competence: the choice of a language becomes a metaphor which defines his estrangement from both cultures. The tenor of this is echoed by the context of his travels in Europe and the 'stateless sea' perfectly images his cultural ambivalence. Although his novels and other poems touch on more familiar themes of cultural conflict and change, the sense of estrangement dominates despite a novel such as *The Murder of Aziz Khan* (1968) where the protagonist stands for traditional peasant values threatened by the new order in the persons of the Shah brothers. In essence the story is a traditional one—the despoilment of the simple man by the powerful—but he makes it a moral fable of contemporary Pakistan.

Exile haunts Ghose's writing: as Aziz Khan is exiled from his home so Ghose's own character and himself are estranged from self, home and identity. In order to appreciate his work it is necessary to read his autobiographical *Confessions of a Native Alien* (1965) which recalls both his life as a sensitive youth in Bombay and the experience of being a Muslim in a culture where religious and nationalist ideologies lay a claim upon him. The West is part of his cultural being and yet he remains an outsider and, moreover, uncertain whether he is Indian or Pakistani.

Taufiq Rafat

A poet whose work has been anthologised with other Pakistani poets writing in English—Kaleem Omar (*b*. 1937), Maki Kureishi in *Wordfall* (1975) and Zulfikar Ghose, M.K. Hameed, Shahid Hosain (*b*. 1934), Adrian Husain (*b*. 1942), Nadir Hussein (*b*. 1939), Omar and Salman Tariq Kureshi (*b*. 1942) in *Pieces of Eight* (1971)—Taufiq Rafat (*b*. 1927) is haunted by melancholy. The poem 'Circumcision' gives form to this pervasive feeling:

> ... by the act
> of a pull and downward slash,
> they prepare us for the disappointments
> at the absence of golden birds
> life will ask us to look at
> between our circumcision and death.

Rafat's poems provide, in short, a series of thoughtful meditations on the frailty of the human condition through a human landscape where tragedy and brevity of experience seem the norm, and death, whether by freak accident or the inevitability of time, takes all.

Against this, his landscape poems celebrate warmth, colour and the vitality of life—as in his poem 'Arrival of the Monsoon'—and the landscape itself is something against which the poet hones his imagination to discover himself. A good example of this aspect is 'The Stonechat'. In the unpromising 'eroded hills' Rafat finds himself challenged by the environment and provoked into reflection; 'To understand this waste, I must try and know myself'. By chance he spots a stone-chat, 'his tail vibrating with excitement' and the bird becomes the metaphor through which he learns acceptance:

Intolerant of excuse, he calls
this place home, has learnt to distinguish
between the various shades of grey
till the neighbourhood is a riot of colour,
and a ragged patch of wheat sufficient
cause to be mellifluous about.

Bangladesh: a note

M.M. Datta (1824–73) can serve as a paradigm for the development of Bengali poetry: initially he wholly adopted European modes and then, at the age of thirty-four, turned to Bengali literature and language to create a poetry that demonstrated how traditional language and writing could be enriched by fusion with European literature. His example was followed by writers such as Ananda Coomaraswamy, Akshay Kumar Datta, Ram Mohun Roy and Iswarchandra Vidyasagar. To these writers M.M. Datta's poem on the Bengali language offers a choice:

The spirit of your house in a vision called me then:
'O my child, unnumbered treasures are in your mother's hoard.
Why then as a beggar are you wandering abroad?
Turn back, misguided child, and find your home again.'

Modern Bengali poets such as Shamsur Rahman, Sakti Chattopadhyay, Al Mahmud, Nirendranath Chakravarty, Jibananda Das, Sibnarayan Ray, Ajit Datta and Subash Mukhopadhyay are usually well translated, and their themes cover the traditional spectrum—love, death, parting, the landscape—but explore, too, the violence, poverty and urban social and political themes that characterise contemporary experience. By comparison, for those poets who do write in English, for example Razia Khan in his *Argus under Anaesthesia* (1976), there is often some difficulty in breaking away from the social and cultural context of this well-established Bengali literature and the force of Yeats's reminder to Indian writers 'no man can think or write with music and vigour except in his mother-tongue' gains a qualified credibility.

Sri Lanka

Sri Lankan writing in English issues from the social and cultural tensions symbolised by the country's three principal languages, Tamil, Sinhala and English, and its three main religions, Buddhism, Hinduism and Christianity. English was introduced in the eighteenth century and its colonial origins have prejudiced its role in a national literature when it has been too often a political instrument and status symbol. Traditional literature in Sinhala and Tamil has persisted and encouraged writers in vernaculars to persist in developing a contemporary idiom while the quality of traditional verse can be gauged by the poet and painter George Keyt's translations into English of Sinhalese folk poetry in 1938. Although English has provided the most useful tool for writers who wish to reach a wide readership the position of the language declined during the period of intense nationalism and postcolonial tensions of 1956–76. The feeling of this era is forcefully expressed by Lakdasa Wikkramasinhe's (1941–78) declaration in *Lustre Poems* (1965) that 'to write in English is a form of cultural treason' for it is to use 'the tongue of the most loathsome and despicable people on earth'. Tension, bitterness, as well as the varied inheritance of Sri Lankan life and his familiarity with European culture, have given Wikkramasinhe's poetry 'muscle'; here biculturalism has released energy and he uses European culture and language as an instrument and a foil for his Sri Lankan awareness—as in the poem 'Don't Talk to Me About Matisse'.

The development of the literature

As an instrument of colonial administration English was introduced to Sri Lanka through generations of school children who were taught to admire the literature of the Augustans, Romantics and Victorians, even to imitate their diction and themes, at the expense of the traditional literatures with their roots in village, court and monastery. It is ironic that the first serious Sri Lankan works in English were written by planters, administrators and settlers: first was William Knighton's *Forest-Life in Ceylon* (1854) which merged tropical reminiscence with a Buddhist ethos; second was Leonard Woolf's *The Village in the Jungle* (1913). An Assistant Government Agent, Woolf drew upon his experiences to provide material for an outstanding fictional study of a rural community. Jungle and village form a violent, fatalistic microcosm where Silindu's half-wild family is destroyed by the influences of 'civilisation' personified by the corrupt village leaders—such as Fernando, the Mudalali, who is 'a typical town man, cunning, unscrupulous, with a smattering of education'. Woolf's disenchantment with the colonial enterprise pervades the novel to make it, in his own words, a 'symbol of the anti-imperialism which had been growing upon me more and more in my last years in Ceylon'.* Village life and the

* L.S. Woolf, *Beginning Again*, Hogarth Press, London, 1968, p.47.

Veddahs, the primitive jungle communities, recur in J. Vijayatunga's evocation of rural life, *Grass for My Feet* (1935), while, a little earlier, S.J.K. Crowther's novel *The Knight Errant* (1928), began to explore the consequences of colonial English education and the replacement of a traditional hierarchy by a colonial one.

The Second World War marked a turning-point as Sri Lankan writers began to assert a heightened critical self-awareness. For example, there was a resurgence of Sinhala literature. Led by Martin Wickramasinghe's novels *Gamperaliya* (1944) and *Viragaya* (1956), there was a marked responsiveness to European modernism: techniques of realism and the avant-garde were drawn upon, and the 'Colombo School' of poets abandoned traditional idiom and sought an appropriate diction for contemporary themes. In England, the Ceylonese poet M.J. Tambimuttu (1915–1983) edited the influential journal *Poetry London* while George Keyt's translations and original poetry—*Poems* (1936), *Image in Absence* (1937), *The Darkness Disrobed* (1937)—embodied a new bicultural confidence. The full strength of this new feeling emerges in the work of the poets Lakdasa Wikknamasinhe (*d.* 1978) and Patrick Fernando (*d.* 1982) and the writer of fiction, Punyakante Wijenaike (*b.* 1934), whose works—two collections of short stories, *The Third Woman* (1963), and *The Rebel* (1979), and two novels *The Waiting Earth* (1966) and *Giraya* (1971)—are firmly rooted in Sri Lanka's divided culture and explore the struggle for authentic individuality in unfavourable circumstances.

Drama in an English medium is lacking in substance. The most successful dramatist, Ernest MacIntyre (*b.* 1934), now lives in Australia. He shows a talent for comedy in *The Education of Miss Asia* (1971), a comic-serious examination of cultural confusion in a post-colonial society, while his two short plays, *The Loneliness of the Short-Distance Traveller* (1971) and *A Somewhat Mad and Grotesque Comedy* (1972) demonstrate skills in comic poetry. A recent play, *Dark Dinkum Aussies or Let's Give Them Curry* (1981) focuses upon the experience of a migrant Sri Lankan family in Australia.

Critics and recent history have both played an influential role in the appreciation and development of Sri Lankan literature in English. In Australia, Yasmine Gooneratne (*b.* 1935) has been an acute and prolific critic and editor as well as a poet, the author of *Word, Bird, Motif* (1970) and *The Lizard's Cry* (1972). The violence between Tamil and Sinhalese communities in April 1971 is a traumatic experience in Sri Lankan fiction: it recurs in *Curfew and a Full Moon* (1978) by Ediriweera Sarachchandra, an influential figure in the Sinhala cultural revival, and in Wijenaike's short story 'The Rebel' where the fate of Kumani symbolises that of 'the betrayed and the innocent' to whom the book is dedicated.

Lakdasa Wikkramasinhe

Lakdasa Wikkramasinhe's (1941–78) contribution to Sri Lankan writing epitomises a bicultural and bilingual sensibility. Versed in European letters, he provides an indigenous voice and perspective. His 'To My Friend Aldred' employs an assured literary humour: 'in this Kandyan weather there is no shame in having in your bed a servant maid'—and he cites Tecmessa and Briseis—'Being classical in our traditions'. The catalogue of Josie's charms further accords with the noble ancestry required for true female beauty by Sanskrit tradition, makes various contemporary allusions and ends with a boisterous bawdy conclusion:

And lastly,
in this matter of praise, in your fortune—
thick black coils of hair on her head, and Elsewhere—
I mean, all's well
that ends there
And all roads lead to Rome!

'Stones of Akuratiye Walauwa' expresses the sense of desolation at a culture deprived of its history. Here there is no space for anger—as in 'Don't Talk to Me About Matisse'—but only for sorrow:

There is only the fallow smell of obliterated fields.
And the twenty-one windows of the house
That looked inwards into poetry, into the courtyard
And the grain, drying in the sun, is perhaps
The last memory
Witnessed, before emptiness pervades
Forgotten time.

Against the loss of tradition and history which the broken structure of these lines presents, the poet offers only a fading individual memory. This pessimism is polemical as much as descriptive. In the poem where he describes his craft, 'The Poet', he clearly declares himself a radical who is concerned with change in the depths of the reader's imagination. He is

the one that, tossing a bomb into
The crowd, takes notes;
The one who, from an unseen distance
Levels on the tripod that black rifle
With sights that see as far as his soul . . .

The poet is the bomb in the city,
Unable to bear the circle of the
Seconds in his heart,
Waiting to burst.

This social orientation is demonstrated from a different perspective in the poem 'O Regal Blood'. Here his cultural sensitivity to ancestry responds to the underprivileged casualties of Sinhalese society:

Ashanti was different and I don't know
how many she'd given herself to
to keep alive—
and a two-year old kid she had; but yesterday
I heard she'd drunk acid, raising a great
marsh-howl inside the old house as it burnt
her insides and she died, a seven-month baby
in her belly . . .

The gifts of tone and linguistic vitality are obvious, while at the same time there emerges a humane perspective which presses beyond issues of tradition and cultural conflict to a shared human condition of universal relevance.

Patrick Fernando

Patrick Fernando's (*d.* 1982) poetry is further removed from a Buddhist or Hindu literary tradition than that of almost any other Sri Lankan poet, so much is his work steeped in a Catholic and classical European education. Wry wit, civilised irony and an intense religious vision characterise his poems. This last quality is readily demonstrated by the poem 'One Flock, One Shepherd' where Christ, 'A thorough and efficient person', 'still Abides with us', to feed

thousands with one
Parable of swift unambiguous plot whose power
Expels all doubts and burns the traitorous dark.

Here Christ's triumph is to outwit the great 'Adversary' who is imagined as a wolf. Tone and language relieve the weight of religious clichés. Humour prevails with intelligence and sensitivity in 'The Late Sir Henry':

Two candles light the still impressive head,
Two more the feet, once of a scampering boy.
Sustained with eau-de-cologne the daughters shed
Tears wrung from memories of childhood joy.

Like disciples before Resurrection—
Bankers, brokers, objective though distraught,
Assessed the impact of the sudden loss upon
Politics, trade, industry, Church and sport.

Certain features are striking. The language Fernando uses here is standard English, not a Sri Lankan spoken English idiom such as Yasmine Gooneratne has experimented with in *The Lizard's Cry*. Fernando is too committed to the English medium to be troubled by accusations of 'cultural treason'. Instead he is moved by the incongruity and vulnerability of human experience, for example the detailed contrast between 'the feet' and the reminder, 'once of a scampering boy'. The light touch is characteristic, and the emphasis an endearingly human one. He moved beyond the elegiac moment to contrast the fact of this death with the world that remains utilitarian: observant, ironic, his description is, nevertheless, free of malice.

While this awareness of human frailty and inconstancy links Fernando with a major tradition of European letters it demonstrates again that writers in the new literatures share the common interest of writers everywhere. To stress only patterns of conflict and identity is to obscure the humanity and creative individuality of the writer. In the poem 'The Return of Ulysses' Fernando celebrates humanity through a Ulysses and Penelope who affirm the wonder of human experience which intimates 'transcendence' through its finite, vulnerable, being:

> ...grieving over their god fallen, then gently stooped,
> Gathered the scattered bits reconstructed out of these,
> Secure against destruction, a figure less delicate,
> > less divine,
> But ineffably beautiful.

Chapter 5

Malaysia and Singapore

Malaysia

The political boundaries of contemporary Malaysia are misleading since a Malay-Muslim character is shared by most of the Malay Peninsula, Indonesia and Borneo. Over much of the region Malay has served as a lingua franca although no one great culture has been dominant while Sinic, Indic and Islamic contributions are prominent in the cultural mosaic. The region had never been formally annexed by Britain but governed through Malays, and the ready fall of Malaya to Japanese forces in 1942 showed the lack of political coherence in the region and demonstrates that, even on the Malay Peninsula, Malaya as a nation barely existed.

History and politics

Malaya's colonial history was dominated by commerce. From the sixteenth century it was a crucial link in the spice trade between East and West: Arabs, Portuguese, Dutch, and British sought to gain control of the trade route. During the nineteenth and early twentieth centuries large numbers of Chinese and Indian immigrants worked in the tin mines and rubber plantations, and these communities, now equal in size to the Malays, inevitably gave cultural and economic tensions an ethnic focus. Rural Malay Islamic culture dominates government, and the civil service; the Buddhist urban Chinese community is commercially powerful; while the Indians, mainly Hindu Tamils, are based on the rubber estates. The Federation of Malaysia was declared in 1963 and in 1969 riots erupted in Kuala Lumpur: Malays were angered by Chinese economic dominance, while Chinese were aggrieved by Malay political power.

Language

Although with English there are four main language groups, Bahasa Malaysia has become the national language and the instrument of administration and power. Always associated with an elite, English literature never took root in Malaysia whereas literature from the Islamic world was translated into Malay. As English power has declined in Malaysia so has the English language, and to write in any one of the sectional languages—including English—is to imply political disaffection.

The development of Malay literature

Vernacular Malay literature is normally divided into classical and modern. The former has both oral and written forms which reflect its different contexts—village and court. Its influence is still substantial: the epic *Hikayat Hang Tuah* is admired for Hang Tuah's traditional Malay feudal values and his combat with Hang Jebat has been taken to symbolise the conflict between old and new values.

Modern Malay literature begins with Abdullah bin Abdul Kadir Munshi's nineteenth-century 'autobiography', *Hikayati Abdullah*, which inaugurated a new self-consciousness in Malay writing. In the early twentieth century Syed Sheikh Al-Hady wrote the first Malay novel: set in Cairo, it was a Malay reflection of the Islamic reform movement concerned with traditional morality, patriotism and sexual ethics. While Egyptian popular literature—penny novels, adventure stories and thrillers—was also translated into Malay and influenced Malay writers such as Abdula Rahim Kajai to produce stories with a social, political or religious import, serious modern Malay literature began at the time of the Japanese occupation when Malay nationalism followed the Indonesian example. Whereas pre-war literature tended toward romanticism, post-war Indonesian writing, especially in short stories, demonstrated a realism in accord with the times. In Malay literature also during the nineteen-fifties a realistic, graphic mode concentrated upon urban and social themes; the most important was the group *Angkatan Sasterawan 50* (Generation of Young Writers of the Fifties), usually abbreviated to Asas 50. These writers were school teachers, journalists and civil servants, all based in Singapore and many of them graduates of the Sultan Idris Training College where the first courses in Malay literature had been taught and a translation unit established for translating major works of English literature into Malay for school children. Asas 50 defined the purpose of modern Malay writing and related it to Malay nationalism: its leaders were political activists and fought for the use of Malay as the national language both before and after independence. The slogans 'Language is the soul of the people' and 'Art for society' symbolise the aspirations of the movement demonstrated by writers such as Keris Mas and Usman Awang who expose social problems and voice patriotic themes, concerns echoed in the social moralising of modern Malay drama.

Singapore

Although the literary developments of Malaysia and Singapore need to be considered together, the contrasts are obvious. Since Singapore is an island-city with no local traditional literature, its people and cultures are all 'immigrants', and its industrialised, entrepreneurial, busy English-speaking Chinese society sharply contrasts with that of Malaysia. Singapore's modern history began in 1819 when it was acquired by Raffles for the East India Company as a free port to tap the trade of the Indonesian archipelago and the China Sea. It became a separate Crown Colony in 1946, joined the Federation of Malaysia in 1963, but in 1965 broke away from the Federation to become an independent city-state.

Language

Singapore's multi-cultural population speaks about twenty-five languages and dialects but English is one of the two official languages although not specific to any of the dominant ethnic groups—Tamils, Malays, Chinese. Here English provides coherence, it is what Edwin Thumboo (b. 1933) has called a 'bridge language', and in this complex social mosaic there is no stigma in its use.

Singapore's language and history render identity uncertain, a problem which Malaysia has attempted to resolve by stressing Malay-Muslim values. In Singapore where all are immigrants, in what language is the 'soul' of the people defined when Tamil, Chinese and Malay literary traditions can be invoked? Since no cultural forms are unique to Singapore its remarkable openness to diverse cultural influences is a defining characteristic.

Allied to this, in Singapore English still carries a certain middle-class value and raises the familiar issue of the writer and 'commitment'. Chandran Nair has made the point in his introduction to *Singapore Writing*:

> The writer in English seems more concerned at this moment, with discovering an image of the individual self, of extrapolating human experience. The social milieu of the English educated is a middle class one and they have middle class pretensions.*

The problem has been refined by Edwin Thumboo in his introduction to the anthology *The Second Tongue* (1976) where he points out that Singapore differs from other Third World countries by lacking a hinterland of exploited people for the intellectual elite to seek to speak

---

* Chandran Nair (ed.), 'Creative Writing in Singapore', *Singapore Writing*, Woodrose Publications (for the Society of Singapore Writers), Singapore, 1977, p.1.

for. Instead he suggests that since there is only a hinterland of ideas the search for a national identity primarily has been intellectual.

Development of literature

Whereas modern Malay literature began in the nineteen-twenties with a culture to support it, Singapore writing in English is recent, not clearly defined, and can, for practical purposes, include Malay writing in English since for the region's writers in English the starting point was a shared one, Raffles College, which subsequently became the University of Malaya in Singapore along with King Edward VII Medical College (established 1907).

Three stages characterise the development of this literature. The first stage was imitative and influenced by British education and attitudes, while the second stage has been satirised by one of its representative figures, Ee Tiang Hong (*b*. 1933). It coincided with the rise of Malay nationalism and was dominated by contrived local imagery: as Ee Tiang Hong expresses it, the poetry of the fifties 'was not just wholesale adoption . . . but with local substitutes wherever possible' and he provides a 'model':

Full many a *bunga* was born to blush unseen
And waste its sweetness in the *kaumpung* air.

This question for Singaporean or Malayan themes led to the proposal for a synthetic language 'Engmalchin' derived from English, Malay, and Mandarin; although the proposal lapsed it marks the uncertainties of writers in the nineteen-fifties and sixties and contrasts with the stylistic assurance and mastery of language which characterises the region's contemporary writers. Prose developed in the sixties with writers such as Robert Yeo (*b*. 1940), Dudley de Souza, Arthur Yap (*b*. 1943) and Wong May Pheng, while through the support of the Literary Society of the University of Singapore, writers such as Muhammad Haji Salleh (*b*. 1942), Chandran Nair and Goh Poh Seng (*b*. 1936) began to change the direction of the literature as a whole. Style and technique were honed and the formation of a Society of Singapore Writers in 1976 provided a new forum and an additional impetus. The short stories of Catherine Lim, Shirley Lim's poems, and the presence of energetic and young critical forces in the region, for example Kirpal Singh, suggest that this impetus has not been lost. Thumboo's words apply to more than poetry: 'The present bilingual push . . . could perhaps produce bilingual poets, but, more certainly, encourage poets to become aware of a second, perhaps third, culture as resources for their own poetry'.*

* Edwin Thumboo, *The Second Tongue* (1976), p.xxxv.

Wang Gungwu

In a recent essay Wang Gungwu (*b*. 1930) has commented on the role
of the writer amidst contemporary Asia's rapid social change:

> Not least, there are the creators of memorable literature whose
> imagination captures an inner truth about their society's changes
> and enriches not only their own people but also readers elsewhere.
> For all of them ... there is the remaking of language to match the
> new reality and the painful responsibility to communicate while at
> the same time pushing at the boundaries of comprehension.*

These words define Gungwu's own contribution to the region's literature in English: as a Malaysian historian who has held posts in Malaya
and Australia, Gungwu's influence upon a nascent nationalism and
literature is characterised by a comprehensive Asian awareness. As he
says, 'I have lived in a society with many complex ethnic and religious
groups. To me the idea of homogeneity seems idealistic, abstract and
quite unreal.' A leader in the efforts to establish a regional literary identity in the nineteen-fifties, he comments on 'the contradiction between
our search for *Malayan* poetry and our decision to base that search on the
English verse forms. We used English because it was convenient and we
were in a hurry. We were impatient to write Malayan poetry which we
thought needed only to consist of Malayan images and sentiments.'†

Initially Gungwu's poetry was acclaimed as an advance on previous
verse but while *Pulse* (1950) was a disciplined collection with a varied
diction, it now appears limited and Thumboo only includes one poem
in his anthology. 'Moon Thoughts', while carefully shaped, echoes the
literary diction inherited from English literature and demonstrates the
laboured attempts at a Malayan context:

> The moon, impure as ever, like tea leaves,
> Coffee dregs, on a cup of cream, cleaves
> Onto drooping leaves of rubber trees,
> ... the same
> That shone on ancient heroes born.
> Thought loiters among the glorious shades,
> And martyrs and lovers, alike they came,
> Welcome as dewdrops onto the evening lawn:
> How they embalm the thought cells,
> How they sweeten the deepest depths of mind's own dells.

---

* Wang Gungugu, 'Race, Religion and Nationalism in Asia', *Westerly*, No. 3, Septem-
ber 1971, p. 61.
† See H. Aveling, 'Singapore Malaysian Poetry', *South Pacific Images* (ed. C-R.
Tiffin), SPACLALS, Brisbane, 1978, p.87.

Ee Tiang Hong

Born in Malacca in 1933, Ee Tiang Hong attended the University of Malaya in Singapore from 1951 to 1956, taught in Malaysia and migrated to Western Australia in 1975 to become an Australian citizen in 1979. Ee has published three volumes of poetry, *I of the Many Faces* (1960), *Lines Written in Hawaii* (1973), and *Myths for a Wilderness* (1976) and belongs to the 'first generation' of writers which includes Edwin Thumboo and, later Wong Phui Nam (*b*. 1935), who assembled at the University of Malaya in Singapore. Many of the poems in the first collection reflect the social, political and cultural crisis of this period, as, for example, 'Address':

Riding on air in American car comfort
So big you will not even feel a stir,
Will your coxcomb ever bend again
To the wonder of the people?

Current political messages sustain poems such as 'Retreat' and 'Patriotism' which voice the post-independence disenchantment brought about by events such as the race riots of 1969. 'Retreat' reads:

Those who in quadrangle, hall and common room
Tabled their dreams in angry eloquence,
And saw the mob's rejection and the compromise,
Have shifted from their premises,
Sealed their ambitions in a grip
Of tight cockles dumb within
Dungeons of granite shells
And a soundlessness of mud.
Exile where they may they will encounter
The same creatures riding on the crest
And backwash of the same wave
Rolling in complacent measure,
See how futile it is to shed
One anger against the world.

Ee's poetry is replete with allusions to places—Singapore, Kuala Lumpur, Malacca, Hawaii—which give an assurance of identity while the poems mark an acute, alienated self-awareness. At a more obvious level the reflections on places allow opportunity for reflections on society and history, particularly in the Malacca poems with their poignant contrasts of past and present—in, for example, 'Tranquerah, Malacca':

Endurance is the hallmark of the stone
That bears the fickle traffic,
The purposes unfulfilled, coming and going.

More substantial is his reflection in 'Heeren Street, Malacca', where he recalls the Babas' past with their triumphant adaptation of Chinese origins, Malay context and British loyalty:

> Here in the good old days
> The *Babas* paved
> A legend on the landscape . . .

Against this past he sets the crass and sordid present where change has overtaken former glory:

> Newcomer urchin strides the gutter,
> Reeking cockroach, rat and faeces.
> On *charpoy jaga* fast asleep.
>
> Beneath antique lanterns,
> The *Babas*, comfortable on old benches,
> Gaze at Fords and Mercedes
>
> While swallows shrill
> Shriek in the twilight
> Stealing over the obscurity of eaves.

This use of irony and understatement marks a secure poetic identity despite the stressful resonance. Ee's control of language, its freedom from rhetoric and obscurity while firmly rooted in a genuine concern for social issues, reflect his consistent concern for craftsmanship. 'On Writing a Poem' expresses this:

> To be simple is to be involved
> In a whole chaos, the claims and counterclaims
> Of mind, heart, word, a universe
> on fire—and the final sacrifice

In short, here the poet is a mediator. His Baba background has made him sensitive to cultural mix and change, and his terse, wry lines express a dispossession which, while doubtless initiated in personal experience, moves into the wider domains of general human estrangement.

Edwin Thumboo

Now Professor of English at the National University of Singapore, Edwin Thumboo (*b.* 1933) was at the centre of the first group of poets who established the region's literature in English during the first phase of self-conscious literary nationalism. His first collection of poems, *Rib of Earth* (1956), was the most substantial, and subsequently his poetry, criticism and anthologies have been formative contributions. His volumes of verse are *Gods Can Die* (1977) and *Ulysses by the*

Merlion (1979) while his anthologies include *Seven Poets: Singapore and Malaysia* (1973) and *The Second Tongue: An Anthology of Poetry from Malaysia and Singapore* (1976).

As a critic Thumboo has placed Singaporean and Malaysian writing in an historical, literary and international perspective, provided arguments for maintaining the use of standard English in Singapore, and imaginative strategies for coping with cultural complexity and change. Thumboo has related geographical size to the nature of Singaporean English: it is 'such a hospitable language, it has survived words like "pukka", and if we can add a few of ours, why not? But the *grammar* has to be stable... because a small country never has its language learned by other people.'* Yet the loss of myth in a once myth-oriented society can be compensated for in its languages and he remarks: 'You can *tap* the myth because the myth has shaped the language and if you learn the language, its dominant symbols enter into you.'†

Implicit in these comments is Thumboo's conservatism. Social themes and stylistic innovations are placed within 'the main creative tradition in English' while his own poetry demonstrates his preference for reticence, irony and an international style. 'Words' is indicative of the man:

Words are neither valid, merciful nor bad,
in themselves, nothing unless used, urged,
Imported into dialogue,
Becoming part-anger, part-laughter, bruised,
Adding to the mood and gesture.
Words are words. Except for us
They are not personalities.

This is not to dismiss his social commitment. In his own words the heady experiences of the nineteen-fifties and meetings with Wang Gangwu and Beda Lim helped him to see at the outset 'that politics was important'. Yet his chief achievement has been to clarify issues and find strategies. In his own words:

The search for an idiom is ongoing. I picked the most international of languages, one upon which the sun never sets... I wish to stay within its grammer but take lexical liberties.**

In short, for Thumboo language and literary tradition have formed a bridge by means of which he achieves and mediates unity in a complex

---

* Interview with Peter Nazareth in *Pacific Quarterly Moana* 7: 2, 1982, pp.99–101.
† Ibid., pp.99–101.
** Edwin Thumboo, 'The Search for Style and Theme: a Personal Account', *The Writer's Sense of the Contemporary* (ed. B. Bennett, Ee Tiang Hong, R. Shepherd), Centre for Studies in Australian Literature, Perth, 1982, p.5.

society while the urbane control of his poetry communicates this *modus vivendi.*

> We are flexible, small, a boil
> On the Melanesian face.
> If it grin or growl, we move—
> To corresponding place,
> Keeping sensitive to trends, adapting,
> To these delinquent days.

Wong Phui Nam and Omar Mohammed Noor

Wong Phui Nam's (*b*. 1935) collection of poems, *How The Hills Are Distant* (1963), is a sequence of twenty poems which represents a major advance in the region's poetry. Richness of language and a complex style provide the means through which Wong attains a vibrant and comprehensive poetic statement. His verse paragraphs build upon a landscape that is partially in the poet's mind and yet also external. A welter of sensual detail and a network of allusion provide a luminous world in which a new understanding seems imminent; the technique is almost cinematographic, often the lines are crammed and tense. In manner and mood he recalls other poets in the new English Literatures such as Derek Walcott and Nissim Ezekiel. Where he finds the environment isolated, vacuous, he uses language to engage it, penetrate it and provide a private landscape which has public significance for his generation of Malaysians. The last lines of his sequence demonstrate this:

> There are no shrines.
> Inland, the terrain is locked in salt
> where the beasts and fowls of the air
> lay down their bones by bitter lakes.
> There are no pilgrimages but into the rocks' madness
> at noon or their whimpering in the chill by night.
> Let the shadows upon the rocks
> number among losses. This is a time to endure
> camping upon the lonely beaches,
> content not to take much stock
> by shooting stars, auguring the advent of sails.

By contrast with Thumboo's work his poetry appears less disciplined, but against the loss of an absolute clarity and control must be set the gains: this montage, its blurred distinction between actual and image, excites. Where Thumboo appears a diagnostician, Wong Phui Nam acts as a prophet, an intellectual outcast who indicts his society's failure to comprehend itself.

Wong Phui Nam's sustained attempt at epiphany is in direct contrast with the style adopted by his younger contemporary, Omar Mohammed Noor whose 'international' diction echoes Philip Larkin (*b*. 1922) and e.e. cummings (1894–1962). This direct spare style represents another technique in the Singapore—Malaysia context. 'Three Layers' demonstrates its strength:

there are three layers of rural areas
the first became towns and cities a half-generation ago
the second now becoming towns
with yellow electricity and greyish pipe-water
here some of the characteristics of jungles are intact
the third is still a jungle by itself
only the electricity of the sun permeates it
the stars compensate for the lack of light
by shining extremely brightly
as they never do in towns
which mock their services.

Muhammad Haji Salleh

Muhammad Haji Salleh's (*b*. 1942) sensibility is rooted in traditional Malay culture; he speaks for its rural foundation and recalls a heritage stretching beyond the boundaries set by colonial powers. For example, 'Blood' affirms the Malay-Indonesian connection:

The blood in me has travelled the centuries
flowed in unknown veins
crossed swampy rivers and proud swamps
the loins that have borne my beginnings
stood in their past
the great-grandfather who stood in piety
had filtered his purity into his dutch-hating son
who walked with him and with god
they dominated their communities and their traditions
purified the ancestral mud to clean earth
and grew in its clutch children of faith

much as i owe, i am
i am both branch
and remote stalk of this tree.

The poetic self here is always in the lower case, his identity deliberately subordinate to the larger purpose of illustrating the implications of his people's fate. At the same time his search for identity and origins reflects a consistent theme in Malay-Singaporean literature.

Rural experience and poverty are emphases which stress both his antipathy to urban life and his implicit belief that in these rural communities lies a centre of value bound by courtesies, traditions and ceremonies. 'Tropics' is an example:

here,
they still dance and sing graceful
with hands and voices that reach the heart.

Yet this village life is threatened and 'Quiet Village' voices anger at the destruction of rural communities tied to an economy where 'the rubber tree is no factory, prices come from businessmen' and 'industry is only a mark of the satiated'. A poem where rural and urban contexts are juxtaposed is 'the traveller' and it serves as a parable of the search for identity in the midst of social change:

some night when the city is asleep
i'll walk out quietly along your cruel streets
through the suburban edge and into the dawn forests.
somewhere, perhaps near where the sun rises,
i can sit down,
and sometimes perhaps, i can tell myself,
here, i am a man.

While Haji Salleh's first volume of poetry, *Time and Its People* (1978), reflected his travels and studies in England, Singapore, Indonesia and the United States and the influence of his mentors, D.J. Enright (*b*. 1920) and Edwin Thumboo, it demonstrated his capacity to establish coherence and identity: 'They are legitimate worlds and I do not disown them. I find them in my experiences as well as in my works. They are the first and last sources for these poems and I try to work out an existence in contemporary predicaments.'

Johnny Ong and Goh Poh Seng

Only in the nineteen-sixties did worthwhile fiction appear. This reflects both the superficial impact of English literature upon the cultures already established in Malaysia and Singapore, and a reluctance to employ a realistic mode where sources of potential conflict were so near the surface.

Johnny Ong's *Sugar and Salt* (1964) was launched in London and acclaimed by Anthony Burgess and others who considered it an accomplished portrayal of life and characters in tropical Malaya. Flaws were readily put down to Ong's youth (he was only nineteen) and the fact that there were really no literary models for him to follow. Naivety and clichés marred its fluent style and freshness while its descriptive passages were of most interest to an overseas readership, although the plot, based upon an inter-racial love affair between Chinese and Indian, was superficial. Nonetheless, in its place and time it has historical significance.

Goh Poh Seng (b. 1936) is one of the most prolific writers in the region. A medical practitioner, he has, since 1958, published poems, plays and several novels and short stories. With Lim Lok Ann, Goh Poh Seng established Centre 65 which provided him with a theatre for his plays: *The Moon is Less Bright* (1964), *When Smiles Are Done* (1965), *The Elder Brother* (1966). Goh's novels marked the next stage in his literary career: *If We Dream Too Long* (1972), *The Immolation* (1977), which were succeeded by his collections of poetry, *Eyewitness* (1976) and *Lines from Batu Ferringhi* (1978).

Like his protagonist in the short story *Temple Bells*, Goh is characterised by his resolve to 'work hard'. Earnestness betrays him: his prose verges on social documentation and its language clogs, as for example in the tedious description of the protagonist's thought sequences in *If We Dream Too Long*. Unfortunately this lack of discipline extends to Goh's poetry, and rhetoric mars *Eyewitness*:

A castaway, whose identity was
Finally unconcealed:
Me! Me! Me!

Lloyd Fernando

Formerly Professor of English at the University of Malaya, now a lawyer, Lloyd Fernando (b. 1926) has published an anthology, *Twenty-Two Malaysian Stories* (1968), as well as numerous critical articles and a novel, *Scorpion Orchid* (1976). These represent major developments in the literature of the region. Set in the nineteen-fifties, the years of great changes for Singapore and Malaysia, *Scorpion Orchid* mixes different modes of writing with unusual and subtle effects. On a primary realistic level the story is concerned with the different perspectives of Malay, Chinese, Indian and Eurasian bohemians, whose speech and aspirations reflect a crisis of experience through their relationship with Sally who, herself of mixed race, is left to be raped by a mob. Inserts of history, fable, and stream-of-consciousness narrative, suggest processes independent of the characters themselves: for example some of the extracts from the older literature of the region subtly disclose undesirable aspects of colonialism while they illuminate tensions and attitudes in the dominant characters.

Scorpion Orchid is a bold examination of latent racial tensions. As the plot unfolds, so areas of cultural friction are clarified, and although written in the nineteen-seventies about events twenty years earlier, it makes disturbing reading. Peter, a displaced Portuguese Eurasian, is singled out by his awareness of estrangement. The burning of a Eurasian in a street riot, one of the most horrifying events in the book, images the more subtle destruction of identity imposed by the obligation to learn Malay. The final discussion between Sabran and Peter makes the point:

> I was born in Malacca speaking Portuguese . . . then because the British had ousted the Dutch, I learnt English and forgot Portuguese. It was like taking out the parts and organs of my body and replacing them with others. Then the Japs came and we were told forget English, learn Japanese. So once more I began taking out parts and putting in new ones—unlearning my language and learning another. Now it seems I must unlearn it once more and learn Malay . . . I've gone through the process so many times, I can't any more. Say I'm a colonial creature because I speak English . . . You want to unlace all my nerves and tie them up in a different set of knots. How many times? . . . The process is simply repeating itself, why can't it stop?

Lee Kok Liang

A lawyer, educated in Chinese and English, practising in Penang, Lee Kok Liang uses the background of the neighbourhoods of Penang and Ipoh for most of his writing. He has produced the most sophisticated fiction in English in the region, particularly in the short story genre as his collection *Mutes in the Sun* (1964) demonstrates. In both these stories and in the recent novel *Flowers in the Sky* his sense of place dominates and the complex variety of the Malaysian scene is both source and setting.

'Return to Malaya' demonstrates Lee's adroit handling of the short story genre. For reasons suggested by the title, impressions matter, and related to them are themes which recur in his other works: the ear for the sound of a language, the sense of the landscape, colonialism, change, the alienation of the protagonist. These themes recur elsewhere in his writing, their treatment shaped by Lee's wit and instinct for irony.

Most of Lee's fiction is set in the contemporary world, that is from 1950 to the present, and 'Return to Malaya' celebrates Malay place and character. For example the sound of language in the streets as the protagonist overhears the children and the comments of the card players. A good writer, Lee is not troubled by a dialect form of language and the sound and rhythm are vivid:

> *'I saw a rat to-day-lah.'*
> *'A big fat rat with a long tail-lah.'*

'Oo-ee oo-ee oo-ee' (A sharp whistle sounded).
'One two som, la-la-li-tum-bong.'
... They spoke in a sort of Hokkien Chinese [towns in Malaya are dominated by different Chinese dialects] with a few Malay and English expressions thrown in. Their conversation was not the lazy dingdong dialogue. It was more a ringing of voices than anything else; a sudden release of exultant feelings. Somehow they all wanted to talk at the same time and succeeded in doing so. Like starlings, twittering and wheeling in a mass, they filled the night with their high voices. Night-time was talking time for them.

Elsewhere the climate and landscape at evening impart a vivid quality to the inhabitants—'who strolled gently about in brilliant clothes'—and release sensuality, 'hidden desires'. This theme recurs in *Flowers in the Sky* but Lee contrasts this exciting cultural milieu with the behaviour of the Europeans who even walk differently, for example, in the evening in the marketplace:

Suddenly, striding down the alley, a belated theatrical figure made his appearance: tall, fearsome, high in the nose, with stormy sunset complexion, wearing a bow-tie and flowing nylon shirt; and, without turning his head, bore himself like a dreadnought through the crowds as though he had a mission to fulfill, or as if, a neighbour commented, he was hunting for the lavatory. In other words, an Englishman had walked by.

The subversion achieved here, through the mock-heroic anti-climax, underscores the estrangement of the colonial power and its agents from the life of the community. This is subsequently stressed further through the amusement of villagers at soldiers playing football in the heat, while the strange appearance of the 'sullen-eyed Home Guard boys' brings a reminder of the changing social fabric: the fact of the Emergency and indigenes who are separated from their own people.
Change is painted in through the use of a subtly pervasive technique. A street hawker is a 'gradually vanishing tribe'; there are New Villages 'as attractively planned as a poultry farm'; an old bridge is to be pulled down and replaced with 'a new million dollar bridge' while, more generally, 'Western democracy was beginning to seep through the town'. Yet this is more than documentation on a social level: the change in society is seen through the eyes of a protagonist who, as we realise ever more clearly, is himself estranged from his society. The method is oblique: for him the tropical rain is refreshing, 'like having points of sunlight on one's face on a cold winter's morning, say in London', but between him and his society there is now mainly silence. He visits old friends: 'A few more desultory remarks and I left them.' His predicament worsens as he visits his wife or former mistress to find her in

poverty with a disease which has rendered her barely able to speak. The protagonist can only speak in clichés and evades further responsibility by leaving abruptly. The individual aspect of experience is never forgotten. Lee exposes the pretensions of the protagonist by an incisive but unobtrusive irony while the title of the collection, *Mutes in the Sun*, symbolises the limitations of human behaviour and the breach wrought in traditional life.

Silence almost dominates *Flowers in the Sky* where Lee brings together two dominant and two subordinate plots which act like a series of mirrors to reflect a central theme: the contradictions of flesh and spirit and the religious means which can most adequately do justice to human reality. So, at the centre, is the Buddhist monk Hung, who is troubled by the tension between his training in China and his desire for the mute girl Ah Lan. Hung is at the hospital, the 'Marvellous Cure Centre' managed by the Ceylonese surgeon Mr K who, while disciplined as a surgeon, is pre-eminently a man of sensual indulgence and is nevertheless fascinated by Hung with whom he can only converse through dumb-show signs or interpreters. These expatriates move toward self-awareness against the backdrop of the rich variety of Malaysia itself. Some of this variety is to be found in the first half of the novel in the minor story of Inspector Gopal, torn between his sense of duty and his religious-sexual passion for a *shakti* on whom and through whom his meditations will be focused. His inability to disperse a crowd which has gathered to revere a statue of Ganesh enables him to achieve a comic reconciliation of sexual and spiritual elements which counterpoints both Hung and Mr K. In the second half of the novel the story of Ah Looi with her fear of death and her ultimate defeat by cancer presents the basic human need for religious faith against the contradictions of religious practice. Here tragedy and irony come together.

There are human predicaments. Hung, for example, brings his Chinese Buddhism to the very different climate of Malaysia, and finds the situation a testing one:

> What he was not warned against was the heat of this country . . . He found himself sweating as he had never sweated in his life . . . corroding him, reminding him . . . of . . . his private parts and of the impermanence and corruption of the body.
>
> (*Flowers in the Sky*, p.33)

Here is an old cultural tradition transplanted and in practice liable to become distorted. It is an exquisite irony that Hung leaves the hospital in a status symbol of the new culture, a Mercedes with the number plate 666 which has ambiguous symbolic meaning—joy in Cantonese but diabolism for Christians. At the same time individual predicaments remain. At the centre is silence: the mute girl Ah Lan can only communicate her feelings through her paintings, and Hung does not allow her to do this. Again, as in *Mutes in the Sun*, social and individual perspectives are implied. Although in Malaysia religion is a sensitive social indicator of the measure of understanding and incomprehension—and this is a basic aspect of the novel—Lee manages to blend with this the individual perspective which can involve suffering but also, as in Gopal's case, fulfilment. His use of irony points out the contradictions, but with details that suggest a possibility of happiness. In this sense he not only reflects his society but illuminates key elements for its future.

Various writers: Lee Tzu Pheng, Chandran Nair, Robert Yeo, Arthur Yap

---

Lee Tzu Pheng (*b.* 1946) is arguably one of the finest of the region's poets in a generation which has been spared the turbulence, anxiety and social urgency with which Thumboo and Goh Poh Seng had to come to terms. With this change in time different approaches became appropriate and Lee Tzu Pheng demonstrates a more private mode of address. For example, in the urbanised multi-cultural milieu of Singapore she has expressed a new sense of rootlessness in words which have been often quoted:

> My country and my people
> are neither here nor there, nor
> in the comfort of my preferences,
> if I could even choose.   ('My Country and My People')

The qualities to be singled out here are directness, fluency and a capacity to use cadences to capture an atmosphere, the sensibility of a moment. For example the use of 'even' in the last line introduces a calculated hesitancy. The device recurs in her poem 'Because I Only Write' where the personal strain dominates:

> because I only write,
> not knowing where and how to bring
> these feelings to your doorstep,
> my hands hold no order,
> transfer no look, no grace,
> cannot contain the red pulse of the heart,
> only the blue throb over the page;
> small, drying in ways not mine.

Also of Tzu Pheng's generation, Chandran Nair demonstrates how the search for identity endures in the necessity to test values, relationships and to express selfhood. Nair tends to write in an almost contorted fashion as he probes the pain of cultural dislocation:

I have broken from the past,
history etched in ancestral blood,
bodies sword torn, shields hacked
to hands that have turned to writing
and dashed across my throat dry words.　　　　　('Dry Words')

Invariably what is at stake in these various approaches is the question
of human survival. Not necessarily physical survival but emotional
wholeness, and the poetry is an instrument which establishes order in
an environment where the individual is uncertain. The 'younger' poets
have resorted to different, often slick tones. For example, Arthur Yap
(*b.* 1943) records the substance of social change, and evokes its emotional consequences through flat statement.

so what if this is
your grandfather's house
his ghost doesn't live here anymore
your family past is
superannuated grime
which increases with time
otherwise nothing adds or subtracts
the bricks and tiles
until re-development

which will greatly change
this house-that-was
dozens like it along the street
the next and the next as well
　　　　　　　　　　　　　　　('Old House at Ang Siang Hill')

Related to this, but taking up a disenchanted, more political stance, are
Robert Yeo's (*b.* 1940) comments in 'Out of Changi' (Changi being a
prison built by the British and used by the Japanese occupation forces
and, since independence by the Singapore government):

The elected
In their difficence
Had shut you up,
Now in their confidence
Have released you,

Having meantime secured the house,
Evicted legally S. Kee
His landlords and his tenants,
Efficiently removed other eyesores
That platformed your protest
And renovated and overhauled with new ideas . . .

> No doubt they will further construct and expand
> With you along.

These poets reflect the complexity of changes in the region, whether an elementary loss of identity, of tradition, the demolition of loved buildings or a lost political ambition, they give shape to vital but barely expressed feelings in their society, while the work of more recent poets such as Chung Yee Chong and Sng Boh Khim indicate that poetry in the region will continue to perform this prophetic function.

A note on the drama: Edward Dorall and other playwrights

Various factors have limited the growth of drama in English in the literature of Malaysia and Singapore. In Malaysia traditional dramatic forms such as Ma'yong, Manorah and shadow play are no longer appreciated by urban audiences while new drama has been constrained by the emphasis upon Bahasa Malaysia. While Singapore lacks a strong base for drama, political and class considerations have been even more detrimental: rigorous censorship laws, a sensitive mix of races, cultures, languages, and the fact that the writers tend to come from middle and upper-middle classes often with overseas educational experiences which separate them from their society and reflect racial divisions. These are crucial considerations in so public a genre and the consequences are reflected in the limited scope, depth and range of Malaysian-Singaporean drama in English.

A Singaporean lawyer, Lim Chor Pee was the first to write plays in English set in Singapore: *Mimi Fan* (1962), *A White Rose at Midnight* (1963), *An Affair with Pearl* (1970). Although in the first two plays the gulf between education in English-medium and Chinese-medium schools is a dominant theme, it provides a more comprehensive concern—the Singaporean search for an identity which Chan Fei-Loong articulates in *Mimi Fan* alongside the tension between traditional values and the demand for change:

> It's a sickness. We call this the local mentality. Before I came back from England I told myself one day I would change all this sickness. Then I discovered that I too am becoming sick inside. No, we must first grow up ourselves. We must learn the hard way and find our own identity.

In Malaysia Lee Joo For has established a reputation with about forty plays for stage and radio as well as many short stories and two novels. *Son of Zen*, which was produced in the United States, develops the quest for an Asian identity in the central character—Kenzo—who draws his powers from the traditions symbolised by Zen Buddhism. In his quest cultural and universal elements are synthesised and Kenzo becomes an Everyman, but his dilemma remains unresolved.

Patrick Yeoh's (*b.* 1940) plays include: *Father*, *The Clay Model*, *Gamble or The Rules of the House*, *Bajar*, *Stools*, *The Need to Be* and *When All the Winds Blow*. *The Need to Be* is a naturalistic study of the poor of Malaysian society. It concerns a squatter family in Kuala Lumpur awaiting the return of their eldest son who has studied law in England. Despite the sacrifices made for him by his family Kok Keong does not return and the family breaks up without the play reaching a decisive conclusion. This departure from a middle-class background gives the play a special place in Malaysian English-language drama, despite the fact that Yeoh uses a flat standard English with inserts from Malay Cantonese, and the dialogue lacks the characteristic Malaysian idiom which the best of Dorall's plays achieve.

Goh Poh Seng's plays need special mention: *The Moon is Less Bright* (1964), *When Smiles Are Done* (1965), *The Elder Brother* (1967) have all been performed in Singapore and *When Smiles Are Done* has been produced in Kuala Lumpur under a title from the last line of the play, *Room with Paper Flowers*. The popularity of this last play is perhaps due to its theme—the problems created by inter-racial marriages and class prejudices. The action centres about Raju, an Indian who marries Jenny Wong, a Chinese, and Wong Chong Kit who has impregnated Mary Ho, a bar girl.

Edward Dorall's earliest plays were designed for production as school plays and reflect his earlier profession as a teacher: *The Young Must Be Strong* (1965), *Arise O Youth* (1966), *A Tiger is Loose in Our Community* (1966) and *A Time for a Man to Say No* (1967–8). Obvious ancillary public issues are included: mixed marriages and the pressures of the inherited colonial examination system are especially stressed. The preface to *Arise O Youth* indicates Dorall's special interest in the problem of a dramatic literary Malay-English:

> The real problem of my play . . . is linguistic, not educational. I have chosen my central characters from the lower middle class of Malaysian society and I have put into their mouths a selection of the language which people in their social class would actually use. The problem that arises is whether the resulting pidgin English, with tenses limited, or absent altogether, pronouns confused, plurals often ignored, vocabulary unadventurous, and the whole punctuated by 'ah's, 'la's and 'wah's—the problem is whether this crippled but colourful dialect can be used extensively in drama, not only for comic and realistic effects, but also for pathos and tragedy.

Dorall demonstrates that this language can be used to good effect for pathos and tragedy. It is not just that Malaysians invest examinations with enormous emotional importance, but here, when Kong Leong's father hears of his son's failure, the broken idiom accords with the shattering emotional experience:

> What I do now? What I do? I got nothing. (*Sadly*) No more hope. No more happy. All finish. I don't want even hit you. I don't want do anything.

Here at least is one clear effective example of the variety of English idioms in the region—Dorall is a master of the Chinese form—and it remains for other dramatists to use the different racial idioms creatively in a literature which has at its heart the problem of communication in a society where race, culture and language still divide and define identity.

Chapter 6

The Philippines

SET AT THE CROSSROADS between Asia and the Pacific, the cultural and racial mix of Philippine life has shaped its literature. From Borneo, according to Visayan epics, came waves of migrations which forced Negrito aborigines of the Philippines into the mountains and established a Malay dominance. From China came other waves of settlers and on top of these were later imposed Spanish and American cultural influences. In 1521 the coming of Magellan brought the Spanish rule and, with it, western civilisation and Christianity. A harsh colonial power, Spain united the loose conglomeration of Philippine tribes into one nation and its regime was marked by sporadic revolts which culminated in the great revolution of 1896 and the inauguration of the First Philippine Republic in 1898 and 1899. In 1898 the American presence was established in the Philippines and with this came democracy and, crucial for the later literature, the English language. Despite economic and political advantages the American presence has made the Philippines a market for American culture and consumer goods to the detriment of indigenous cultural resources. Against this ambiguous background of diverse influences the English-medium literature of the Philippines has emerged.

Pre-Hispanic literature

Language is a crucial issue in the Philippines because the literature is written in many languages. When the Spaniards arrived they discovered a literate people: the Tagalogs, Visayans, Ilocanos and other ethnic groups had an alphabet, and their songs, poetry and stories still remain.

The Spanish presence (*c*. 1565—*c*. 1782)

Under the Spanish political and religious influence Filipino writing gradually abandoned its traditional literary forms and became primarily religious, imitating Spanish forms and themes. Much of the secular literature was poetry and Fernando de Bagongbanta is generally regarded as the father of Tagalog poetry; his poems which date from about 1606 were among the first publications in the region and were followed by a variety of religious poems. The *corrido* (eight syllables to the line) and the *awit* (twelve syllables to the line) were forms used for legends in verse. Both evolved from European romances and the Spanish introduction of this form culminated in the awit *Florante at Laura* by Francisco Baltazar (1788–1862) which, set in Albania to escape the Spanish censor, gave expression to the nascent Filipino nationalism.

The last decade of the nineteenth century is the era of Jose Rizal (1861–96) and his contemporaries. This has been called the Golden Age of Philippine literature and includes poets such as Fernando Guerrero, Cecilio Apostel, Claro Recto, Manuel Bernabe, and, above all, Rizal himself. Born in Calamba, Luzon, in 1861, Rizal experienced the disadvantages of being a Tagalog under colonial rule and he went to Europe to study. A frequent traveller between Europe and the Philippines, he was regarded in official quarters as a *filibustero*, a revolutionary. His first book *Noli Me Tangere* (1887) pointed out the abuses of the colonial rule while his second work, *El Filibusterismo* (1891) is more political. Rizal was executed for his views and became a martyr for Philippine nationalism: his poem *Mi Ultimo Adios* ('My Last Farewell') is said to have been written on the eve of his execution.

Drama

Drama has for a long time been used in the Philippines as an expression of Filipino consciousness and indigenous forms have continued to be used. The *duplo* and the *karagatan* are debates in rhyme: the former is staged by professionals as entertainment during a wake, the latter by amateurs for recreation. The *moro-moro* is a huge performance at an annual fiesta and is like a staged *awit* but is written by a local writer for his community. Others are the *zarzuela* and the *Pasion* and some of these works reflect anti-Spanish and anti-American sentiments from the late nineteenth century onward. Again these are forms of entertainment which reflect local circumstances, and one of the great examples of this was the explosion of vernacular theatre in Iloilo City from about 1903 to 1930 when about seventy *zarzuela* were produced in Ilongo, one of the eight major Filipino languages. The *zarzuela* was inspired by frustrated nationalism and through it the stage became an urban entertainment with an intense didactic purpose.

The American presence

From 1896 to 1902 revolutionary armies led by members of the Filipino elite fought both the Spanish and American colonial regimes. By 1898 the Spanish had been defeated, but the Filipinos had to come to terms with the Americans, who promised a greatly liberalised colonial administration and had occupied Manilla in 1898. The Americans removed censorship regulations, permitted the formation of political parties, trade unions and non-Catholic religious organisations. During the period of American colonialism (1900–41) English became the popular language and school teachers from the United States so americanised the school system that a literature in English was rapidly produced which rivalled that hitherto written in Spanish and the vernaculars. The commonly accepted pattern of literary development from 1898 to 1945 assumes three distinct stages:

1. *Apprenticeship* (1898–1930): Little was published in English before 1910 since during the first years of American colonisation the Filipinos were preoccupied with adapting to an alien tongue. Pioneer work in literature in English began about 1910 through *College Folio*, a journal devoted to literature in English and sponsored by the University of the Philippines. It was the first of an impressive number of such journals which included: *The Philippine Review*, *The Philippine Columbian Notes*, *The Philippines Free Press*, *The Philippines Herald*, *The Philippines Magazine*. Essays and ideas abounded while in creative writing the short story dominated although encumbered with messages and moralising. The best of the writers was probably a woman, Paz Marquez-Benitz, whose first story was published in 1920. Her restrained style and discriminating vocabulary are demonstrated in 'Dead Stars' with its portrayal of human indecision and disillusionment.

2. *Emergence* (1930–44): By 1930, when the Commonwealth of the Philippines was established, writers were influenced by essayists and American teachers who stressed the particular traditions of Philippine society and argued that writers should record barrio life and rural virtues, retell legends and folk tales. Writers of the period include Jose Garcia Villa (*b*. 1914) whose claims for artistic autonomy vied with the Philippine Writers' League's manifesto which read:

> All writers worthy of the name are, whether they are conscious of it or not, workers in the building up of culture. Since economic injustice and political oppression are the enemies of culture, it becomes the clear duty of the writer to lend his arm to the struggle against injustice and oppression in every form in order to preserve those cultural values which generations of writers before him have built up with slow and painful effort.

Salvador P. Lopez (*b*. 1911) was one whose literary commitment epitomised the movement of many Filipino writers against romanticism and toward realism at a time of rapid changes, particularly urbanisation, industrialisation. Where Villa stressed the claims of art, Lopez stressed social responsibility and these complementary influences were reflected in the maturity of the literature produced by writers such as Carlos Bulosan (*d*. 1956), N.V.M. Gonzalez (*b*. 1915) and Manuel Arguilla (*b*. 1911). Although the Japanese occupation of the Philippines delayed literary development the course was set and its national awareness established. In the drama there were Carlos Romulo (*b*. 1898), Vidal Tan, Wilfred Guerrero and Severino Montano who organised the Arena Theatre and took a contemporary Filipino drama to the people.

3. *The Japanese period* (1941–5): Some writers were executed by the Japanese and during this period most of the writing in English was by expatriates: Villa and Bulosan were in America while Carlos Romulo and Bienvenido Santos (*b*. 1911) were also outside the Philippines. The influence of the occupation is evident still in works written after the war such as, for example, Stevan Javellana's *Without Seeing the Dawn* (1947) and Edilberto Tiempo's *Watch in the Night* (1953) and *More Than Conquerors* (1964). These highlight the way Philippine literature is directly related to a struggle against forms of colonialism. In the words of Lucila Hosillos:

> Modern Philippine literature can be said to have its ancestry in the protest literature of the nineteenth century against Spanish colonial rule. Then, at the turn of the century, Filipino playwrights were resisting colonialism with the incendiary 'seditious plays' which helped protract nationalist struggle and undermined American policy of 'benevolent assimilation'. During the Japanese occupation, the Filipino writer's vision of the contemporary used drama as the most effective form in satirising the invaders and keeping alive the resistance to foreign rule and hopes for freedom and democracy. Post-independence realities, particularly the widening gap between the rich and the poor, the breakdown of moral values, the injustices and exploitation of the lower classes, and the worsening of the economic conditions of the country imposed themselves on the writer's sense of the contemporary.*

Jose Garcia Villa

Villa (*b*. 1914) left the Philippines for the United States soon after he had found his Whitmanesque poems (1929/30) unacceptable at the University of the Philippines. His short stories, collected under the title *Footnote to Youth* (1933), marked his future devotion to poetry, and his status as the premier Filipino poet is widely accepted although his poetry is hostile to his country's most revered images – fathers and

* Lucila Hosillos, 'Breaking Through the Wayang Screen'; *The Writer's Sense of the Contemporary* (ed. B. Bennett, Ee Tiang Hong, R. Shepherd), Centre for Studies in Australian Literature, Perth, 1982, p.60.

homeland. His publications of poetry include *Many Voices* (1939), *Selected Poems and New* (1958), *Poems 55* (1962) and *Poems in Praise of Love* (1962).

While Villa made annual selections of the best Filipino short stories in English from 1926 until 1940 and these, more than any other single activity, defined and directed the course of this genre, poetry is central to his work. 'The short story humanised me,' he said, 'But I willed to be a poet. I willed to be a poet because a poet is the highest thing, the hardest thing to be. There is nothing else I would rather be.' Villa's first poems were included in the first two volumes published by the Philippine Book Guild but international recognition only came after Dame Edith Sitwell's acclaim: 'The best of these poems are amongst the most beautiful written in our time.' His 'style' is experimental, 'revolutionary', designed to liberate Filipino poetry from colonial models. Yet Villa does not always acknowledge his dependence upon poets such as e.e. cummings, Ezra Pound or Robert Lowell (1917–77), and his originality suffers by the comparison. His 'comma' poems, with the use of a comma after every word are, for example, reminiscent of e.e. cummings—except that Villa tends to be more mechanical and his method of rhyming, what he calls 'reversed consonants', whereby, for example, 'sing' is a mirror-image of 'begins' despite the difference in sounds, seems unduly ingenious though much admired. With these reservations his combative verse commands attention while his constant reliance on reversals, negatives and reductives pricks the reader to tease out the meaning—such as there is. One example will suffice:

The, bright, Centipede,
Begins, his, stampede!
O, celestial, Engine, from,
What, celestial, province!
His, spiritual, might,
Golding, the, night—
His, spiritual, eyes,
Foretelling, my, Size;
His, spiritual, feet,
Stamping, in, heat,
The, radium, brain,
To, spiritual, Imagination.

Manuel E. Arguilla

For those theorists during the period of Emergence such as Jorge Bocobo and Salvador P. Lopez, who had wished Filipino writers to voice a traditional rural spirit and champion the cause of injustice, Manuel Arguilla (*b.* 1911) very nearly fulfilled their hopes. His early stories are set in the barrios of Ilocandia; the atmosphere is economically but evocatively described in 'Morning in Nagrebcan':

> In the gray shadows of the hills, the barrio was gradually awakening. Roosters crowed and strutted on the ground while hens hesitated on their perches among the branches of the camachile trees. Stray goats nibbled the weeds on the sides of the road, and the bull carabaos tugged restively against their stakes.

Here familiarity with the village life is obvious and vivid, the virtues of an agrarian culture are evoked but with restraint. Youthful narrators are a recurrent device, as the title story of Arguilla's *How My Brother Leon Brought Home a Wife and Other Stories* (1940) demonstrates. Here with wonder and shyness the young Baldo watches the love between Leon and his city wife Maria. The technique is deceptively simple and through it Arguilla blends intimacy and objectivity. Later stories concern the socially oppressed in Manila and their characters are generally weak, failed beings such as Alfredo Santos in 'Caps and Lower Case', caught between the editor of the magazine he works for and the foreman of the press. While not overwhelmed by socialist doctrines and abstractions such as the 'masses' these stories evoke compassion for the oppressed and demonstrate how Arguilla's writing spans the movements associated with the emergence of Philippine letters.

Carlos Bulosan

It is ironic that Carlos Bulosan (*d*. 1956), once thought the successor to Rizal, has been remembered primarily as a humourist. A letter written in 1955 presents a more accurate view of his short stories.

> Let me remind you that *The Laughter of My Father* is *not* humour; it is satire; it is indictment against an economic system that stifled the growth of the primitive, making him decadent overnight without passing through the various stages of growth and decay.

Embedded in *The Laughter of My Father* (1944) is a protest at the near-penal conditions imposed by the economic structure, and Bulosan's Ilocanos endure floods, war, land-grabbing, child-labour and similar privations. This subtle complaint becomes more pronounced in his later writing while his own attempt to explore his history and ideas, the fact of his estrangement, *America is in the Heart* (1946) demonstrates the same humane vision and warmth.

N.V.M. Gonzalez

N.V.M. Gonzalez's (*b*. 1915) literary career started as a member of the Veronicans—a literary group headed by Francisco Arcellana which used this name because it was their aim to make their writing bear the imprint of the face of the Philippines, just as the cloth of St Veronica is said to bear the imprint of the face of Christ. Gonzalez's novels reflect the folk life of the Philippines, his restraint evoking the slow but often desperate way of life experienced by Filipino peasants.

The Winds of April (1941) has the simple style and structure of a semi-autobiographical piece and is Gonzalez's first novel. He traces different levels of Philippine society, emphasises social environment rather than evolution of character, and while the setting is static and dreamlike, language and style foreshadow the accomplished technique of his later works.

Two collections of short stories show Gonzalez perfecting a prose style which evokes a way of life while defining suffering. *Seven Hills Away* (1947) is about *kaingin* life in the hills of Mindoro. Here description dominates as the sequence traces the life of the *kainginero*, what ties him to the *kaingin* he has cleared, his debts to the landlord, his loneliness and fears; all these establish an elemental world of struggle with sun and soil in which individual character still remains unimportant. The same primitive quality is notable in the next collection, *Children of the Ash-Covered Loam* (1954) but with an increased attention to character. Stories such as 'The Blue Skull and the Sark Palms' with the lonely school-teacher Miss Inocencio, or Mrs Bilbao the active but vacuous socialite in 'Where's My Baby Now?', are concerned with the ironies and dilemmas of the human condition.

A Season of Grace (1956) again concentrates upon the *kaingineros*; the novel is shaped by the cycle of ploughing, planting and harvesting as events mirror one another, and the time sequence is blurred as the narrative proceeds through the recollections of the characters. At the centre are Sabel and Doro who have chosen to make their way in the *kaingin* and whose personal goodness enables them to pass through the cycle of the seasons and attain fulfillment. By conveying the narrative through the characters, Gonzalez has also provided opportunity for the use of an idiomatic English that suggests the dialect and provides a foil against which we can observe Doro grow through stress toward maturity.

The Bamboo Dancers (1959) is a more ambitious novel with its cosmopolitan artist protagonist, Ernie Rama and the geographical panorama against which the action is set—New York, Vermont, Montreal, Tokyo, Hiroshima, Taipeh, Sipolog. Loneliness and exile characterise Rama himself while more generally misunderstandings, silence, emotional barrenness and betrayal recur through the book. Beneath this Rama's uncertainty about his identity and his estrangement from Filipino culture and its traditions give symbolic force to the title of the book since the *tinikling*, or bamboo dance, is the national dance of the

Philippines: the bamboo dance Rama can no longer perform reflects the cultural heritage he has disowned. Yet the end is not negative. Rama comes to understand his predicament and moves toward a new social commitment, remarking in a letter, 'the amazing thing is that here, on this soil, and in this climate, anything grows'.

Ricaredo Demetillo and Alejandrino G. Hufana

Both Ricaredo Demetillo (*b.* 1920) and Alejandrino Hufana (*b.* 1929) explore the many facets of Filipino identity through their poetry. Demetillo's collection *No Certain Weather* (1956) is a bitter protest, rebelling against constraint, which is essentially continued in the long poem *La Via: A Spiritual Journey* (1958). These works, showing the influence of Villa, acted as a catharsis which enabled Demetillo to achieve *Bartar in Panay* (1961), his adaptation of the folk epic *Maragtas*. In this account of an ancient journey and conflict he finds a symbolic structure for the journey to authentic social awareness and emotional commitment. Through it he establishes origins and responsibilities:

> The place from which we come is called Brunei,
> One of two cities in a distant land
> Of inlets, bays and valleys by the sea.
> Great forests brood along the mountain-sides.
> The people there, divided into tribes,
> Are loosely ruled by Makatunaw, king
> And tyrant, too, for through his treachery,
> *Datus* have lost their valued properties.

Hufana is certainly a more accomplished poet than Demetillo, but he too suffers from a confusion of images, symbols, and jumbled syntax in *Sickle Season* (1959) which, like Demetillo's work, searches for a past that will sustain the present. *Poro Point: An Anthology of Lives* (1961) extends this through a desperate sifting of ancestors and contemporaries.

Bienvenido N. Santos

Born in 1911 in Antonio Rivera—the Sulucan of his stories—Bienvenido N. Santos in his fiction goes beyond the imagery of return used by Hufana. For example, the stories in *Brother, My Brother* (1960) are framed by Sulucan: the collection opens with a story about a return to Sulucan and it closes with 'A Visit to Sulucan'. The purpose that underwrites this use of a homecoming theme is not sentimental but confessional; Santos discovers the truth of his identity through what has happened to others.

Three periods can be distinguished in Santos's life for the impact they have made upon his writing: the Sulucan years in the Tondo slums as a youth; exile in America during the Second World War; the return to the Philippines and the shock of their devastation. His poems in the collection *The Wounded Stag* (1956) trace an essential history which is more than autobiography, rather a probing of waste and spiritual drought.

In *You Lovely People* (1955), a collection of short stories where the dominant image is anguish (the title that was originally planned was 'The Hurt Men'), he examines the pain of Filipinos exiled from their roots and subject to an unconscious patronage in America. In these stories Santos articulates the anguish of a thwarted Filipino dream, and stories such as 'The Prisoners', 'The Door', 'Brown Coterie', 'Scent of Apples', 'Accept the Homage' are outstanding reflections of the root-lessness of the Filipino in America. The homecoming theme links these stories to *Brother, My Brother* and through the first-person narrator Santos enters into a multiplicity of characters while discriminating irony and honed details keep him from sentimentality. The return theme again dominates his first novel *Villa Magdalena* (1965). Here the old mansion is effectively an image of the Philippines: it is the place of origin where communion and mutual support are possible and the self can be renewed.

Gregorio Brillantes

A graduate of the Ateneo de Manila in 1952, Gregorio Brillantes quickly won acclaim for his ability in literary competitions and became accepted as representative of a new generation of Filipino writers. His stories are based in Manila or the provinces and their personae come from the relatively organised affluent middle classes—a background very different from those writers who had previously focused upon rural simplicity, suffering and poverty. Yet again alienation is at the centre of his collection of short stories, *Distance to Andromeda and Other Stories* (1960). While each story appears separate gradually the connections become apparent. Barriers divide families in 'The Living and the Dead', 'The Exiles', 'A Wind over the Earth' and such parallels can be instanced through the collection to demonstrate an imagination which has the capacity to unify disparate experiences without denying the individual integrity of each occasion.

Nick Joaquin

A sense of the past is Nick Joaquin's (*b.* 1917) characteristic contribution to the problems of Filipino identity but it is in no simple sense; for

Joaquin the past is an expression of the ultimate reality of Philippine life. In an early essay, written originally in 1943 and published in the *Philippines Review*, Joaquin indicates why he feels in this way about history in general and Filipino-Spanish history in particular:

> To accuse the Spanish, over and over again, of having brought us all sorts of things, mostly evil, among which we can usually remember nothing very valuable 'except perhaps' religion and national unity, is equivalent to saying of a not very model mother that she has given her child nothing *except* life.

Disenchanted with his vocation in a religious order, Joaquin combines in his work a dense poetic style reminiscent of Wilson Harris with a historical, metaphysical and theological apprehension of the world. Stories such as 'May Day Eve', 'The Summer Solstice' and more overtly religious ones such as 'The Legend of the Virgin's Jewel', 'The Legend of the Dying Wanton', 'The Mass of Sylvester' and 'Dona Jeronima' demonstrate a mythological approach which reorders experience.

The Christian and pagan values upon which Joaquin draws are clear in his *Prose and Poems* (1952) and *La Naval de Manila* (1964). Physical regeneration and superstition here run together in the blend of lust, violence and cultic mystery which attracts his interest. A comment from one of his essays demonstrates what he discerns to be the common elements of Christianity and paganism: 'Strip a Western Christian legend—the Quest of the Holy Grail, for example—and what do you get? Pagan myth and ritual.' This fusion of past and present, the carrying over into the present of the past is strikingly demonstrated in Joaquin's play *A Portrait of the Artist as Filipino*, in *Prose and Poems*. Here the Aeneas myth is the main symbol for this almost autobiographical play (Aeneas escaped from Troy carrying his aged blind father Anchises on his shoulders and eventually founded what was to become Rome). By having a painting of Aeneas as the central motif but giving Anchises the face of an old Don Lorenzo and Aeneas the face of a young Lorenzo, Joaquin makes a dramatic statement. Here the writer is responsible for his own ancestor and he carries the past, present and future.

In his novel *The Women Who Had Two Navels* (1961) the flight of Connie Escobar from the duplicity and immorality of the Philippines brings her into contact with estranged members of her family and other Filipino exiles in Hong Kong. At the same time Joaquin refuses to let any single character be the spokesman for the novel: the human situation is too ambiguous, and there are repetitions and parallels which ironically disclose that Connie's version of the truth leaves much untold. History here only highlights the difference between dream and reality when—in Concha's words to Manson—he evokes a splendid past with the comment that 'people like your father were my conscience walking around in elegant clothes'.

It is clear that the two 'navels' of Connie are her two cultural legacies —Spanish and American: again the question of Filipino identity. The decadence, evil and sense of nightmare which pervade the novel become then the morbid consequences of the ambiguities of Philippine culture. For example, Don Paco remains in Hong Kong as an exile loyal to Philippine-Spanish culture, disillusioned by the destructive influence of America upon the Philippines. In this Joaquin demonstrates a spiritual and stable traditional way of life in the Spanish ethos and attributes the confusion of Filipino life to rejection of this tradition in favour of American materialism.

Origins cannot be discounted and the coherence of Joaquin's writing reflects his generation. His father a colonel in the revolutionary war against the Spanish, he himself is immersed in the nationalism of the first ill-fated Philippine Republic that was destroyed by the United States. The opening scene of *A Portrait of the Artist as Filipino* embodies the nostalgia and the conflict which haunt his works:

> BITOY: Intramuros! The old Manila. The original Manila. The Noble and Ever Loyal City . . .
>
> To the early conquistadores she was a new Tyre and Sidon; to the early missionaries she was a new Rome. Within these walls was gathered the wealth of the Orient—silk from China; spices from Java; gold and ivory and precious stones from India. And within these walls the Champions of Christ assembled to conquer the Orient for the Cross. Through these old streets once crowded a marvellous multitide—viceroys and archbishops, mystics and merchants; pagan sorcerers and Christian martyrs; nuns and harlots and elegant marquesas; English pirates, Chinese mandarins, Portuguese traitors, Dutch spies, Moro sultans, and Yankee clipper captains. For three centuries this medieval town was a Babylon in its commerce and a New Jerusalem in its faith—
>
> Now look: this is all that's left of it now. Weeds and rubble and scrap iron. A piece of wall, a fragment of stairway—and over there, the smashed facade of old Santo Domingo . . . .

Conclusion

Filipino writing in English continues to be concerned with the definition of a cultural identity and for that reason to be heavily biased towards social concerns. The collection of short stories by Pacifico N. Aprieto and Andres Cristobal Cruz *Tondo by Two* (1961) employs obvious symbols in juxtaposition, slums and decay on the one hand, nature on the other, to illuminate the loss and contradictions in modern Filipino urban experience. Edith L. Tiempo's works, particularly *A Blade of Fern* (1953) and *Abide, Joshua* (1964), are beset by a sense of death and desperate efforts at some sort of commitment in their characters. A similar sense of claustrophobia troubles the protagonists in the stories of Antonio Reyes Enriquez (*b*. 1936), *Surveyors of the Liguasan Marsh* (1981), Francisco Sionil José's numerous short stories and novels such as *Wayawa* (1980), and Ninotchka Rosca's *The Monsoon Collection* (1983) in which the familiar mix of place, nostalgia and brutal history are formative ingredients.

Chapter 7

Oceania

SET IN THE PACIFIC OCEAN, Oceania encompasses a vast area with over twelve hundred indigenous languages apart from English, French, Spanish, Hindi and various types of pidgin. Though only influenced by European culture since the eighteenth century, the region has been settled for thousands of years and this slowly changing traditional world has been protected from outside interference by its isolation from large centres of population. Among the countries the region includes are the Solomon Islands, Kiribati, the Republic of Nauru, Niue, Fiji, the Cook Islands, Tokelau, the Kingdom of Tonga, Tuvalu, Western Samoa and Vanuatu. While Papua – New Guinea's literature can be separated from Oceanic writing, convenience and the occasional assertion of 'a Pacific way' would justify its inclusion even if the network of mutual interests among Oceanic writers did not require it.

The colonial perspective and beyond

Oceania has long influenced the European imagination. With French and English exploration from the eighteenth century the penetration of the Pacific produced overheated legends of Edenic bliss and beautiful women. Here J.J. Rousseau's (1712–78) hypothesis about 'the noble savage' seemed likely to be fulfilled and, even before colonial powers moved in, missionary societies actively competed for converts and demolished the structures of traditional life. While European dominance was mainly accomplished during the nineteenth century, in this century independence was achieved during the sixties and seventies. Although independence has reversed the arbitrariness of boundaries defined by colonial powers the more substantial effects of colonialism remain. On the one hand the racial composition of the islands is now very mixed: with the partial exception of Papua – New Guinea, Europeans, Chinese, Indo-Fijians and various mixes of these groups have penetrated the ethnic homogeneity of the region. As missionary activity, technology, and new social factors have made their impact, fragmentation has occurred at all levels of traditional life.

The development of a literature

Factors common to all the new literatures have contributed to the development of literature in English in Oceania. Since colonialism here has been less violent than in, say, Africa, the developing literary consciousness has avoided ideological extremes such as negritude. There have been three broad areas of shared experience: oral traditions, colonialism and the English language. These common factors do not eliminate national differences within the region—Samoan, Tongan, Fijian, and so on—but enable a broad regional cultural identity to be set against a constrictive nationalism.

Writers have helped to form this regional consciousness which has evolved alongside other regional institutions such as the South Pacific Forum, the South Pacific Bureau for Economic Co-operation and the University of the South Pacific. For literature the last of these has been most influential in the Polynesian sector of Oceania, just as the influence of the University of Papua – New Guinea has been decisive in Papua – New Guinea. In Oceania these institutions have catered for and created an educated elite from which writers have been drawn. In Polynesia, for example, most of the writers of the region are, or have been, on the staff of the University of the South Pacific which serves eleven countries and has thereby fostered a sense of the region as a whole.

In this the significance of a writer of the stature of Albert Wendt (*b.* 1939) must not be underestimated. Wendt has not only been the most productive writer, the most assured in his critical stance and the most stimulating, but he has also been the most influential figure for a whole generation of new writers. In a seminal article, 'Towards a new Oceania' (1976), Wendt began to define a new cultural identity and self-awareness which affirmed a common tradition against the tutelage imposed by the West. In this he sounded a 'call to arms' for literature in Oceania by showing connections and trends across the region as a whole:

In the last few years what can be called a South Pacific literature has started to blossom. In New Zealand, Alistair Campbell, of Cook Island descent, is acknowledged as a major poet: three Maori writers —Hone Tuwhare (poet), Witi Ihimaera (novelist), and Patricia Grace (short stories) have become extremely well-known. In Australia, the aboriginal poets Kathy Walker and Jack Davis continue to plot the suffering of their people. In Papua New Guinea, *The Crocodile* by Vincent Eri—the first Papuan novel to be published— has already become a minor classic. Also in that country poets such as John Kasaipwalova, Kumalau Tawali, Alan Natachee, and Apisai Enos, and playwrights like Arthur Jawodimbari are publishing some powerful work. Papua New Guinea has established a very forward looking Creative Arts Centre, which is acting as a catalyst in the expressive arts movement, a travelling theatre, and an Institute of Papua New Guinea Studies. *Kovave* magazine, put out by a group of Papua New Guinea writers, is already a respected literary journal.*

He went on to stress the way in which being part of a small community of writers in the region overcame differences. Implicit in this was a recognition of the writer as part of an educated elite; and the consequences of this—isolation from the wider community and the writer as part of a community still unborn—are embedded in his writing:

> Our ties transcend barriers of culture, race, petty nationalism, and politics. Our writing is expressing a revolt against the hypocritical/ exploitative aspects of our traditional/commercial/ and religious hierarchies, colonialism and neo-colonialism, and the degrading values being imposed from outside and by some elements in our societies. This artistic renaissance is taking us through a genuine decolonialisation; it is also acting as a unifying force in our region. †

Clearly these polemical sentiments reflect an educated elite already partly estranged from its original culture, yet such writers' works are not regional—but local: in the words of André Gide, 'It is by becoming national that a literature takes its place in humanity and acquires significance in its assembly'. Comparison with the development of West Indian writing provides some interesting parallels as Wendt works from specific, local experiences—particularly in Samoa—while an Indo-Fijian writer such as Raymond Pillai reflects the anxieties of his community.

Tradition and estrangement

Answering the charge of elitism Wendt has argued that serious writing is always an elitist activity, drawing upon a traditional Oceanic cultural assumption, that of *mana*. The word denotes a creative energy which can emanate from the gods or specially gifted human beings. While Chiefs are supposed to have *mana* Wendt is also aware that the creative individual can attain it. In his essay 'The Artist and the Reefs Breaking Open' (1978) he shows how the elitist artist is still tied to his community and its thought forms as he ushers in the new.

> Like a sensitive plant, the artist, through an unconscious process of osmosis, draws his mana (his artistic and imaginative energy) from everything surrounding him like a birth sac, from different sources —the aesthetic and cultural traditions into which he is born, his personal relationships, even the food and drink he consumes, and so

* A. Wendt, 'Towards a New Oceania', *Mana Review*, I,1, January 1976, p.59.
† Ibid.

forth. This mana he transmits back into his community in a reconstituted form. How well he does this depends on his talents and the ability of his society to receive his painting, or poem, or song, or whatever form he has encapsulated his mana in.*

One of the influences that the writer absorbs from his cultural surroundings is, of course, oral traditions. Wendt admits his awareness of an oral literature:

> Samoa was and still is extremely rich in its oral traditions, and I was lucky to have the grandmother I had . . . She was steeped in Samoan culture and the Bible, and spoke fairly fluent English. Every night she would reward us with *fagogo*. I didn't realise until I read Aesop's fables and Grimm's fairy tales in English years later that some of grandmother's stories were from these collections, but she was telling them the *fagogo* way in Samoan. Her style and versions of these stories were better than the originals.†

Implicit in this account is the author's recognition of culture as something not fixed but fluid, liable to change. This insight accords with studies by Ruth Finnegan in the relationship between oral literature and writing in Oceania. She talks about an 'overlap' between oral and written literature and rejects the romanticism that hopes for a 'primitive and unspoiled original state':

> . . . it is fascinating to study how once-foreign ideas and stories (from the Christian tradition especially) have been taken over by the Pacific islanders and moulded accordingly to local styles and insights into truly Pacific literary genres. It is impressive too to study how poets and narrators have not been content just to take over word-for-word verbalisation from the past but have also worked with new ideas and developed new forms built on the old. It seems unfortunate that the romantic search for 'the primitive' has so often blinded investigators to the fascination of contemporary and developing forms of Pacific literature and to the richly creative ways in which new ideas have been moulded into Pacific culture.**

This insight sets Wendt's writing in a wider perspective. His fables, anecdotes, proverbs, epics, folk tales and jests come from a tradition which, because it has been open to changes, enables him to hope for his own role as artist in a new situation. In his own words: 'In their

---

* A. Wendt, 'The Artist and the Reefs Breaking Open', *Mana* (a South Pacific Journal of Language and Literature), 3,1, October, 1978, p.107.
† Interview, 'Samoa's Albert Wendt, Poet and Author', *Mana* (Annual of the South Pacific Creative Arts Society), 1973, p.45.
** Ruth Finnegan, 'Oral Literature and Writing in the South Pacific', *Pacific Quarterly Moana*, 7, 2, 1982, p.22.

individual journeys into the Void, these artists, through their work are explaining us to ourselves and creating a new Oceania.'*

Beginnings (Polynesia)

The origins of contemporary Polynesian writing in English are essentially post-colonial. There was a limited amount of indigenous writing during the colonial period, principally of a moral and religious nature such as *Joel Bulu: The Autobiography of a Native Minister in the South Seas* (1871), but it was the establishment of the South Pacific Literature Bureau in the late nineteen-fifties which marked the self-conscious beginnings of secular literary production while creative literature in English emerged from the Polynesian sector of Oceania in the early nineteen-seventies. The South Pacific Creative Arts Society and Mana Publications borrowed Ulli Beier's approach to publishing in Papua – New Guinea: by 1976 Mana Publications had published four anthologies of poetry, a volume for each of the regions—the Solomon Islands, New Hebrides, Fiji and Western Samoa, while the *Mana Review* a literary biennal, provided a future forum for both writing and criticism. With the publication of the first novel by a Polynesian, Albert Wendt's *Sons for the Return Home* (1973), the literature gained a writer of international repute.

The strongest genre has been poetry which includes the work of such writers as Konai Helu Thaman (*b.* 1947, Tonga), Sano Malifa (Samoa), Satendra Nandan (Fiji), Veramu Seri (Fiji), and Makiuti Tongia (*b.* 1953, Cook Islands) as well as Wendt's own verse. Verse from the Solomons and New Hebrides has tended to express nuances of cultural conflict in stereotyped and superficial ways, although Mildred Sope (New Hebrides) and Celestine Kilagoe (Solomons) have produced original and satisfying poetry. In Fiji and Samoa the literary situation is more firmly established. Sano Malifa, Albert Wendt, Eti Sa'aga and Ruperake Petaia have castigated their Samoan society, its apathy, its religious milieu, and the forms of education, government and business which determine its future. Veramu Seri is the most controversial Fijian poet. While his anger at the complacent façade of Fijian society has lacked depth, it provides an example of a young writer under stress in a young society and contrasts with the urbane control of Satendra Nandan's concern with the dilemma of his Indo-Fijian community.

Given that sustained prose fiction has been achieved primarily by Albert Wendt, much has been achieved in the short story genre by other writers—in particular by Vanessa Griffen and Raymond Pillai of

* A. Wendt, 'Towards a New Oceania' *Mana Review*, I, 1, January 1976, p.59.

Fiji. Pillai discloses the rhythms and anxieties of Indo-Fijian life while Vanessa Griffen in her story 'The Concert' (1973) is adept at delineating emotions and the embedded attitudes which determine human relationships. Marjorie Crocombe's sketches—'Nero' (1969), 'The Healer' (1970), 'Bush Beer' (1974)— are sharp and effective realisations of Cook Islands life.

Drama remains relatively weak in Polynesia—by contrast with Papua – New Guinea. Prophetic is Vilsoni Tausie's (*b.* 1954) of Rotuma *Don't Cry, Mama* (1977), a three-act play which was published by Mana Publications. Tausie exposes the dissolution of a traditional Rotuman family as they submit to the commercial and social pressures of Suva. Jo Nacola of Fiji, a lecturer in English at University of the South Pacific, has also had his three dramatic sketches published by Mana—*I Native No More* (1976).

From about 1976 the literary development of the South Pacific has included the indigenous languages. The South Pacific Creative Arts Society has fostered this, as has the decentralisation of the University of the South Pacific with its eight regional centres. These centres have organised creative writing workshops and sponsored publications in the vernacular languages: for example in *Mana*, the Samoan-language literary periodical, established in 1977, and in *Faikava*, the journal of the Tonga Centre, which publishes literature in both English and Tongan. These efforts both reaffirm a cultural identity which has been under threat from western influences (if not already substantially eroded) and foster literary talents that might otherwise have been lost. Wendt in his introduction to *Lali: A Pacific Anthology* comments on the conscious shift toward these expressions of distinct national consciousness:

> Journals like these are providing publishing avenues for our writers who write in the mother tongues, and we are anticipating a steady growth in vernacular literature and the active participation of our peoples in the scientific study and teaching of their own languages.

Beginnings (Papua – New Guinea)

Independent since 1975, Papua – New Guinea lacks the ethnic tensions of Malaysia – Singapore or Fiji: here Europeans and Chinese form small enclaves, transient in nature, and the bulk of the population is Melanesian in its varying shades of brown from the black of the Bouganvilleans to the light brown of Motu. Linguistic variations are far more complex but alongside the numerous vernaculars are two pidgins: Police Motu, a traditional trading pidgin, and Pidgin English. While the vernaculars with traditional rivalries of communities and interest groups remain, these two pidgins with the English which is the language of the educated elite dominate practical affairs and written literature. The richness of Papua – New Guinea Pidgin has been enhanced by a standardised orthography and it has already become a medium in newspapers and journals, and creative writers have been able to use it effectively for subtle forms of narrations whereas creoles not so standardised—as in West Africa and the Caribbean—have been relatively constrained and inconsistent. As urban communities have developed in Papua – New Guinea so new cultural expressions have evolved and the dynamic linguistic development has become a source of enrichment.

In this a consequence for the writer is that he or she will be trilingual. It is likely that a writer will have a 'trivial' language or dialect—of which there are about seven hundred different groups—then English as the main language of education and informed literary communication, and Pidgin as 'the common tongue'. The creative potential of Pidgin has been realised by writers, particularly in drama. Rabbie Namaliu and Kumalau Tawali (*b*. 1947) have used Pidgin for immediate dramatic effect with an audience already very willing to ignore stage illusion, and a similar technique has been effective in film drama. Pidgin has particularly established itself as the superior literary medium for satire, comedy and depiction of 'low life'. Poets such as Bede Dus Mapun and Jerry Kavop, whose poster poems in Pidgin became household words, concentrated upon urban subjects—a new element in the consciousness of Papua – New Guinea. From the anti-colonial dramas of Hannet (*b*. 1941) in the late nineteen-sixties, where Pidgin was an effective rhetorical instrument, its use has continued in the dramatic social satires of Rabbie Namaliu (*b*. 1947) and J.B. Rokome in the nineteen-seventies. A small illustration of the way Pidgin can crystallise an image is the title of Russell Soaba's (*b*. 1950) novel *Wanpis* (1978): derived from the English words 'one piece' it has evolved to an image—freighted with assertive pride—for an isolated, resourceful and defiant individual.

Educational resources are a formal influence in defining the origins of the literature in English of Papua – New Guinea. Its seeds were sown by the Australian school teachers of the nineteen-sixties/seventies who may have imparted a few less formal ideas about the nature of poetry, its form and rhyme. With the establishment of the University of Papua – New Guinea, however, and the arrival in the late nineteen-sixties of Ulli Beier (who was to conduct creative writing classes) there began a literature which for the first four or five years was primarily concerned with decolonisation: to exorcise bitterness, to identify cultural conflicts. In Beier's words: 'Much of it will probably date, but that is beside the point. It had a liberating effect on the minds of that generation, and this was needed and healthy.'

Beier quickly established the Papua Pocket Poets; *Kovave*, Papua –

New Guinea's first literary magazine; supported the establishment of a Creative Arts Centre and, later, became the director of the Institute of Papua – New Guinea Studies. This was a 'hothouse' atmosphere for literature to grow in, especially with visits by African writers such as Taban lo Liyong and Wole Soyinka. Moreover Beier's tertiary-level creative writing courses propelled students toward productivity and perhaps inclined them to short literary forms—which may account for the fact that there are only two Papua – New Guinean novels.

The earliest genre for Papua – New Guinean writing was autobiography. Beier's influence is especially obvious in the production of the first autobiography, Albert Maori Kiki's *Kiki: Ten Thousand Years in a Lifetime* (1968) which Beier 'edited' from taped interviews. Kiki's concerns reflect those of other writers in this genre: they too were moving away from traditions and there was the need to preserve, define areas of conflict and assert an identity. Writers such as Tawali, Hannet and Jawodimbari (*b.* 1949) were among the first autobiographers and provided a basis from which the short story could grow.

Russell Soaba and Kama Kerpi (*b.* 1953) are particularly worthy of notice for their contribution to the development of the short story in Papua – New Guinean literature. Both use it in a sustained sequence (trilogies) although their contexts for the conflict between an educated protagonist and the society about him differ greatly. By contrast with this essentially tragic sense, the stories of Jawodimbari and Kasaipwalova stand out for their humourous and ironic vision of things.

In the first five years, however, the major developments in Papua – New Guinean writing were in drama and poetry. The poems of Kumalau Tawali were collected in *Signs in the Sky* (1970), as were those of Apisai Enos (*b.* 1946), *High Water* (1971), and John Kasaipwalova, *Reluctant Flame* (1971), and *Hanuabada* (1972). In *Five New Guinean Plays* (1971), which included plays by John Waiko (*The Unexpected Hawk*), M. Lovori (*Alive*), K. Tawali (*Manki Masta*), Jawodimbari (*Cargo*) and Leo Hannet (*The Ungrateful Daughter*), Ulli Beier commented on the background to this productivity:

> The five plays in this volume were produced by students in the creative writing class of the University of Papua and New Guinea. They do not represent the whole picture, because a group of Pidgin plays is not included here. Of the latter, Leo Hannet's short sketch, *Em Rod Bilong Kago* ... represents the real beginning of New Guinean drama in the western sense. Rabbie Nammaliu wrote three Pidgin plays: a farce about an innocent labourer who is pursuing a prostitute; a skit on European tourism ... and a semi-historical play, *Maski Kaunsel*, which deals with the conflict between a Talai village and the administration over the establishment of a council—Peter Malala has written a skit on elections in New Guinea.

Beier's summary of developments indicates the creative energy which was so quickly expressed in drama and poetry. The plays in an English medium in these early years clearly formulated anti-colonial sentiments but also went on to define cultural confusion, traditional legends, city life and the establishment of a new identity. Waiko's *The Unexpected Hawk* showed villagers expelled from their homes which were then burned on the order of the *Kiap* (government officer) to compel them to move to another area. Leo Hannett's *The Ungrateful Daughter* is an allegory about independence and therefore lacks subtle characterisation: in it Ebonita (the adopted daughter) is engaged to Sidney Smith, a representative Australian, but at the last minute she tears off her wedding clothes and joins her countrymen in a wild victory dance which scatters all the whites on the stage. As in most allegorical forms the names, characters, language and situations are contrived to establish an allusive structure. The other anti-colonial plays use white stereotypes—but not in an allegorical manner—while few manage subtle treatment of the complexities of the colonial situation. Jawodimbari's *The Old Man's Reward* (1973) and Kasaipwalova's *Kanaka's Dream* (1971) demonstrate an ability to use anti-colonial themes while making observations on human frailty but it was the anti-colonial interest which proved successful with audiences.

From students at the Goroka Teachers' College came plays which primarily reflected cultural confusion. While these were contemporary with the anti-colonial plays from the University of Papua – New Guinea it is likely that at Goroko a different milieu tackled colonialism in different terms: so John Kaniku's *Cry of the Cassowary* (1970) explored familiar dilemmas—the conflict between generations, urban and rural, the educated and the uneducated. Plays by Kambau Namaleu Lamang—*The Rock is Tall but Papua is Even Taller* (1972)—and Peter Kama Kerpi—*Voices from the Ridge* (1974)—dealt with the tensions between Christianity and traditional religion while John Kaniku in his play *Kalawai Kwasina* (unpublished but first performed in 1972) shows how both religious interests co-exist: he had Christianity for the day and the night for the traditional gods.

History as a means of affirming identity under the stress of westernisation was also explored by the Goroka writers. Turuk Wabei's *Kulubob* (1970) reinterpreted a Melanesian myth, and traditional material is also central to Bernard Narokobi's *Death of Muruk* and Jawodimbari's *The Sun* (1970) as they reflect the fusion of diverse elements in an evolving society. Explorations of city life and the search for identity feature in Soaba's work: *Wilma Wait* (unpublished, first performed 1974) voices disillusionment; its bitter presentation of the new urban black elite marks both his innovative style and a possible development in future drama. Soaba's other play, *Scattered by the*

Wind (1973), shows a Papuan Anglican priest whose doubts reflect Soaba's astringent criticism of his own society. At the other end of this range of themes are Narokobi's affirmations of Papua – New Guinean village life *When the Eagle Dies* (1973) and *Strangers are My People*; and Namaliu's comedy of urban low-life in *The Good Woman of Konedobu* (1970).

By contrast with the dramatic rituals of traditional Papuan – New Guinean society these playwrights tend to write for the educated urban elite. However, as the writers seek a wider audience, so there is the need to popularise the drama and establish rapport with unsophisticated audiences through dance and mime. The dangers of failing to do so have been clearly expressed in *Kovave* (1972) by Apisai Enos: 'We are creating an "unpopular" literature for an elitist culture.'

The development of poetry marks regional interests and reflects stereotyped images. Kumulau Tawali's 'The Bush Kanaka Speaks' stereotypes the *kiap* in negative terms while village life is celebrated as honourable, beautiful and simple. This essentially serious attitude is reflected in the social and moral expectations of the individual which underpin the poetry of Apisai Enos and John Kasaipwalova. Highland poets such as Kama kerpi in *Call of the Midnight Bird* (1973) and Henginike Riyong in *Nema Namba* (1974), have tended to be more concerned with traditional village life and its spiritual milieu than the coastal poets who have generally been more westernised and have concentrated upon aspects of cultural conflict. Of these Soaba's poems are one example, others are Arthur Jawodimbari's *Return to My Land* (1974) and Jack Lahui's *Gamblers Niugini Style* (1975).

Makiuti Tongia

Born in 1953, a graduate of the University of the South Pacific and a lecturer at the Teachers' Training College in Rarotonga (Cook Islands), Tongia has published a collection of poems, *Korero* (1977). These brief, poised statements delineate his sense of cultural loss without bitterness. The influence of the missionaries is suggested by the title: *korero* denotes the lost traditions, as in, for example, the poem 'Burning in Hell' which casts an ironic glance on the new religion:

I am no more Chief Taratoa's son,
no more the torch of his pagan *mana*.
Those ancient and highly esteemed
tribal honours of my ancestors are
stripped off me.
Now I am the torchbearer
    of my Christian saviour.

He will carry me on his white
    chariot to heaven
And crown me a chiefly son
    of Jehovah.
Then my *mana* would be great
unlike those of my ancestors'
burning in hell.

Other poems such as 'If I Were to Marry', 'Lost Soul' and 'Jesus Is Our Beer' trace different aspects of cultural displacement and confusion. 'Beware of Dog' strikes a new note. In this poem there is a clear social orientation which moves away from colonial colour-line distinctions and operates on the basis of contrast between wealth and poverty as traditional Cook Islands mores have been abandoned by those who ought most defend them. In a traditional society this critique of the hierarchy highlights the changing values:

As I walk this rich suburb
    full of white and black chiefs'
I hear the barking of a dog
I listen to its calls
    knowing I am that dog
    picking what it can
    from the overflowing rubbish tins

I say to you chiefs
    bury the scraps you can't eat
So no hungry dog will come to eat
    at your locked gate

Chiefs beware of hungry
    dogs!

Alongside regret and anger there are also affirmation and lyrical celebration of place and people. In 'Spirit of the Land' he images the unity of the poet with place in simple, controlled lines which adjust lengths to the weight of the words:

This land is my home
where I'll live alone until
    my hair grows white
    and my bones grow old
then I'll hang my spirit on tree tops
to provide a cushion of coolness
for children who gather round
evening fires.

Pillai, Subramani and Nandan: the Indo-Fijian experience

Raymond Pillai is one of the three dominant Indo-Fijian writers and critics, the others being Satendra Nandan and Subramani, who are haunted by the experience of the Indian community in Fiji. During the nineteenth century Indians were indentured labourers for the sugar cane plantations and despite the hopes of a 'promised land' found bitter disappointment. A religious mix of Hindus and Muslims, the Indo-Fijian community has had to fight for an identity against the prejudice of colonial authorities and indigenes. Pillai's stories dissect the urban milieu in a didactic, almost analytical manner. Yet his style can vary: in 'To Market, To Market' he provides idiomatic speech and withering irony as Meena's mother unconsciously contradicts herself after having forced her eldest daughter into a marriage:

> What else can I think of? It isn't easy to arrange a decent marriage nowadays. You can't treat your daughters like cattle to be sold in the market. We women have our pride too, you know.

The religious rhythms of Indian culture inform a story such as 'Laxmi' with its claustrophobic juxtaposition of two couples during 'Deepawali, the Festival of Light, the traditional Indian New Year'. The story, even more clearly than 'To Market, To Market', shows Pillai's tendency to construct a type of parable. Beneath the surface of the narrative is a sense of Indo-Fijian life as a fragmented existence and of the story as a structure which can enlighten and even assist in the creation of order.

The second of the three Indo-Fijian writers to be discussed here is Subramani. His two short stories in Wendt's anthology *Lali* are an indication of Subramani's highly cerebral, almost 'detached', approach to the Indo-Fijian inheritance. Sautu, meaning in Fijian 'peace and plenty', is the name of a village in which Dhanpat, an indentured labourer, struggles with the soil. Readings from the Gita open up another culture and call forth a sense of the metaphysical void which provides an ironic counterpoint to the Fijian world and reminds us of the sadness of Indo-Fijian history. With care and economy the narrative records Dhanpat's gradual mental disintegration.

It is difficult to avoid a comparison of Subramani with V.S. Naipaul. Both seem to have been equally possessed by their Indian identity and yet forced to live and write outside it as expatriates. The character of Dhanpat reflects this predicament. His reading of the Gita's ascetic counsels counterpoints his insubstantiality. When he takes out his suitcase and finds a mirror, his face reminds him of a 'mask of death'. Soon Dhanpat enters the void: he is declared insane and the story ends affirming his essential estrangement—'Dhanpat was taken away for observation. And the chief took possession of his land'.

Satendra Nandan's collection of poems *Faces in a Village* (1976) studies Indo-Fijian history through the village communities of indentured labourers and their descendants. The poem 'the old man and the scholar' voices the unpalatable dilemma:

> authentic history cannot be written
> with words from living mouths.

Without reliable living voices Nandan draws upon early memories, especially his father's account of the voyage from India, and he centres on these in the opening poem, which is the longest in the collection:

> his eyes withdrew into himself:
> 'the dark waters and the blind winds
> the landless sea forever raging.
> it was *narak*, many died; i survived.
> what retribution for leaving a loving home
> and the cows grazing beside the *mandir*
> my friends playing *gullidanda*.
> sleeping and eating we arrived.'
>
> that's how he remembered
> the passage of one life into another.

This sense of dislocation pervades the whole collection and is most commonly expressed by allusions to a past—'shattered dreams, cracked memories create chaos in the mind'—and to the land—'this bitter cruel promised land'. It is hard to find a poem which does not define some aspect of cultural estrangement or seek to overcome it. 'Two Waves' is one of the few poems using rhymed couplets, and it attempts to affirm a future by identifying the malaise:

> yet homeless, nameless between earth and sky
> a race without a place must forever die;

This urgent, strained tone is characteristic of Nandan's poetry. The attempt to overcome displacement by studying 'the ancestral face' does not resolve the thwarted millennial expectations of previous generations, and this sadness of disappointment is never absent from Subramani's and Nandan's work; Pillai, on the other hand, remains less interested in penetrating the essence of Indian experience, less haunted by the past and more alert to the drama of life in Suva's urban context.

Albert Wendt

Apart from Albert Wendt's (*b.* 1939) formative role in criticism and the formulation of a 'Pacific way', he has written novels which are linked by his continual probing at a cluster of key ideas, experiences and concerns. In particular there is a metaphysical consciousness and psychic displacement which derive from seminal experiences in childhood and adolescence; his writing uses reflective and mythopoetic strategies to image and imaginatively resolve the dilemma. These gather substance as his fiction develops. This can be simply demonstrated by the fact that his first two works, *Sons for the Return Home* (1973), a novel, and *Flying-Fox in a Freedom Tree* (1974), a collection of short stories, had their inception in brief sketches published in 1963 and 1965 respectively. Elements from these works, more particularly from *Flying-Fox*, are to be found in his later novels, *Pouliuli* (1977) and *Leaves of the Banyan Tree* (1979), where they are developed further.

Wendt's thirteen-year stay as a child and then as a university student in New Zealand—after which he returned to Western Samoa—seems to have initiated a profound sense of cultural dislocation which contributed to an even more acute metaphysical anxiety; hence, for example, his castigation of materialism and reference to 'the intellectual solitude so peculiar to the disinherited souls of the west'. In *Sons for the Return Home* the protagonist reflects situations and contexts Wendt was very familiar with and he is attracted to desolate places which, it would seem, image his spiritual condition: 'There was need of desolate places, deserts, tapu areas, he thought, where the mind and heart could find solitude—the sacred fire that warmed and made the self whole again' (*Sons*, page 108). This symbolic disassociation from his *aiga*, or village community, presages the protagonist's eventual flight from Samoa and its customs. For Wendt this marks an initial rejection of his own culture which enabled later reassessment: the break frees him and then impels him, as he has put it for other artists, 'through the Void', and he returns to Samoan culture with a heightened consciousness.

In *Sons for the Return Home*, his first novel, Wendt shows a young Samoan's response to New Zealand society as a child and as a young man. His evolving consciousness is lightly sketched in his relationship with a European girl whom his mother forbids him to marry. There are scenes which demonstrate cultural confusion, prejudice and mutual incomprehension but central to the work is a sense of absurdity. The hero lacks a spiritual centre and his education and understanding of life in Samoa are mutually unrelated. A perception which hints at the presence of the Void lies behind the hero's remark to his girlfriend that 'the absurdity in life was at the core of all Polynesian myths'.

The theme of his second novel, *Pouliuli*, is symbolised in the title's image of 'darkness'. The first paragraph condenses a society and a metaphysical condition:

Early on a drizzly Saturday morning Faleasa Osovae—the seventy-six-year-old titled head of the Aiga Faleasa, faithful husband of a devoted Felefele, a stern but generous father of seven sons and five obedient daughters, and the most respected alii in the village of Malaelula—woke up with a strange bitter taste in his mouth to find, as he looked out to the rain and his village, and then at his wife snoring softly beside him in the mosquito net, and the rest of his aiga (about sixty bodies wrapped in sleeping sheets) who filled the spacious fale, that everything and everybody that he was used to and had enjoyed, and that till then had given meaning to his existence, now filled him with an almost unbearable feeling of revulsion . . .

From this the narrative unfolds through a movement back in time which can be compared with the summaries and flashbacks Wendt used earlier in *Flying-Fox*. The hospital scene symbolises a futility which the protagonist goes on to explore in recollections and to which he consistently returns: 'the two old men stoking the fire . . . now and then they throw white parcels into the fire. Stink of burning meat, guts, bits and pieces of people from the surgery department' (*Flying-Fox*, page 103). Here, then, is a metaphysical vacuum which Wendt has sensed within Samoan society and which he has shaped by a careful use of metaphors and analogies. His protagonists at this level embody a spiritual malaise, the resolution of which is the underlying concern of Wendt as an artist.

Above all this purpose is realised in *Leaves of the Banyan Tree* where the fourfold structure enables Wendt to use history, myth, and a variety of perspectives. The first book appears biographical and the character of Tauilopepe dominates the cluster of themes which reflect the conflict between the old and the new, in particular the questions of values, traditional life and the ownership of the land. While the history goes back to his remote ancestors the principal action does not go back beyond 1900. Tauilopepe stands as one tied to the past by obligations which he breaks and his betrayal of the Sapepe community forms the basis of Books Two and Three.

As Tauilopepe strives for power the novel traces the disintegration of the culture which he dominates through his adoption of western ideas. In turn he defeats himself. His son Pepe marks a new consciousness and so embodies social change. His emotional centre is now Vaipe, not traditional village life, and through this change Wendt introduces nuances of conflict within Pepe: town against country and the tension between two generations. Here, in the fragmented life of urban Samoa, Pepe is accompanied by Tagata, the maimed dwarf who embodies this vulgar, fractured culture and who serves as his alter ego.

In Samoan 'Tagata' means 'man' and this misshapen character who indulges in anarchic actions—such as burning down the church hall and looting Tauilopepe's shop—embodies a symbolic and mythic statement about life as Wendt perceives it. Tagata embraces absurdity and by doing so is liberated from the fear of the void. His final action, hanging himself, can be compared with the Maui myth when Maui enters the vagina of the death-goddess and is killed.

In the final section of the novel the dominant new figure to emerge is Galupo, who embodies Tauilopepe's energy and Pepe's creativity. He begins to show a way out of the impasse that concludes Book Two. Galupo returns to Sapepe as a stranger, an action which evokes associations with epic and folklore, and he claims affinity both with Tauilopepe and Pepesa as he begins to reorganise the Sapepean economy. Where Tauilopepe demonstrated a freedom that was a betrayal when he favoured his plantation rather than the mountain and his spiritual heritage, and where Pepe seemed unable to act, Galupo can be free and act honestly. Yet at the same time he inhabits something of the darkness of *Pouliuli*: he reads Albert Camus's *The Myth of Sisyphus* and we need to understand that he too is troubled by the absurdity of life, and acts despite it. In this he embodies the 'intellectual solitude' which Wendt identified first in New Zealand society and which is never entirely absent from his fiction. In short, the novel represents Wendt's most sustained diagnosis of Samoan society's spiritual malaise. Its historical and mythical elements when juxtaposed with his estranged outlook pave the way to an imaginative fusion of past, present and future.

Finally Wendt's collection of poems *Inside Us the Dead* (1976) illuminates essential features of his fiction. The 'Conch Shell' is a poem which uses the symbolic artifact to evoke a past tradition which is now inaccessible to Wendt but which he, unlike his daughter, cannot forget. Implicit here is the cultural aspect of the metaphysical void and impotence which permeates his fiction. His mind is drawn:

to the palm grove deserted, the sinnet
thread dangling headless in the Void,
and I drown in the dreaming
of a priest without hands.

Mildred Sope and Albert Leomala

Both these poets write a more radical and political poetry aimed at reviving their culture than most other Polynesian poets attempt. Yet they are not revolutionaries. Both are tied to their traditional culture in the New Hebrides. Various symbols mark this: Sope's use of the land in 'Motherland' is particularly expressive and her affection for the New Hebrides obvious:

Do I mean anything to you mother
Won't you listen to me for once
I can't bear this burden any longer
Where are we going mother
What is our destination

Leomala's anger at the destruction of tradition is well defined in the poem 'Kros' (Cross) where the Pidgin marks his dissociation from western intrusion:

Kros me no wandem you
Yu kilim me
Yu sakem aot ol
We blong mi
Mi no wandem yu Kros

(Cross I hate you
You are killing me
You are destroying
My traditions
I hate you Cross)

At the same time Leomala's verse is not a mere reaction against colonialism. The traditions of New Hebridean oral literature, music and dance are reflected in his translations of New Hebridean songs, and chant rhythms penetrate his writing through repetitions and stylised language, as, for example, in the first lines of 'My Home':

father father of mine
mother mother of mine
sister sister of mine
and you brother of mine
why did you leave me father
why are you so far away mother
why do you hate me sister
why don't you see me brother

Eri, Kasaipwalova, Tawali, Soaba and Enos

In his novel *The Crocodile* (1970) Vincent Eri (*b.* 1936) one of the first graduates of the University of Papua – New Guinea, provides a compact description of Papuan village life before the Second World War. Its language is a spare, almost standard English with little figurative expression, almost no pidgin, and erratic use of local idiom. At the centre is the hero, Hoiri, a young Papuan who has been drawn into the European world by education and religion but denied full access to it.

As an example of this, the Papuans serve as soldiers but after the war are referred to as 'kanakas' once again.

Hoiri remains an alienated hero caught between two worlds and unable to find fulfilment in either. Although the title of the book comes from the hunt for a crocodile which supposedly took his wife at the instigation of a hostile sorcerer, it symbolises his inability to cope with his cultural predicament: while he can kill the crocodile he is cut off from the cultural resources to deal with the 'sorcerer'. The real subject is therefore Hoiri's progress toward defeat and exhaustion after all 'the wasted years of carrying the white man's cargo'.

Born in the Trobriand Islands, John Kasaipwalova has a prophetic stature in Papua – New Guinean writing comparable with that of Wendt in Polynesia and Soyinka in West Africa. When he was a student of great promise at the University of Papua – New Guinea his academic 'failure' signalled his opposition to authority of almost any sort, which his writing has made plain. His poetry, short stories, drama and poetic drama demonstrate a language unfettered by usage, in which nouns are created and adjectives put to work as verbs.

Thematically his writing centres upon the destructive consequences of colonialism. The influences of Beier and Taban lo Liyong may be traced in his freedom from parochialism: not tied to issues of local consciousness, he writes as part of the Third World and a wider black experience. Corroboration of this is that *Reluctant Flame*, a collection of his verse, was published almost simultaneously in Nigeria and in Papua – New Guinea.

Prolific though he is, *Reluctant Flame* remains his best-known work, probably because it seems most fully to arouse and express an indigenous political consciousness. In this work the confrontation with colonialism is given an imaginative coherence through the controlling imagery of heat and chill; a control which the violence of his language, as he seeks to exorcise the paralysis of will effected by colonialism, makes necessary. Naturally the chill symbolises white rule and western culture: a cold wind that grows to pervade all—'What is this chill, where is the flame to warm and melt me? The chill is killing the flame, it is everywhere.'

Against this chill, the essential identity of Papua – New Guineans, however stifled by the colonial experience, is asserted and revived. For this he turns, as so many Third World writers have, to pre-European history and the later surging release and assurance issue from this source: 'Inside, Inside, where our minds do not now recognise there is a living memory! A flame alive from its ignition and its fuel.'

Kumalau Tawali's poetry reflects the concerns of coastal Papua – New Guinean writers with aspects of cultural confrontation. *Signs in the Sky* (1970) contains 'The Bush Kanaka Speaks' with its expression of early anti-colonial feeling. Tawali has also written a later collection of poetry, *Tribesman's Heartbeat*, and a play, *Manki Masta*.

Also a product of the University of Papua – New Guinea and contemporary with Kasaipwalova, Tawali affirms the integrity of indigenous culture by showing its strengths when contrasted with a stereotyped image of white rule. Against the accusations 'you are ignorant', 'you are dirty' he shows the weakness of a culture dependent upon technology rather than personal experience. His reflective monologue counterpoints the shouts of the *kiap* (government officer) to dramatise the conflict:

> He says: you are ignorant,
> but can he shape a canoe,
> tie a mast, fix an outrigger?
> Can he steer a canoe through the night
> without losing his way?
> Does he know when a turtle comes ashore
> to lay its eggs?

In literary terms Russell Soaba's contribution to Papua – New Guinean writing, although it includes the novel *Wanpis*, some plays (*Scattered by the Wind*, *Wilma Wait*) and a collection of poetry, *Naked Thoughts*, belongs to the late nineteen-sixties. Coming from the small Anuki community, he shows both urbanity and deep concern for traditional life as his poem 'Mass Mania' demonstrates in its reflection on the execution of an Anuki tribesman for the rape of a white child. While Soaba sees the incident as a martyrdom founded upon mutual cultural misunderstanding he castigates the black elite. The voice of the narrator is controlled, cultivated, whereas the elders, the elite, use a sterotyped idiom which satirises their moral crassness. A similarly alienated protagonist is portrayed in his short stories. 'A Portrait of the Odd Man Out' (1971), 'A Glimpse of the Abyss' (1972) and 'The Victims' (1972) have isolated rebellious heroes and satirise a corrupt society where, 'Thus reigned our elders, forever supreme, boasting of luxury gained from their Aussie wives'.

Apisai Enos comes from Rabaul and three collections of poetry have established his reputation (*High Water*, *Tabapot*, *Warbat*). His work is exceptionally free from preoccupation with colonial themes but reflects the relationship between Papua – New Guineans and the metaphysical quality of their landscape. The title poem of *Highwater* presents a social awareness within the lyrical natural imagery:

> and the water echoes
> the rhythm of rushing feet
> like a long column of marching men
> seeking the life in the cities below ...

Epeli Hau'ofa and Konai Helu Thaman

Urban, well-educated, Epeli Hau'ofa (*b.* 1939) in his short stories and poems gently mocks acceptance of western values in his native Tonga. In 'The Winding Road to Heaven' the opening image defines the subject for the story: '"Religion and Education Destroy Original Wisdom" cry the letters on the back of Manu's shirt. "Over Influenced" says the front of the same garment.' A similar technique is used in 'Old Wine in New Bottles' where Hiti's aged BSA bicycle reflects the incongruity of technology in a traditional society. While both stories move on from details to stress nuances of social irony, his poetry is less witty but more savage. If the poems begin with restraint they end bitterly as in 'Blood in the Kava Bowl' which marks both the inaccessibility of Tongan culture to the westerner and the poet's sense of deprivation when he is left with only memories of a past. Again 'Our Fathers Bent the Winds' offers a similar contrast between the lost past and an unsatisfactory present:

> But the Sands of Sopu are gone,
> broken beer bottles strew the Sacred Shore,
> the tennis court from Salt Lake City marks the grave
> of Salote's lawn,
> and the one-time nation of givers,
> dreaded jaws of the ocean,
> begs for crumbs from the Eagle and the Lion.
> Yesterday Tangaloa made men,
> but the God of Love breeds children.

You, The Choice of My Parents (1974), Konai Helu Thaman's first collection of poems, offers similar criticism of her society for its inability to resist the erosion of traditional ways. The title poem defines this through her own experience, the pressure of her parents that imposed upon her an education which estranged her from her own past. Most of her poems tend to comment on this central experience. Although elements of social criticism are obvious—she castigates bureaucrats, politicians and academics for their self-interested imitation of the west— her images focus upon personal alienation: she is an onlooker caught between worlds. 'In Session' is another poem which focuses upon the social and political milieu, and the sense of psychic estrangement from traditional life in Tongan politics. 'Elite' crystallises this sense of loss:

> He cannot be himself again
> And feels the ground
> Which weeps for his dismemberment.

Sa'aga, Petaia and Malifa

While Eti Sa'aga has provided a socially relevant and unique model for poetry in 'Little Fale' both he and his fellow Western Samoan, Ruperake Petaia, sound the familiar themes of cultural dislocation. Sa'aga shows imaginative sympathy in both 'Me, the Labourer' and 'Him Fella Saviour' with their use of local idiom. The former contrasts poverty and wealth in the dignity and simplicity of the subject:

I does my work hard
and think of me.
Is good to have me
think of me
for there's no one to
think of me but me.

Petaia's poem 'Kidnapped' ingeniously attacks western education by presenting it as a forced and costly extortion with his parents and himself as victims:

Each time
Mama and Papa grew
poorer and poorer
and my kidnappers grew
richer and richer
I grew whiter and whiter

Apart from Wendt's the poetry of Sano Malifa provides some of the most accomplished writing in English in Western Samoa. Parallels with Wendt are inevitable, for Malifa's work shows the same consciousness of a literary tradition and influence. He too was acquainted with the New Zealand poet James K. Baxter, and 'Belching Flame' pays tribute to that relationship. Again, as with Wendt, the influence of the New Zealand educational system recurs in Malifa's work, in poems such as 'Question and Answer'. In *Looking Down at Waves* (1975) the division into places—Wellington, Samoa, Honolulu and Washington—denotes through the structure an isolation that permeates the author's experiments with sonnet forms and dramatic monologue. Often these, as in 'To the Woman Selling Handicrafts Outside Burns Philip's Doors (a word to the tourist)', carry familiar social comments. Yet Malifa remains haunted by his cultural isolation and his need of relationships; in his own words, 'The art of travelling teaches the true meaning of loneliness'.

Bibliography

GENERAL

Reference and anthologies

FERRES, J.H. AND TUCKER, M. (EDS.): *Modern Commonwealth Literature: A Library of Literary Criticism*, F. Ungar, New York, 1977.

GOODWIN, (ED.): *National Identity*, Heinemann, London/Australia. 1970.

KING, BRUCE: *The New English Literatures: Cultural Nationalism in a Changing World*, Macmillan, London, 1980.

LARSON, C.R.: *The Novel in the Third World*, Inscape Publishers, Washington, D.C., 1976.

MCLEOD, A.L.: *The Commonwealth Pen: an Introduction to the Literature of the British Commonwealth*, Cornell University Press, New York, 1961.

MOORE, GEOFFREY (ED.): *The Chosen Tongue: English Writing in the Tropical World*, Longman, London, 1969.

NIVEN, ALASTAIR (ED.): *The Commonwealth Writer Overseas: Themes of Exile and Expatriation*, Didier, Brussels, 1975.

PRESS, JOHN (ED.): *Commonwealth Literature: Unity and Diversity in a Common Culture*, Heinemann Educational, London, 1965.

WALSH, WILLIAM (ED.): *A Manifold Voice: Studies in Commonwealth Literature*, Chatto & Windus, London, 1970.

—: *Readings in Commonwealth Literature*, Oxford University Press, London, 1973.

—: *Commonwealth Literature*, Macmillan, London, 1979.

Journals

ACLALS BULLETIN (Bulletin of the Association for Commonwealth Literature and Language Studies).

ARIEL: A Review of International English Literature.

CRNLE Reviews Journal, Centre for Research in the New Literatures in English, Flinders University, South Australia.

The Journal of Commonwealth Literature.

KUNAPIPI (Bulletin for EACLALS: the European branch of the Association for Commonwealth Literature and Language Studies).

Moko: Newsletter (Bulletin for the Canadian branch of the Association for Commonwealth Literature and Language Studies.

New Literature Review, Canberra.

SPAN (Bulletin for SPACLALS: the South Pacific branch of the Association for Commonwealth Literature and Language Studies).

WLWE (World Literature Written in English).

CARIBBEAN

General

JAMES, L. (ED.): *The Islands In Between*, Oxford University Press, London; 1968.

KING, B. (ED): *West Indian Literature*, Macmillan, London, 1979.

RAMCHAND, K.: *The West Indian Novel and Its Background*, Faber, London, 1970.

SANDER, R.W.(ED.): *From Trinidad: An Anthology of Early West Indian Writing*, Hodder & Stoughton, London, 1978.

Writers

ANTHONY, MICHAEL (Trinidad and Tobago): *The Games Were Coming*, Deutsch, London, 1963.

—: *The Year in San Fernando*, Deutsch, London, 1965.

—: *Green Days by the River*, Deutsch, London, 1967.

—: *King of the Masquerade*, Nelson, Sunbury-on-Thames, 1976.

BRAITHWAITE, EDWARD (Barbados): *The Arrivants: A New World Trilogy*, Oxford University Press, London, 1973. Contains *Rites of Passage, Masks, Islands*, first published 1967, 1968, 1969 respectively.

—: *Other Exiles*, Oxford University Press, Kingston, 1977.

—: *Days and Nights*, Caldwell Press, Kingston, 1977.

—: *Mother Poem*, Oxford University Press, London, 1977.

CLARKE, AUSTIN (Barbados): *The Survivors of the Crossing*, Heinemann, London, 1964.

—: *Amongst Thistles and Thorns*, Heinemann, London, 1965.

—: *The Meeting Point*, Heinemann, London, 1967.

—: *Storm of Fortune*, Boston, 1973.

—: *The Bigger Light*, Boston, Brown, 1975. (These three works form a trilogy).

—: *The Prime Minister: A Novel*, General Publishing Co., Don Mills, Ontario, 1977.

DE LISSER, HERBERT (Jamaica): *Jane's Career: A Story of Jamaica*, Methuen, London, 1914.

—: *Susan Proudleigh*, Methuen, London, 1915.

—: *Triumphant Squalitone: A Tropical Extravaganza*, F.L. Myers & Son, Kingston, 1916.

—: *Revenge: A Tale of Jamaica*, The Author, Kingston, 1919.

—: *The White Witch of Rosehall*, E. Benn, London, 1929.

—: *Under The Sun: A Jamaican Comedy*, E. Benn, London, 1937.

—: *Psyche*, E. Benn, London, 1952.

—: *Morgan's Daughter*, E. Benn, London, 1961.

—: *The Cup and the Lip: A Romance*, E. Benn, London, 1956.

—: *The Arawak Girl*, Pioneer Press, Kingston, 1958.

HARRIS, WILSON (Guyana): *Palace of the Peacock*, Faber, London, 1960.

—: *The Far Journey of Oudin*, Faber, London, 1961.

—: *The Whole Armour*, Faber, London, 1962.

—: *The Secret Ladder*, Faber, London, 1963. (These four works form the Guiana Quartet.)

—: *Heartland*, Faber, London, 1964.

—: *The Eye of the Scarecrow*, Faber, London, 1965.

—: *The Waiting Room*, Faber, London, 1967.

—: *Tumatumari*, Faber, London, 1968.

—: *Ascent to Omai*, Faber, London, 1970.

—: *The Age of the Rainmakers*, Faber, London, 1971 (short stories).

—: *Black Marsden: A Tabula-Rasa Comedy*, Faber, London, 1972.

—: *Companions of the Day and Night*, Faber, London, 1975.

—: *Da Silva da Silva's Cultivated Wilderness & Genesis of Clowns*, Faber, London, 1977.

—: *The Tree of the Sun*, Faber, London, 1978.

JAMES, C.L.R. (Trinidad and Tobago): *Minty Alley*, Secker & Warburg, London, 1936.

LAMMING, GEORGE (Barbados): *In the Castle of My Skin*, Michael Joseph, London, 1953.

—: *The Emigrants*, Michael Joseph, London, 1954.

—: *Of Age and Innocence*, Michael Joseph, London, 1958.

—: *Season of Adventure*, Michael Joseph, London, 1960.

—: *Water with Berries*, Longman Caribbean, London, 1971.

—: *Natives of My Person*, Longman Caribbean, Port of Spain/Harlow, 1972.

MCKAY, CLAUDE (Jamaica): *Home to Harlem*, Harper & Brothers, New York, 1928.

—: *Banjo: A Story Without a Plot*, Harper & Brothers, New York, 1929.

—: *Gingertown*, Harper & Brothers, New York, 1932.

—: *Banana Bottom*, Harper & Brothers, New York, 1933.

—: *A Long Way From Home*, L. Furman, New York, 1937.

MAIS, ROGER (Jamaica): *And Most of All Men*, City Printery, Jamaica, 1942.

—: *The Hills Were Joyful Together: a Novel*, Cape, London, 1953.

—: *Brother Man*, Cape, London, 1954.

—: *Black Lightning*, Cape, London, 1955.

MENDES, ALFRED H. (Trinidad and Tobago): *Pitch Lake*, Duckworth, London, 1934.

—: *Black Fauns*, Duckworth, London, 1935.

MITTELHOLZER, EDGAR A. (Guyana): *Corentyne Thunder*, Eyre & Spottiswoode, London, 1941.

—: *A Morning at the Office*, Hogarth Press, London, 1950.

—: *Shadows Move Among Them*, P. Neville, London, 1951.

—: *Children of Kaywana*, P. Neville, London, 1952.

—: *The Weather in Middenshot*, J. Day, New York, 1953.

—: *The Life and Death of Sylvia*, Secker & Warburg, London, 1953.

—: *My Bones and My Flute: A Ghost Story in the Old Fashioned Manner*, Secker & Warburg, London, 1955.

—: *Kaywana Heritage*, Secker & Warburg, London, 1976.

NAIPAUL, V.S. (Trinidad and Tobago): *The Mystic Masseur*, Deutsch, London, 1957.

—: *The Suffrage of Elvira*, Deutsch, London, 1958.

—: *Miguel Street*, Deutsch, London, 1959 (short stories).
—: *A House for Mr Biswas*, Deutsch, London, 1961.
—: *Mr Stone and the Knight's Companion*, Deutsch, London, 1963.
—: *An Area of Darkness*, Deutsch, London, 1964 (travel in India).
—: *The Mimic Men*, Deutsch, London, 1967.
—: *A Flag on the Island*, Deutsch, London, 1967 (two stories).
—: *In a Free State*, Deutsch, London, 1971.
—: *Guerillas*, Deutsch, London, 1975.
—: *India: A Wounded Civilization*, Knopf, New York, 1977.
—: *A Bend in the River*, Deutsch, London, 1979.
REID, V.S. (Jamaica): *New Day*, Knopf, New York, 1949.
—: *The Leopard*, Heinemann, London, 1958.
—: *Sixty Five*, Longman, London, 1960.
RHYS, J. (Dominica): *Postures*, Chatto & Windus, London, 1928.
—: *Quartet: A Novel*, Simon & Shuster, New York, 1929.
—: *After Leaving Mr Mackenzie*, Cape, London, 1931.
—: *Voyage in the Dark*, Constable, London, 1934.
—: *Good Morning Midnight*, Constable, London, 1939.
—: *Wide Sargasso Sea*, Deutsch, London, 1966.
ST OMER, GARTH (St Lucia): *A Room on the Hill*, Faber, London, 1968.
—: *Shades of Grey*, Faber, London, 1968.
—: *Nor Any Country*, Faber, London, 1969.
—: *J-Black Bam and the Masqueraders*, Faber, London, 1972.
SALKEY, ANDREW (Jamaica): *A Quality of Violence*, New Authors, London, 1959.
—: *Escape to an Autumn Pavement*, Hutchinson, London, 1950.
—: *Hurricane viii*, Oxford University Press, London, 1964.
—: *Earthquake*, Oxford University Press, London, 1965.
—: *Drought viii*, Oxford University Press, London, 1966.
—: *Riot*, Oxford University Press, London, 1967.
—: *The Late Emancipation of Jerry Stover*, Hutchinson, London, 1969.
—: *The Adventures of Catullus Kelley*, Hutchinson, London, 1969.
—: *Joey Tyson*, L'Ouverture, London, 1974.
—: *Come Home, Malcolm Heartland*, Hutchinson, London, 1976.
SELVON, SAMUEL (Trinidad and Tobago): *A Brighter Sun*, Wingate, London, 1952.
—: *An Island is a World*, Wingate, London, 1955.
—: *The Lonely Londoners*, Wingate, London, 1956.
—: *Turn Again Tiger*, MacGibbon & Kee, London, 1958.
—: *I Hear Thunder*, MacGibbon & Kee, London, 1963.
—: *The Housing Lark*, MacGibbon & Kee, London, 1965.
—: *The Plains of Caroni*, MacGibbon & Kee, London, 1969.
—: *Those Who Eat The Cascadura*, D. Poynter, London, 1972.
—: *Moses Ascending*, D. Poynter, London, 1975.
WALCOTT, DEREK (St Lucia): *25 Poems*, Port of Spain, 1948.
—: *Epitaph for the Young*, Barbados, 1949.
—: *Henri Christophe*, Barbados, 1951.
—: *Poems*, Kingston, 1952.

—: *In a Green Night*, Cape, London, 1962.
—: *Selected Poems*, Farrar, Strauss & Giroux, New York, 1964.
—: *The Castaway and Other Poems*, Cape, London, 1965.
—: *The Gulf and Other Poems*, Cape, London, 1969.
—: *Dream on Monkey Mountain and Other Plays*, Farrar, Strauss & Giroux, New York, 1970.
—: *Another Life*, Farrar, Strauss & Giroux, New York, 1973.
—: *Sea Grapes*, Cape, London, 1976.
—: *The Joker of Seville and O Babylon*, Farrar, Strauss & Giroux, 1978 (plays).
—: *The Starapple Kingdom*, Farrar, Strauss & Giroux, New York.

AFRICA

General

AWOONOR, KOFI: *The Breast of the Earth: a survey of the history, culture and literature of Africa south of the Sahara*, Arthur Doubleday, New York, 1975.
BEIER, ULLI (ED.): *An Introduction to Africa Literature: an anthology of critical writing*, Longman, London and New York, 1979.
CLARK, JOHN PEPPER: *The Example of Shakespeare*, Longman, London, 1971.
COOK, D.: *African Literature: a critical view*, Longman, London, 1977.
GAKWANDI, SHATTO ARTHUR: *The Novel and Contemporary Experience in Africa*, Heinemann Educational, London, 1977.
GERARD, ALBERT: *Four African Literatures: Xhosa, Sotho, Zulu, Amharic*, University of California Press, Berkeley, California, 1971.
GRAY, S.: *Southern African Literature: an introduction*, David Phillip, Cape Town, 1979; Rex Collings, London, 1979.
GRIFFITHS, G.: *A Double Exile: African and West Indian Writing between two cultures*, Marion Boyars, London, 1978.
HERDECK, D.E.: *African Authors: A Companion to Black African Writing 1300–1973*, Inscape, Washington, D.C. (bibliography).
HEYWOOD, CHRISTOPHER (ED.): *Aspects of South African Literature*, Heinemann Educational, London, 1976.
KILLAM, GEORGE (ED.): *African Writers on African Writing*, Heinemann Educational, 1972.
LARSON, C.R.: *The Emergence of African Fiction*, Indiana University Press, Bloomington, Indiana, 1972.
LIYONG, TABAN LO: *Thirteen Offensives against Our Enemies*, East African Literature Bureau, Nairobi, 1973 (criticism, essays, poetry).
—: *The Last Word, Cultural Synthesism*, East African Publishing House, Nairobi, 1969.
MAHOOD, MOLLY: *Colonial Encounter*, Rex Collings, London, 1977.
MPHAHLELE, EZEKIEL: *Voices in the Whirlwind, and other essays*, Macmillan, London, 1972.
NAZARETH, PETER: *The Third World Writer: his social responsibility*, Kenya Literature Bureau, Nairobi, 1978.
NGUGI WA THIONG'O: *Homecoming: essays on African and Caribbean literature, culture and politics*, Heinemann Educational, London, 1972.

NKOSI, LEWIS: *Home and Exile*, Longman, London, 1965.

—: *Tasks and Masks: themes and styles of African literature*, Longman, London, 1981.

PALMER, EUSTACE: *The Growth of the African Novel*, Heinemann Educational, London, 1979.

P'BITEK, OKOT: *Africa's Cultural Revolution*, Macmillan Books for Africa, Nairobi, 1975.

PIETERSE, COSMO, AND MONRO, DONALD (EDS.): *Protest and Conflict in African Literature*, Heinemann Educational, London, 1969.

SOYINKA, WOLE: *Myth, Literature and the African World*, Cambridge University Press, London and New York, 1976.

WAUTHIER, CLAUDE: *The Literature and Thought of Modern Africa*, Heinemann Educational, London, 2nd edn, 1978.

ZELL, HANS M., BUNDY, C. AND COULON, V. (EDS.): *A New Reader's Guide to African Literature*, Africana Publishing Co., New York, 1983 (bibliography).

Writers: West Africa

ACHEBE, CHINUA (Nigeria): *Things Fall Apart*, Heinemann Educational, London, 1958.

—: *No Longer At Ease*, Heinemann Educational, London, 1960.

—: *Arrow of God*, Heinemann Educational, London, 1966.

—: *A Man of the People*, Heinemann Educational, London, 1966.

—: *Beware, Soul-Brother*, Nwankwo-Ifejika, Enugu, Nigeria, 1971; reprinted with revisions and additions as *Christmas in Biafra and Other Poems*, Doubleday, New York, 1973.

—: *Girls at War and Other Stories*, Heinemann Educational, London, 1972.

—: *Morning Yet on Creation Day*, Heinemann Educational, London, 1977.

AIDOO, AMA ATA (Ghana): *The Dilemma of a Ghost*, Collier-Macmillan, New York, 1971 (play).

—: *No Sweetness Here, a collection of short stories*, Doubleday, New York, 1971.

—: *Our Sister Killjoy: or reflections from a blackeyed squint*, Nok Publishers, New York, 1977 (novel).

ALUKO, TIMOTHY M. (Nigeria): *One Man, One Matchet*, Heinemann Educational, 1965.

—: *Kinsman and Foreman*, Heinemann Educational, London, 1966.

—: *One Man, One Wife*, Heinemann Educational, London, 1967.

—: *Chief the Honourable Minister*, Heinemann Educational, London, 1970.

—: *His Worshipful Majesty*, Heinemann Educational, London, 1973.

AMADI, ELECHI: *The Concubine*, Heinemann Educational, London, 1966.

—: *The Great Ponds*, Heinemann Educational, London, 1969.

—: *Peppersoup and The Road to Ibadan*, Onibonoje Press, Ibadan, 1977 (plays).

—: *The Slave*, Heinemann Educational, London, 1978.

—: *Dancer of Johannesburg*, Onibonoje Press, Ibadan, 1978 (play).

—: *Fragments*, Houghton Mifflin, Boston, 1970.

—: *Why Are We So Blest?*, Doubleday, New York, 1972.

—: *Two Thousand Seasons*, East African Publishing House, Nairobi, 1973.

—: *The Healers*, East African Publishing House, Nairobi, 1978.

AWOONOR, KOFI (Ghana): *Night of My Blood*, Doubleday, New York, 1971.

—: *This Earth, My Brother*, Doubleday, New York, 1971.

—: *Ride Me, Memory*, Greenfield Review, Greenfield Centre, N.Y., 1973.

—: *The House by the Sea*, Greenfield Review, Greenfield Centre, N.Y., 1978.

BETI, MONGO (Cameroon): *The Poor Christ of Bomba*, (French original 1956; English translation by Gerald Moore), Heinemann Educational, London, 1971.

—: *Mission to Kala*, (French original 1957; English translation by Peter Green), Heinemann Educational, London, 1964.

—: *King Lazarus*, (French original 1958; English translation by Peter Green), Heinemann Educational, London, 1960.

—: *Perpetua and the Habit of Unhappiness*, (French original 1974; English translation by John Reed and Clive Wake), Heinemann Educational, London, 1978.

—: *Remember, Reuben*, (French original 1974; English translation by Gerald Moore), Heinemann Educational, London, 1980.

CLARK, JOHN PEPPER (Nigeria): *Poems, Mbari, Ibadan, 1962.*

—: *Song of a Goat*, Mbari, Ibadan, 1962.

—: *America, their America*, Deutsch, London, 1964.

—: *Three Plays*, Oxford University Press, London and New York, 1964.

—: *A Reed in the Tide*, Longman, London, 1965.

—: *Ozidi*, Oxford University Press, London and New York, 1966.

—: *Casualties: poems 1966/68*, Longman, London, 1970.

—: *The Ozidi Saga*, Ibadan University Press, Ibadan, 1977 (translations of traditional poetry).

DE GRAFT, J.C. (Ghana): *Sons and Daughters*, Oxford University Press, London and New York, 1964 (play).

—: *Through a Film Darkly*, Oxford University Press, London, 1970 (play).

—: *Beneath the Jazz and Brass*, Heinemann Educational, London, 1975 (poems).

—: *Muntu*, Heinemann Educational, Nairobi, 1977 (play).

EASMON, R. SARIF (Sierra Leone): *Dear Parent and Ogre*, Oxford University Press, London, 1964.

—: *The Burnt-out Marriage*, Nelson, London, 1967.

—: *The New Patriots*, Longman, London, 1965.

—: *The Feud*, Longman, London, 1981 (short stories).

EKWENSI, CYPRIAN (Nigeria): *When Love Whispers*, Chuks, Yaba, Nigeria, 1947.

—: *People of the City*, Dakers, London, 1954.

—: *Jagua Nana*, Hutchinson, London, 1961.

—: *Burning Grass*, Heinemann Educational, London, 1962.

—: *Beautiful Feathers*, Hutchinson, London, 1963.

—: *Iska*, Hutchinson, London, 1966.

—: *Lokotown and other stories*, Heinemann Educational, London, 1966.

—: *Restless City and Christmas Gold: with other stories*, Heinemann Educational, London, 1975.

—: *Survive the Peace*, Heinemann Educational, London, 1976.

—: *Divided We Stand*, Fourth Dimension Publishing Co., Enugu, Nigeria, 1980.

EDWURU, A. (Nigeria): *Songs of Steel*, Rex Collings, London, 1979.

—: *Going to Storm*, Nelson, Walton-on-Thames, 1980.

EMECHTA, BUCHI (Nigeria): *In the Ditch*, Barrie and Jenkins, London, 1972.

—: *Second-Class Citizen*, Allison and Busby, London, 1974.

—: *The Bride Price*, Allison and Busby, London, 1974.

—: *The Slave Girl*, Allison and Busby, London, 1977.

—: *The Joys of Motherhood*, Allison and Busby, London, 1979.

—: *Destination Biafra*, Allison and Busby, London, 1981.

—: *Naira Power*, Macmillan, London, 1981.

—: *Double Yoke*, Ogwugwu Afor, London, 1981.

IROH, EDDIE (Nigeria): *Forty-Eight Guns for the General*, Heinemann Educational, London, 1976.

—: *Toads of War*, Heinemann Educational, London, 1979.

NWANKWO, NKEM (Nigeria): *Danda*, Deutsch, London, 1964.

—: *My Mercedes is Bigger than Yours*, Heinemann Educational, London, 1975.

NWAPA, FORE (Nigeria): *Efuru*, Heinemann Educational, London, 1966.

—: *Idu*, Heinemann Educational, London, 1969.

—: *This is Lagos and Other Stories*, Nwamife Publ., Enugu, Nigeria, 1971.

—: *Never Again*, Nwamife Publ., Enugu, Nigeria, 1976.

—: *Wives at War and Other Stories*, Nwamife Publ., Enugu, Nigeria, 1980.

OKARA, GABRIEL (Nigeria): *The Voice*, Deutsch, London, 1964.

—: *The Fisherman's Invocation*, Heinemann Educational, London, 1978.

OKIGBO, CHRISTOPHER: *Heavensgate*, Mbari, Ibadan, 1962.

—: *Limits*, Mbari, Ibadan, 1964.

—: *Labyrinths, with Path of Thunder*, Heinemann Educational, London, 1971.

OUOLOGUEM, YAMBO (Mali): *Bound to Violence*, (French original 1968; translation by Ralph Mannheim), Secker & Warburg, London 1971.

PETERS, LENRIE (Gambia): *Poems*, Mbari, Ibadan, 1964.

—: *The Second Round*, Heinemann Educational, London, 1965 (novel).

—: *Satellites*, Heinemann Educational, London, 1967.

—: *Katchikali*, Heinemann Educational, London, 1971.

—: *Selected Poetry*, Heinemann Educational, London, 1981.

SOYINKA, WOLE (Nigeria): *Three Plays*, Mbari, Ibadan, 1963.

—: *A Dance of the Forests*, Oxford University Press, London and New York, 1963.

—: *The Lion and the Jewel*, Oxford University Press, London and New York, 1963.

—: *Five Plays*, Oxford University Press, London and New York, 1964.

—: *The Interpreters*, Deutsch, London, 1965.

—: *The Road*, Oxford University Press, London and New York, 1965.

—: *Idanre, and other poems*, Methuen, London, 1967.

—: *Kongi's Harvest*, Oxford University Press, London and New York, 1967.
—: *The Trials of Brother Jero, and The Strong Breed*, Dramatists' Play, New York, 1967.
—: *Poems from Prison*, Rex Collings, London, 1969.
—: *Three Short Plays*, Oxford University Press, London and New York, 1969.
—: *A Shuttle in the Crypt*, Rex Collings, London, 1971.
—: *Madmen and Specialists*, Methuen, London, 1971.
—: *The Man Died*, Rex Collings, London, 1972.
—: *Camwood on the Leaves*, Methuen, London, 1973.
—: *The Bacchante of Euripides*, Methuen, London, 1973.
—: *Season of Anomy*, Rex Collings, London, 1973.
—: *Collected Plays*, 2 vols, Oxford University Press, London and New York, 1973–4.
—: *Ogun Abibiman*, Rex Collings, London, 1976.
—: *Aké: the Years of Childhood*, Rex Collings, London, 1981 (autobiography).
TUTUOLA, AMOS (Nigeria): *The Palm-wine Drinkard and his dead palm-wine tapster in the Deads' Town*, Faber, London, 1952.
—: *My Life in the Bush of Ghosts*, Faber, London, 1954.
—: *Simbi and the Satyr of the Dark Jungle*, Faber, London, 1955.
—: *The Brave African Huntress*, Faber, London, 1958.
—: *Feather Woman of the Jungle*, Faber, London, 1962.
—: *Ajaiyi and his Inherited Poverty*, Faber, London, 1967.
—: *The Witch Herbalist of the Remote Town*, Faber, London, 1981.

Writers: East and Central Africa

ANGIRA, JARED (Kenya): *Juices*, East Africa Publishing House, Nairobi, 1970.
—: *Silent Voices*, Heinemann Educational, London, 1972.
—: *Soft Corals*, East Africa Publishing House, Nairobi, 1973.
—: *Cascades*, Longman, London, 1979.
—: *The Years Go By*, Bookwise Ltd, Nairobi, 1980.
BURUGA, JOSEPH (Kenya): *The Abandoned Hut*, East African Publishing House, Nairobi, 1969.
FARAH, NURUDDIN (Somalia): *From a Crooked Rib*, Heinemann Educational, London, 1970.
—: *A Naked Needle*, Heinemann Educational, London, 1976.
—: *Sweet and Sour Milk*, Allison and Busby, London, 1979.
—: *Sardines*, Allison and Busby, London, 1981.
KACHINGWE, AUBREY (Malawi): *No Easy Task*, Heinemann Educational, London, 1966.
KAHIGA, SAMUEL (Kenya): *The Girl from Abroad*, Heinemann Educational, London, 1974.
—: *Flight to Juba*, Longman Kenya, Nairobi, 1979 (short stories).
—: *When the Stars are Scattered*, Longman Kenya, Nairobi, 1979.
KAYIRA, LEGION (Malawi): *I Will Try*, Longman, London, 1965 (autobiography).
—: *The Looming Shadow*, Longman, London, 1968.
—: *Jingala*, Longman, London, 1969.

—: *The Civil Servant*, Longman, London, 1971.
—: *The Detainee*, Heinemann Educational, London, 1974.
KIBERA, LEONARD (Kenya): *Voices in the Dark*, East African Publishing House, Nairobi, 1970.
LESSING, DORIS (Zimbabwe): *The Grass is Singing*, Michael Joseph, London, 1950.
—: *Children of Violence*, MacGibbon & Kee, London, 1952–1969 (5 vols: *Martha Quest*, 1952; *A Proper Marriage*, 1954; *A Ripple from the Story*, 1958; *Landlocked*, 1965; *The Four-Gated City*, 1969).
—: *Retreat to Innocence*, Michael Joseph, London, 1956.
—: *The Habit of Loving*, MacGibbon & Kee, London, 1957.
—: *The Golden Notebook*, Michael Joseph, London, 1962.
—: *A Man and Two Women*, Michael Joseph, London, 1963.
—: *African Stories*, Michael Joseph, London, 1964.
—: *Briefing for a Descent into Hell*, Cape, London, 1971.
—: *The Story of a Non-Marrying Man*, Cape, London, 1972.
—: *The Summer Before the Dark*, Cape, London, 1973.
—: *The Memoirs of a Survivor*, Octagon Press, London, 1974.
LIKIMANI, MUTHONI (Kenya): *What Does a Man Want?*, East African Literature Bureau, Nairobi, 2nd edn, 1974.
LIYONG, TABAN LO (Uganda): *Fixions and other stories*, Heinemann Educational, London, 1969.
—: *Frantz Fanon's Uneven Ribs: poems more and more*, Heinemann Educational, London, 1971.
—: *The Uniformed Man*, East African Literature Bureau, Nairobi, 1971.
—: *Another Nigger Dead*, Heinemann Educational, London, 1972.
—: *Ballads of Underdevelopment*, East African Literature Bureau, Nairobi, 1976.
—: *Meditations of Tabl lo Liyong*, Rex Collings, London, 1978.
—: See also under Africa, general, above.
MAILLU, DAVID G. (Kenya): *Kadosa*, David Maillu Publ., Machakos, Kenya, 1979.
—: *For Mbatha and Rabeka*, Macmillan Educ., London, 1980.
—: *The Equatorial Assignment*, Macmillan Educ., London, 1980.
MANGUA, CHARLES (Kenya): *Son of Woman*, East African Publishing House, Nairobi, 1971.
—: *A Tail in the Mouth*, East African Publishing House, Nairobi, 1972.
MAPANJE, JACK (Malawi): *Of Chameleons and Gods*, Heinemann Educational, London, 1981.
MAZRUI, ALI (Uganda): *The Trial of Christopher Okigbo*, Heinemann Educational, 1971 (novel).
MBITI, J. (Kenya): *Poems of Nature and Faith*, East African Publishing House, Nairobi, 1969.
MUTSWAIRO, SOLOMON M. (Zimbabwe): *Chaminuka: Prophet of Zimbabwe*, Three Continents Press, Washington D.C., 1978.
—: *Mapondera: Soldier of Zimbabwe*, Three Continents Press, Washington D.C., 1978.
MWANGI, MAJA (Kenya): *Kill Me Quick*, Heinemann Educational, London, 1973.

—: *Carcase for Hounds*, Heinemann Educational, London, 1974.
—: *Taste of Death*, East African Publishing House, Nairobi, 1975.
—: *Going Down River Road*, Heinemann Educational, London, 1976.
—: *The Bushtrackers*, Longman Kenya, Nairobi, 1979.
—: *The Cockroach Dance*, Longman Kenya, Nairobi, 1979.
NGUGI WA THIONG'O (Kenya): *Weep not, Child*, Heinemann Educational, London, 1964.
—: *The River Between*, Heinemann Educational, London, 1965.
—: *A Grain of Wheat*, Heinemann Educational, London, 1967.
—: *The Black Hermit*, Heinemann Educational, London, 1968 (play).
—: *This Time Tomorrow*, East African Literature Bureau, Nairobi, 1970 (play).
—: *Secret Lives: and other stories*, Heinemann Educational, London, 1975.
—: *Petals of Blood*, Heinemann Educational, London, 1977.
—: *Devil on the Cross*, Heinemann Educational, London, 1982.
—: See also under Africa, general, above.
—: AND MUGO, MICERE GITHAE (Kenya): *The Trial of Dedan Kimathi*, Heinemann Educational, 1976 (play).
—: AND NGUGI WA MIRII (Kenya): *I Will marry When I Want*, Heinemann Educational, London, 1982.
OCULI, OBELLO (Uganda): *Prostitute*, East African Publishing House, Nairobi, 1968.
—: *Orphan*, East African Publishing House, Nairobi, 1968.
—: *Malak*, East African Publishing House, Nairobi, 1977 (poems).
OGOT, GRACE (Kenya): *The Promised Land*, East African Publishing House, Nairobi, 1968.
—: *Land without Thunder*, East African Publishing House, Nairobi, 1968.
—: *The Other Woman and other stories*, Transafrica, Nairobi, 1976.
—: *The Graduate*, Uzima, Nairobi, 1980.
—: *The Island of Tears*, Uzima, Nairobi, 1980 (short stories).
PALANGYO, PETER (Tanzania): *Dying in the Sun*, Heinemann Educational, London, 1969.
P'BITEK, OKOT (Uganda): *Song of Lawino*, East African Publishing House, Nairobi, 1966.
—: *Song of Ocol*, East African Publishing House, Nairobi, 1970.
P'CHONG, CLIFF LUBWA (Uganda): *Generosity Kills and The Last Sacrifice*, Longman Kenya, Nairobi, 1975 (play).
—: *Words of My Groaning*, East African Literature Bureau, Nairobi, 1976, (poems).
RUBADIRI, DAVID (Malawi): *No Bride Price*, East African Publishing House, Nairobi, 1967 (novel).
RUGANDA, JOHN (Uganda): *The Burdens*, Oxford University Press, Nairobi, 1972.
—: *Black Mamba*, East African Publishing House, Nairobi, 1973.
—: *The Floods*, East African Publishing House, Nairobi, 1980.
RUHENI, MWANGI (Kenya): *What a Life!*, Longman Kenya, Nairobi, 1972.
—: *The Future Leaders*, Heinemann Educational, London, 1973.
—: *What a Husband!*, Longman Kenya, Nairobi, 1974.

—: *The Minister's Daughter*, Heinemann Educational, London, 1975.

RUHUMBIKA, GABRIEL (Tanzania): *Village in Uhuru*, Longman, London, 1969.

SALIH, EL TAYEB (Sudan): *Season of Migration to the North*, Heinemann Educational, London, 1969.

SERUMAGA, ROBERT (Uganda): *Return to the Shadows*, Heinemann Educational, London, 1969.

—: *The Elephants*, Oxford University Press, Nairobi, 1971.

—: *Majangwa and A Play*, East African Publishing House, Nairobi, 1974.

STYLE, COLIN (Zimbabwe): Seven poems in *A World of Their Own*, ed. Stephen Gray, Ad. Donker, Johannesburg, 1977.

—: 'Baobab Street', 25 poems in *Bateleur Poets*, 94, Bateleur, Johannesburg, 1977.

TZODZO, T.K. (Zimbabwe): *The Talking Calabash*, 3 acts, *Opus IV*, April 1971.

WACHIRA, BODWON (Kenya): *Ordeal in the Forest*, East African Publishing House, Nairobi, 1967.

WACIUMA, CHARITY (Kenya): *Daughter of Mumbi*, East African Publishing House, Nairobi, 1969.

WATENE, KENNETH (Kenya): *My Son for My Freedom*, East African Publishing House, Nairobi, 1975 (play).

—: *Dedan Kimathi*, Transafrica, Nairobi, 1974 (play).

—: *Sunset on the Manyatta*, East African Publishing House, Nairobi, 1974 (novel).

WORKU, DANIACHEW (Ethiopia): *The Thirteenth Sun*, Heinemann Educational, London, 1973.

Writers: Southern Africa

ABRAHAMS, PETER (South Africa): *Dark Testament*, Allen and Unwin, London, 1942.

—: *Song of the City*, Crisp, London, 1945.

—: *Mine Boy*, Crisp, London, 1946.

—: *The Path of Thunder*, Harper, New York, 1948.

—: *Wild Conquest*, Harper, New York, 1950.

—: *Return to Goli*, Faber, London, 1953 (essays).

—: *Tell Freedom*, Faber, London, 1954.

—: *A Wreath for Udomo*, Faber, London, 1956.

—: *A Night of their Own*, Faber, London, 1965.

—: *This Island Now*, Faber, London, 1966.

BOETIE, D. AND SIMON, B. (South Africa): *Familiarity is the Kingdom of the Lost*, Cresset Press, London, 1970 (novel).

BRINK, ANDRÉ (South Africa): *Looking On Darkness*, W.H. Allen & Co., London, 1974.

—: *Rumours of Rain*, W.H. Allen, London, 1978.

—: *A Chain of Voices*, Faber, London, 1982.

BRUTUS, DENIS (South Africa): *Sirens, Knuckles and Boots*, Mbari, Ibadan, 1963.

—: *Letters to Martha, and other poems from a South African prison*, Heinemann, London, 1969.

—: *Poems from Algiers*, African and Afro-American Research Institute, Austin, Texas, 1970.

—: *China Poems*, African and Afro-American Research Institute, Austin, Texas.

—: *A Simple Lust*, Heinemann Educational, London, 1973.

—: *Strains*, Troubadour Press, Austin, Texas, 1975.

—: *Stubborn Hope*, Heinemann Educational, London, 1978.

CARIM, ENVER (South Africa): *Golden City*, Seven Seas Publ., Berlin, 1968.

—: *A Dream Deferred*, Allen Lane, London, 1973.

COETZEE, J.M. (South Africa): *In The Heart of the Country*, Secker & Warburg, London, 1977.

—: *Dusklands*, Ravan Press, Johannesburg, 1974.

—: *Waiting for the Barbarians*, Secker & Warburg, London, 1980.

DHLOMO, H.I.E. (South Africa): *An African Tragedy*, Lovedale Press, Lovedale, South Africa, 1928.

DIKOBE, MODIKWE (South Africa): *The Marabi Dance*, Heinemann Educational, London, 1973.

DRIVER, C.J. (South Africa): *Elegy for a Revolutionary*, Faber, London, 1969.

—: *Send War in Our Time, O Lord*, Faber, London, 1970.

—: *Death of Fathers*, Faber, London, 1972.

FUGARD, ATHOL (South Africa): *The Bloodknot*, Somondium, Cape Town, 1963.

—: *Boesman and Lena*, Buren Publications, Cape Town, 1969.

—: *People are Living There*, Buren Publications, Cape Town, 1969.

KANI, JOHN, AND NTSHONA, WILSON (South Africa): *Sizwe Banzi is Dead*, Oxford University Press, London, 1974.

GORDIMER, NADINE (South Africa): *Not for Publication*, Gollancz, London, 1965 (short stories).

—: *The Late Bourgeois World*, Gollanz, London, 1966.

—: *A Guest of Honour*, Viking, New York, 1970.

—: *Livingstone's Companions*, Cape, London, 1972 (short stories).

—: *Some Monday for Sure*, Heinemann Educational, London, 1976.

HEAD, BESSIE (South Africa): *When Rain Clouds Gather*, Simon & Schuster, New York, 1968.

—: *Maru*, Gollancz, London, 1971.

—: *A Question of Power*, Pantheon, New York, 1973.

—: *The Collector of Treasures*, Heinemann Educational, London, 1977.

HUTCHINSON, ALFRED (South Africa): *Road to Ghana*, Gollancz, London, 1960.

—: *The Rain-Killers*, University of London Press, London, 1964.

JABAVU, NONI (South Africa): *Drawn in Colour; African Contrasts*, John Murray, London, 1963.

—: *The Ochre People: Scenes from South African Life*, John Murray, London, 1963.

KATIYO, WILSON (Zimbabwe): *A Son of the Soil*, Rex Collings, London, 1976.

—: *Going to Heaven*, Rex Collings, London, 1979.

KEPPEL-JONES, A. (South Africa): *When Smuts Goes: a history of South Africa from 1952–2010, first published in 2015*, Shuter & Shooter, Pietermaritzburg, 1950.

KGOSITSILE, KEORAPETSE (South Africa): *Spirits Unchained*, Broadside Press, Detroit, 1969.

—: *For Melba*, Third World Press, Chicago, 1970.

—: *My Name is Afrika*, Doubleday, New York, 1971.

—: *The Present is a Dangerous Place to Live*, Third World Press, Chicago, 1974.

—: *Herzspuren*, Schwiftinger Galerie-Verlag, Kirchberg, West Germany, 1981.

KRIGE, UYS (South Africa): *Orphan of the Desert*, Malherbe, Cape Town, 1967.

KUNENE, MAZIZI (South Africa): *Zulu Poems*, André Deutsch, London, 1970.

—: *Emperor Shaka The Great: A Zulu Epic*, Heinemann Educational, London, 1979.

—: *Anthem of the Decades*, Heinemann Educational, London, 1981.

LA GUMA, ALEX (South Africa): *And a Threefold Cord*, Seven Seas Books, Berlin, 1964.

—: *A Walk in the Night*, Heinemann Educational, London, 1967.

—: *The Stone Country*, Seven Seas Books, Berlin, 1967.

—: *In the Fog of the Season's End*, Heinemann Educational, London, 1972.

—: *Time of the Butcherbird*, Heinemann Educational, London, 1979.

MAIMANE, A. (South Africa): *Victims*, Allison and Busby, London, 1976 (novel).

MARECHERA, DAMBUDSO (Zimbabwe): *The House of Hunger*, Heinemann Educational, London, 1978.

—: *Black Sunlight*, Heinemann Educational, London, 1980.

MATSHIKIZA, TODD (South Africa): *Chocolates for My Wife: slices of my life*, Hodder & Stoughton, London, 1961.

MATSHOBA, M. (South Africa): *Call Me Not a Man*, Ravan, Johannesburg, 1979 (short stories).

—: *Seeds of War*, Ravan, Johannesburg, 1981 (novel).

MODISANE, W. BLOKE (South Africa): *Blame Me On History*, Thames & Hudson, London, 1963.

MPHAHLELE, ES'KIA (EZEKIEL) (South Africa): *Man Must Live, and other stories*, African Bookman, Cape Town, 1947.

—: *Down Second Avenue*, Faber, London, 1959.

—: *The Living and the Dead, and other stories*, Ministry of Education, Ibadan, 1961.

—: *In Corner B*, East African Publishing House, Nairobi, 1967.

—: *The Wanderers*, Macmillan, New York, 1971.

—: *Chirundu*, Ravan, Johannesburg, 1979.

—: *The Unbroken Song*, Ravan, Johannesburg, 1981 (miscellany).

MTSHALI, OSWALD MBUYISENI (South Africa): *Sounds of a Cowhide Drum*, Renoster books, Johannesburg, 1971.

—: *Fireflames*, Shuter & Shooter, Pietermaritzburg, 1980.

MULAISHO, DOMINIC (Zambia): *The Tongue of the Dumb*, Heinemann Educational, London, 1971 (novel).

—: *The Smoke That Thunders*, Heinemann Educational, London, 1979.

MUNGOSHI, CHARLES L. (Zimbabwe): *The Coming of the Dry Season*, Oxford University Press, Nairobi, 1972.

—: *Waiting for the Rain*, Heinemann Educational, London, 1975.

—: *The Milkman Doesn't Only Deliver Milk: selected poems,* Poetry Society of Zimbabwe, Harare, 1981.

MUTSWAIRO, SOLOMON M. (Zimbabwe): *Chaminuka: Prophet of Zimbabwe*, Three Continents Press, Washington D.C., 1978.

—: *Mapondera: Soldier of Zimbabwe*, Three Continents Press, Washington D.C., 1978.

MZAMANE, M.B. (South Africa): *Mzala*, Ravan, Johannesburg, (short stories).

—: *The Children of Soweto*, Longman, London, 1981.

NAKASA, NAT (South Africa): *Cross of Gold*, Longman, London, 1981.

NKOSI, LEWIS (South Africa): *The Rhythm of Violence*, Oxford University Press, London & New York, 1964 (play).

NORTJE, ARTHUR (South Africa): *Dead Roots*, Heinemann Education, London, 1973 (poems).

PATON, ALAN (South Africa): *Cry The Beloved Country*, Cape, London, 1948.

—: *Too late the Phalarope*, Cannon (for Cape), Cape Town, 1953.

—: *Tales from a Troubled Land*, Scribner's, New York, 1961.

—: *Hofmeyer*, Oxford University Press, Capetown, 1964.

RIVE, RICHARD (South Africa): *African Songs*, Seven Seas Books, Berlin, 1963.

—: *Emergency*, Faber, London, 1964 (novel).

—: *Selected Writings*, Ad. Donker, Johannesburg, 1976.

SAMKANGE, STANLAKE (Zimbabwe): *The Mourned One*, Heinemann Educational, London, 1975.

—: *Year of the Uprising*, Heinemann Educational, London, 1978.

SEPAMLA, SIPHO (South Africa): *Hurry up to it!*, Ad. Donker, Johannesburg, 1975 (poems).

—: *The Blues Is You In Me*, Ad. Donker, Johannesburg, 1976 (poems).

—: *The Soweto I Love*, David Philip, Cape Town, 1977 (poems).

—: *The Root Is One*, David Philip, Cape Town, 1979.

SEROTE, MONGANE WALLY (South Africa): *Yakhal'inkomo: Poems*, Renoster Books, Johannesburg, 1972.

—: *Tsetlo*, Ad. Donker, Johannesburg, 1974.

—: *No Baby Must Weep*, Ad. Donker, Johannesburg, 1978.

—: *Behold Mama, Flowers*, Ad. Donker, Johannesburg, 1978.

—: *To Every Birth Its Blood*, Ravan, Johannesburg, 1981 (novel).

THEMBA, CAN (South Africa): *The Will to Die*, Heinemann Educational, London, 1972 (short stories).

TLALI, MIRIAM (South Africa): *Muriel at Metropolitan*, Ravan, Johannesburg, 1979.

—: *Amandla*, Ravan, Johannesburg, 1980 (novel).

ZWELONKE, D.M. (South Africa): *Robben Island*, Heinemann Educational, London, 1973.

THE INDIAN SUB-CONTINENT

General

GOONERATNE, Y. (ED.): *Stories From Sri Lanka*, Heinemann, London, 1980.

HOSAIN, S. (ED.): *First Voices: Six Poets from Pakistan*, Oxford University Press, Karachi, 1965.

IYENGAR, K.R. SRINIVASA: *Indian Writing in English*, Asia Publishing House, Bombay, 2nd edn, 1973.

LAL, P.: *Modern Indian Poetry in English: An Anthology and a Credo*, Writers' Workshop, Calcutta, 1969.

MUKHERJEE, MEENAKSHI: *The Twice-born Fiction: Themes and Techniques of the Indian Novel in English*, Arnold-Heinemann, New Delhi, 2nd edn, 1974.

OMAR, KALEEM (ED.): *Wordfall: Three Pakistani Poets*, Oxford University Press, Karachi, 1975.

PARTHASARATHY, R. (ED.): *The Twentieth-Century Indian Poets*, Oxford University Press, Delhi, 1976.

SAID, JUNUS, (ED.): *Pieces of Eight: Eight Poets from Pakistan*, Oxford University Press, Karachi, Dacca, Lahore, 1971.

WILLIAMS, H.M.: *Indo-Anglian Literature 1800–1970: A Survey*, Orient Longman, New Delhi, 1976.

Writers: India

ANAND, MULK RAJ: *The Lost Child and Other Stories*, J.A. Allen & Co., High Wycombe, 1934.

—: *Coolie*, Lawrence and Wishart, London, 1936.

—: *Two Leaves and a Bud*, Lawrence and Wishart, London, 1937.

—: *Lament on the Death of a Master of Arts*, Naya Sansar, Lucknow, 1938.

—: *Untouchable*, Jonathan Cape, London, 1939.

—: *The Village*, Jonathan Cape, London, 1939.

—: *Across The Black Water*, Jonathan Cape, London, 1940.

—: *The Sword and the Sickle*, Jonathan Cape, London, 1942.

—: *The Barber's Trade Union and Other Stories*, Jonathan Cape, London, 1944.

—: *The Big Heart*, Hutchinson, London, 1945.

—: *The Tractor and the Corn Goddess*, Thacker & Co., Bombay, 1947 (short stories).

—: *Seven Summers*, Hutchinson, London, 1951.

—: *Private Life of an Indian Prince*, Hutchinson, London, 1953.

—: *Reflections on the Golden Bed and Other Stories*, Current Book House, Bombay, 1954.

—: *The Power of Darkness*, Jaico Publishing House, Bombay, 1958 (short stories).

—: *The Road*, Kutub Popular, Bombay, 1961.

—: *Death of a Hero*, Kutub Popular, Bombay, 1963.

—: *Morning Face*, Kutub, Bombay, 1969.

—: *Confession of a Lover*, Arnold-Heinemann, New Delhi, 1976.

BHATTACHARYA, BHABANI: *So Many Hungers!*, Hind Pocket Books Kitabs, Bombay, 1947; Victor Gollancz, London, 1947.

—: *Music for Mohini*, Crown Publishers, New York, 1952.

—: *He Who Rides a Tiger*, Crown Publishers, New York, 1954.

—: *Goddess Named Gold*, Crown Publishers, New York, 1960.
—: *Shadow from Ladakh*, Crown Publishers, New York, 1966; W.H. Allen, London, 1967.
—: *A Dream in Hawaii*, Macmillan, New Delhi, 1978.
CHAUDHURI, NIRAD: *Autobiography of an Unknown Indian*, Macmillan, London, 1951.
—: *A Passage to England*, Macmillan, London, 1959.
—: *The Continent of Circe*, Chatto & Windus, London, 1965.
DAS, KAMALA: *Summer in Calcutta*, Everest Press, New Delhi, 1966.
—: *The Descendants*, Writers' Workshop, Calcutta, 1967.
—: *The Old Playhouse and Other Poems*, Orient Longman, Madras, 1973.
—: *Alphabet of Lust*, Hind Pocket Books, New Delhi, 1976 (novel).
DESAI, ANITA: *Cry, The Peacock*, Peter Owen, London, 1963; Rupa, Calcutta, 1964.
—: *Voices in the City*, Peter Owen, London, 1965; Hind Pocket Books, Delhi, 1965.
—: *Bye-Bye Blackbird*, Hind Pocket Books, Delhi, 1971.
—: *Where Shall We Go This Summer?*, Vikas, Delhi, 1975.
—: *Fire on the Mountain*, Harper & Row, New York, 1977.
—: *Games at Twilight and Other Stories*, Heinemann, London, 1978; Allied Publishers, Bombay, 1978.
—: *Clear Light of Day*, Harper & Row, New York, 1980.
DESANI, GOVIND V.: *All About H. Hatterr*, F. Alder, London, 1948.
—: *Hali*, Writers' Workshop, Calcutta, 1967.
DUTT, TORU: *A Sheaf Gleaned in French Fields*, Kegan Paul & Co., London, 3rd edn, 1880 (poems).
EZEKIEL, NISSIM: *A Time to Change*, The Fortune Press, London, 1952.
—: *Sixty Poems*, published privately, Bombay, 1953.
—: *The Third*, The Strand Bookshop, Bombay, 1959.
—: *The Unfinished Man: Poems Written in 1959*, Writers' Workshop, Calcutta, 1960.
—: *The Exact Name: Poems 1960–64*, Writers' Workshop, Calcutta, 1965.
—: *Hymns in Darkness*, Oxford University Press, Delhi, 1976.
GHOSE, SUDHINDRA N.: *And Gazelles Leaping*, New York, 1949.
—: *Cradle of the Clouds*, New York, 1951.
—: *The Vermillion Boat*, New York, 1953.
—: *The Flame of the Forest*, New York, 1955.
JHABVALA, RUTH PRAWER: *To Whom She Will*, Allen & Unwin, London, 1955.
—: *The Nature of Passion*, Allen & Unwin, London, 1956.
—: *Esmond in India*, Allen & Unwin, London, 1958.
—: *The Householder*, Allen & Unwin, London, 1960.
—: *Get Ready for Battle*, Allen & Unwin, London, 1962.
—: *A Backward Place*, John Murray, London, 1965.
—: *An Experience of India*, John Murray, London, 1966 [1971?] (short stories).
—: *A New Dominion*, John Murray, London, 1972; and as *The Travellers*, Harper & Row, New York, 1972.

—: *Heat and Dust*, John Murray, London, 1975.
—: *How I Became a Holy Mother and Other Stories*, John Murray, London, 1976.
JUSSAWALLA, ADIL: *Missing Person*, Clearing House, Bombay, 1976.
KOLATKAR, ARUN: *Jejuri*, Clearing House, Bombay, 1976.
KUMAR, SHIV K.: *Articulate Silences*, Writers' Workshop, Calcutta, 1970.
—: *Cobwebs in the Sun*, Tata McGraw-Hill, New Delhi, 1975.
—: *The Last Wedding Anniversary*, Macmillan, Delhi, 1975.
—: *Subterfuges*, Oxford University Press, New Delhi, 1976.
—: *The Bone's Prayer: A Novel*, Arnold-Heinemann, New Delhi, 1979.
MALGONKAR, MANOHAR: *Distant Drum*, Asia Publishing House, Bombay, 1960.
—: *Combat of Shadows*, Hamish Hamilton, London, 1962.
—: *The Princes*, The Viking Press, New York, 1963.
—: *A Bend in the Ganges*, Hamish Hamilton, London, 1964.
—: *Bombay Beware*, Hind Pocket Books, New Delhi, 1975 (short stories).
—: *Open Season*, Orient Paperbacks, New Delhi, 1979.
MARKANDAYA, KAMALA: *Nectar in a Sieve*, John Day Co., New York, 1955.
—: *Some Inner Fury*, John Day Co., New York, 1956.
—: *A Silence of Desire*, Putnam & Co., London, 1960; John Day Co., New York, 1960.
—: *Possession*, John Day Co., New York, 1963.
—: *A Handful of Rice*, Hamish Hamilton, London, 1967.
—: *The Coffer Dams*, Hamish Hamilton, London, 1969.
—: *The Nowhere Man*, John Day Co., New York, 1972.
—: *Two Virgins*, Chatto & Windus, London, 1973; John Day Co., New York, 1973.
—: *The Golden Honeycomb*, Chatto & Windus, London, 1977; T.Y. Crowell, New York, 1977.
—: *Pleasure City*, Chatto & Windus, London, 1982.
MORAES, DOM: *A Beginning*, Parton Press, London, 1957.
—: *Poems*, Eyre & Spottiswoode, London, 1960.
—: *John Nobody*, Eyre & Spottiswoode, London, 1965.
—: *Poems: 1955–1965*, Macmillan, New York, 1965.
NANDY, PRITISH: *Of Gods and Olives: 21 Poems*, Writers' Workshop, Calcutta, 1967.
—: *I Hand You In Turn My Nebbuk Wreath: Early Poems*, Dialogue, Calcutta, 1968.
—: *On Either Side of Arrogance*, Writers' Workshop, Calcutta, 1968.
—: *Rites for a Plebian Statue: An Experiment in Verse Drama*, Writers' Workshop, Calcutta, 1969.
—: *From The Outer Bank of the Brahmaputra*, New Rivers Press, New York, 1969.
—: *Masks to be Interpreted as Messages*, Writers' Workshop, Calcutta, 1970.
—: *Collected Poems*, Oxford University Press, London, 1973.
NARAYAN, RASIPURAM KRISHNASWAMI: *Swami and Friends*, Indian Thought Publications, Mysore, 1944, [first published 1935].
—: *The Bachelor of Arts*, London, 1937.

—: *The Dark Room*, Macmillan, London, 1938.

—: *The English Teacher*, Eyre & Spottiswoode, London, 1946. Published in the U.S.A. with the title *Grateful to Life and Death*, 1955.

—: *An Astrologer's Day and Other Stories*, Eyre & Spottiswoode, London, 1947.

—: *Mr Sampath*, London, 1949.

—: *The Financial Expert*, London, 1952; Indian Thought Publications, Mysore, 1958.

—: *Lawley Road*, Indian Thought Publications, Mysore, 1958 (short stories).

—: *Waiting for the Mahatma*, London, 1955; Indian Thought Publications, Mysore, 1958.

—: *The Guide*, New American Library, New York, 1959.

—: *The Man-Eater of Malgudi*, Bodley Head, London, 1961.

—: *The Vendor of Sweets*, Bodley, London, 1967; Indian Thought Publications, Mysore, 1967.

—: *A Horse and Two Goats*, Bodley Head, London, 1979.

—: *The Painter of Signs*, Viking, New York, 1976.

—: *The Mahabharata: A Shortened Modern Prose Version of the Indian Epic*, Viking, New York, 1978.

PARTHASARATHY,R.: *The First Step, Poems 1956–66*, 1967.

PATEL, GIEVE: *How Do You Withstand, Body*, Clearing House, Bombay, 1976.

RAJAN, BALCHANDRA: *The Dark Dancer*, London, 1959.

—: *Too Long in the West*, London, 1961.

RAMANUJAN, A.K.: *The Striders*, Oxford University Press, New York and Bombay, 1966.

—: *Relations*, Oxford University Press, New York and Bombay, 1971.

—: *Selected Poems*, Oxford University Press, Madras, 1976.

—: *Selected Poems*, Oxford University Press, (Three Crowns Books), Delhi, 1976.

RAO, RAJA: *Kanthapura*, George Allen & Unwin, London, 1938. Indian edition, Oxford University Press, Champak Library, Bombay, 1947.

—: *The Cow of the Barricades and Other Stories*, Oxford University Press, Champak Libary, Bombay, 1947.

—: *The Serpent and the Rope*, John Murray, London, 1969.

—: *The Cat and Shakespeare*, The Macmillan Company, New York, 1965.

—: *Comrade Kirillov*, Hind Pocket Books, New Delhi, 1976 (novel).

SINGH, KUSHWANT: *The Mark of Vishnu and Other Stories*, The Saturn Press, London, 1950.

—: *Train to Pakistan*, Grove Press, New York, 1956.

—: *The Voice of God and Other Stories*, Jaico, Bombay, 1957.

—: *I Shall Not Hear the Nightingale*, John Calder, London, 1959.

—: *A Bride for the Sahib and Other Stories*, Orient, Delhi, 1967.

—: *A History of the Sikhs, Vol.1, 1469–1839, Vol.2, 1839–1964*, Princeton U.P. and Oxford U.P., Princeton and Oxford, 1963, 1966.

VENKATARAMAN, S.K.: *Murugan the Tiller*, 1927.

—: *The Next Rung*, 1928.

—: *Kandan the Patriot*, 1932.

—: *Jatadharan and other stories*, 1937.

Writers: Pakistan and Bangladesh

ALI, AHMED: *Twilight in Delhi*, Hogarth Press, London, 1940.
—: *Ocean of Light*, Peter Owen, London, 1964.
FAROOQI, NISAR A.: *The Naked Light*, Vintage Press, New York, 1965.
—: *Sadness at Dawn*, Vintage Press, New York, 1965.
GHOSE, ZULFIKAR: *Jets from Orange*, Macmillan, London (poems).
—: *The Contradictions*, Macmillan, London, 1967.
—: *The Murder of Aziz Khan*, Macmillan, London, 1968.
—: *The Incredible Brazilian/The Native* (Pt.1 of trilogy *The Incredible Brazilian*), Macmillan, London, 1972.
—: *The Violent West*, Macmillan, London, 1972 (poems).
—: *The Beautiful Empire*, (Pt.2 of trilogy), Macmillan, London, 1975.
—: *Crump's Terms*, Macmillan, London, 1975.
—: *A Different World* (Pt.3 of trilogy), Macmillan, London, 1979.
KHAN, RAZIA: *Argus under Anaesthesia*, Khoshroz Kitab Mahal, Dacca, 1976 (poems).
—: *Cruel April*, Lutfur Tahman, Dacca (poems).
SAID, Y.: *Death by Hanging and Other Stories*, Falak Pblrs., Karachi, 1964.
SELJOUK, M.A.: *Corpses*, Duckworth, London (short stories).
SIDHWA, B.: *The Crow Eaters*, Illmi Press, Lahore, 1978.
—: *The Bride*, Cape, London, 1983.

Writers: Sri Lanka

FERNANDO, PATRICK: *The Return of Ulysses*, The Hand and Flower Press, Aldington, 1955.
—: Poems in *Poems from India, Sri Lanka, Malaysia and Singapore*, ed. Y. Gooneratne, Heinemann Educational (Asia), Hong Kong, Singapore, Kuala Lumpur, 1979.
GOONEWARDENA, I.: *A Quiet Place*, de Silva, Colombo, 1968 (novel).
—: *The Awakening of Dr Kirthi and Other Stories*, Lake House Investments, Colombo, 1976.
GOONERATNE, YASMINE: *Word, Bird, Motif: 51 Poems*, privately published, Kandy, 1970.
—: *The Lizard's Cry and Other Poems*, privately published, Kandy, 1972.
MACINTYRE, ERNEST: *The Education of Miss Asia*, 1971.
—: 'The Loneliness of the Short-Distance Traveller', *New Ceylon Writing 1971*.
—: 'A Somewhat Mad and Grotesque Comedy', *New Ceylon Writing 1973*.
—: *Dark Dinkum Aussies or Let's Give Them Curry*, first performed 1982.
SARACHCHANDRA, EDIRIWEERA: *Curfew and a Full Moon: A Novel About Sri Lanka*, Heinemann Educational (Asia), Hong Kong, Singapore, Kuala Lumpur, 1978.
—: 'Sinhabahu', a four-act play, written in Sinhala in 1961, translated into English by Lakshmie de Silva, 1983, in *New Ceylon Writing 1984*.
WIJENAIKE, PUNYAKANTE: *The Third Woman and Other Stories*, Salman Publishers, Colombo, 1963.

—: *The Waiting Earth*, Colombo Apothecaries' Co., Colombo, 1966.
—: *Giraya*, Lake House Investments, Colombo, 1971.
—: *The Rebel*, Lake House Investments, Colombo, 1979.
WIKKRAMASINHE, LAKDASA: *Fifteen Poems*, privately published, Kandy, 1970.
—: *Nossa Senhora dos Chingalas*, Praja Pblrs, Colombo, 1973.
—: *O Regal Blood*, privately published, Maradana, 1975.

MALAYSIA AND SINGAPORE

General

BENNETT, B. ET AL (ED.): *The Writer's Sense of the Contemporary*, Centre for Studies in Australian Literature, Perth, 1982.
FERNANDO, L. (ED.): *Twenty-Two Malaysian Stories: An Anthology of Writing in English*, Heinemann Educational (Asia), Singapore, Kuala Lumpur & Hong Kong, 1968.
—: (ED.): *New Drama One*, Oxford University Press, Kuala Lumpur, 1972.
—: (ED.): *New Drama Two*, Oxford University Press, Kuala Lumpur, 1972.
GOONERATNE, YASMINE (ED.): *Poems from India, Sri Lanka, Malaysia and Singapore*, Heinemann Educational (Asia), Singapore, Kuala Lumpur & Hong Kong, 1979.
NAIR, C. (ED.): *Singapore Writing*, Woodrose Publications (for the Society of Singapore Writers), Singapore, 1977.
THUMBOO, EDWIN (ED.): *The Second Tongue: An Anthology of Poetry from Malaysia and Singapore*, Heinemann Educational (Asia), Singapore, Kuala Lumpur & Hong Kong, 1976.
—: (ED.): *The Flowering Tree: Selected Writings (Verse and Prose) from Singapore and Malaysia*, Educational Publications Bureau, Singapore, 1970.
—: (ED.): *Seven Poets: Singapore and Malaysia*, Singapore University Press, Singapore, 1973.
WANG, GUNGWU ET AL. (EDS.): *Society and the Writer: Essays on Literature in Modern Asia*, Australian National University Press, Canberra, 1981.
WIGNESAN, T. (ED.): *Bunga Emas: An Anthology of Contemporary Malaysian Literature (1930–63)*, Rayirath (Raybooks) Publications, Kuala Lumpur, 1964.
YEO, R. (ED.): *Singapore, Short Stories, Vols. 1 and 2*, Heinemann Educational (Asia), Singapore, Kuala Lumpur and Hong Kong, 1978.
—: (ED.): *ASEAN Short Stories*, Heinemann Educational (Asia), Singapore, Kuala Lumpur and Hong Kong, 1981.

Writers

DORALL, EDWARD N.: *A Tiger is Loose in Our Community*, New Drama One, ed. L. Fernando, Oxford University Press, Kuala Lumpur, 1972.
—: *The Hour Of The Dog, New Drama Two*, ed. L. Fernando, Oxford University Press, Kuala Lumpur, 1972.
EE TIANG HONG: *I of the Many Faces*, Wah Seong, Malacca, 1960.

—: *Lines Written in Hawaii*, East-West Culture Learning Institute, Honolulu, 1973.

—: *Myths for a Wilderness*, Heinemann Educational (Asia), Singapore, Kuala Lumpur and Hong Kong, 1976.

FERNANDO, LLOYD: *Scorpion Orchid*, Heinemann Educational (Asia), Singapore, Kuala Lumpur and Hong Kong, 1976.

GOH POH SENG: *If We Dream Too Long*, Island Press, Singapore, 1972.

—: *Eyewitness*, Heinemann Educational (Asia), Singapore, Kuala Lumpur & Hong Kong, 1976.

—: *The Immolation*, Heinemann Educational (Asia), Singapore, Kuala Lumpur and Hong Kong, 1977.

—: *Lines from Batu Ferringhi*, Island Press, Singapore, 1978.

—: *Room With Paper Flowers*, (produced in 1970).

LEE DING FAI: *Running Dog*, Heinemann Educational (Asia), Singapore, Kuala Lumpur and Hong Kong, 1980 (novel).

LEE JOO FOR: 'Son of Zen', *Three South East Asian Plays*, Tenggara, Kuala Lumpur, 1971.

LEE KOK LIANG: *The Mutes in the Sun and Other Stories*, Rayirath Publications, Kuala Lumpur, 1964.

—: *Flowers in the Sky*, Heinemann Educational (Asia), Singapore, Kuala Lumpur and Hong Kong, 1981.

LEE TZU PHENG: *Prospects for a Drowning*, Heinemann Educational (Asia), Singapore, Kuala Lumpur and Hong Kong, 1977.

LIM, CATHERINE: *Little Ironies: Stories of Singapore*, Heinemann Educational (Asia), Singapore, Kuala Lumpur and Hong Kong, 1978.

—: *Or Else, The Lightning God & Other Stories*, Heinemann Educational (Asia), Singapore, Kuala Lumpur and Hong Kong, 1980.

LIM, CHOR PEE: *Mimi Fan*, Singapore, 1962 (mimeographed).

—: *A White Rose at Midnight*, Singapore, 1963 (mimeographed).

LIM, SHIRLEY: *Crossing the Peninsula and Other Poems*, Heinemann Educational (Asia), Singapore, Kuala Lumpur & Hong Kong, 1980.

MUHAMMAD, HAJI SALLEH: *Time and Its People*, Heinemann Educational (Asia), Singapore, Kuala Lumpur & Hong Kong, 1980.

NAIR, CHANDRAN: *Once The Horseman and Other Poems*, University Education Press, Singapore, 1972.

—: *After The Hard Hours, This Rain*, Woodrose Publications, Singapore, 1975.

ONG, JOHNNY: *Sugar and Salt: A Novel of Malaysian Life*, Times Press, Isle of Man, 1964.

—: *Run Tiger Run*, Times Press, Isle of Man, 1966.

—: *The Long White Sands*, Syarikat Pesaka, Kuala Lumpur, 1977.

SINGH, KIRPAL: *Twenty Poems*, P. Lal, Calcutta, 1978.

THUMBOO, EDWIN: *Rib of Earth*, Strait Printers, Singapore, 1956.

—: *Gods Can Die*, Heinemann Educational (Asia), Singapore, Kuala Lumpur and Hong Kong, 1977.

—: *Ulysses by the Merlion*, Heinemann Educational (Asia), Singapore, Kuala Lumpur & Hong Kong, 1979.

WANG, GUNGWU: *Pulse*, B. Lim, Singapore, 1950.

WONG PHUI NAM: *Toccata On Ochre Sheaves: A Long Poem*, Raffles Society, Singapore, 1958.
—: *How The Hills Are Distant*, Rayirath Publications, Kuala Lumpur, 1963.
YAP, ARTHUR: *Only Lines*, Federal Publications, Kuala Lumpur, 1971.
—: *Commonplace*, Heinemann Educational (Asia), Singapore, Kuala Lumpur & Hong Kong, 1977.
—: *Down The Line*, Heinemann Educational (Asia), Singapore, Kuala Lumpur & Hong Kong, 1980.
YEO, ROBERT: *Coming Home Baby: Poems*, Federal Publications, Kuala Lumpur, 1971.
—: *And Napalm Does Not Help*, Heinemann Educational (Asia), Singapore, Kuala Lumpur & Hong Kong, 1977.
YEOH, PATRICK: 'The Need To Be', *New Drama Two*, ed. L. Fernando, Oxford University Press, Kuala Lumpur, 1972.

PHILIPPINES

APRIETO, PACIFICO N. AND CRUZ, ANDRES CRISTOBAL: *Tondo by Two*, Filipino Signatures, Manila, 1961.
ARGUILLA, MANUEL: *How My Brother Leon Brought Home a Wife and Other Stories*, Philippine Book Guild, Manila, 1940.
BRILLANTES, GREGORIO: *The Distance to Andromeda and Other Stories*, Benipayo, Manila, 1960.
BULOSAN, CARLOS: *The Laughter of My Father*, Harcourt, Brace, New York, 1944.
—: *America is in the Heart*, Harcourt, Brace, New York, 1944.
DEMETILLO, RICARDO: *No Certain Weather*, Guinhalinan, Quezon City, 1956.
—: *La Via: A Spiritual Journey*, University of the Philippines, Quezon City, 1958.
—: *Barter in Panay*, University of the Philippines, Quezon City, 1961.
—: *Lazarus, Troubador*, New Day, Quezon City, 1974.
ENRIQUEZ, ANTONIO REYES: *Surveyors of the Liguasan Marsh*, University of Queensland Press, St. Lucia, Queensland, 1981.
GONZALEZ, N.V.M.: *The Winds of April*, University of the Philipines, Manila, 1941.
—: *Seven Hills Away*, Swallow, Denver, 1947; Halcon House, Manila, 1947.
—: *Children of the Ash-Covered Loam and Other Stories*, Benipayo, Manila, 1954.
—: *A Season of Grace*, Benipayo, Manila, 1956.
—: *The Bamboo Dancers*, Benipayo, Manila, 1960.
HUFANA, ALIJANDRINO G.: *Sickle Season*, Kuwan, Quezon City, 1959.
—: *Poro Point: An Anthology of Lives*, University of the Philippines, Quezon City, 1961.
—: *Sieg Heil: An Epic on the Third Reich*, Tala, Quezon City, 1975.
JOAQUIN, NICK: *Prose and Poems*, Graphic, Manila, 1952.
—: *The Woman Who Had Two Navels*, Regal, Manila, 1961.
—: *Tropical Gothic*, University of Queensland Press, St Lucia, Queensland, 1972 (short stories).

—: *Tropical Baroque*, National Book Store, Quezon City, 1979; University of Queensland Press, St Lucia, Queensland, 1982 (play).
ROSCA, NINOTCHKA: *The Monsoon Collection*, University of Queensland Press, St Lucia, Queensland, 1983.
SANTOS, BIENVENIDO N.: *You Lovely People*, Benipayo, Manila, 1955.
—: *The Wounded Stag*, Capitol, Quezon City, 1956.
—: *Brother, My Brother*, Benipayo, Manila, 1960.
—: *Villa Magdalena*, Erewhon, Manila, 1965.
—: *The Volcano*, Phoenix, Quezon City, 1965 (novel).
—: *The Day The Dancers Came*, Bookmark, Manila, 1967 (short stories).
SIONIL JOSÉ, FRANCISCO: *The Pretenders* (and eight short stories), Regal, Manila, 1962.
—: *The God-Stealers and Other Stories*, R.P. Garcia, Quezon City, 1968.
—: *Mass*, Solidaridad, Manila, 1979.
—: *Waywaya*, Heinemann Educational Books (Asia), Hong Kong, 1980.
—: *Platinum*, ten Filipino stories, Solidaridad, Manila, 1983.
TIEMPO, EDILBERTO: *Watch in the Night*, Archipelago, Manila, 1953.
—: *More Than Conquerors*, Ayuda, Manila, 1964.
—: *To Be Free*, New Day, Quezon City, 1972.
—: *A Stream at Dalton Pass and Other Stories*, Bookmark, Manila, 1970.
TIEMPO, EDITH L.: *A Blade of Fern*, Heinemann Asia, Hong Kong, 1978.
—: *Abide, Joshua and Other Stories*, Florentino, Manila, 1964.
—: *The Tracks of Babylon and Other Poems*, Swallow, Denver, 1966.
VILLA, JOSE GARCIA: *Footnote to Youth: Tales of the Philippines and Others*, Scribner's, New York, 1933.
—: *Many Voices*, Philippine Book Guild, Manila, 1939.
—: *Selected Poems and New*, McDowell, Obolensky, New York, 1958.
—: *Poems 55*, Florentino, Manila, 1962.
—: *Poems in Praise of Love*, Florentino, Manila, 1962.

OCEANIA

General

BEIER, ULLI (ED.): *Voices of Independence: New Black Writing from Papua New Guinea*, University of Queensland Press, St Lucia, Queensland, 1980.
SUBRAMANI: *The Indo-Fijian Experience*, University of Queensland Press, St Lucia, Quensland, 1979.
TIFFIN, C. (ED.): *South Pacific Images*, SPACLALS, St Lucia, Queensland, 1978.
WENDT, ALBERT (ED.): *Lali: A Pacific Anthology*, Longman Paul, Auckland, 1980.

Writers

ERI, VINCENT (Papua–New Guinea): *The Crocodile*, Jacaranda Wiley Ltd, Milton, Queensland, 1970.
KASAIPWALOVA, JOHN (Papua – New Guinea): *Reluctant Flame*,

University Bookshop, Papua Pocket Poets, vol. 29, Boroko, 1971; also in PanAfrican Pocket Poets, Vol.1, Ife, Nigeria, 1971.

MALIFA, SANO (Samoa): *Looking Down at Waves*, Mana Publications, Suva, 1975.

NANDAN, SATENDRA (Fiji): *Faces in a Village*, Deepak Seth, New Delhi, 1976.

PILLAI, RAYMOND: *The Celebration Collection of Short Stories*, Mana Publications and the South Pacific Creative Arts Society, Fiji, 1980.

SOABA, RUSSELL (Papua – New Guinea): *Wanpis*, Institute of Papua New Guinea Studies, Port Moresby, 1978.

—: *Naked Thoughts*, Institute of Papua New Guinea Studies, Port Moresby, 1978.

THAMAN, KONAI HELU (Tonga): *You, The Choice of My Parents*, Mana Publications, Suva, Fiji, 1974.

TONGIA, MAKIUTI (Cook Islands): *Korero*, Mana Publications, Suva, 1977.

WENDT, ALBERT (Samoa): *Sons for the Return Home*, Longman Paul, Auckland, 1973.

—: *Flying-Fox in a Freedom Tree*, Longman Paul, Auckland, 1974.

—: *Inside Us the Dead*, Longman Paul, Auckland, 1976.

—: *Pouliuli*, Longman Paul, Auckland, 1977.

—: *Leaves of the Banyan Tree*, Longman Paul, Auckland, 1979.

—: *Shaman of Visions*, Auckland University Press, Auckland, 1984 (poems).

Index

YORK HANDBOOKS

Further titles

A DICTIONARY OF LITERARY TERMS
MARTIN GRAY

Over one thousand literary terms are dealt with in this Handbook, with definitions, explanations and examples. Entries range from general topics (comedy, epic, metre, romanticism) to more specific terms (acrostic, enjambment, malapropism, onomatopoeia) and specialist technical language (catalexis, deconstruction, *haiku*, paeon). In other words, this single, concise volume should meet the needs of anyone searching for clarification of terms found in the study of literature.

Martin Gray is Lecturer in English at the University of Stirling.

AN INTRODUCTION TO LITERARY CRITICISM
RICHARD DUTTON

This is an introduction to a subject that has received increasing emphasis in the study of literature in recent years. As a means of identifying the underlying principles of the subject, the author examines the way in which successive eras and individual critics have applied different yardsticks by which to judge literary output. In this way the complexities of modern criticism are set in the perspective of its antecedents, and seen as only the most recent links in a chain of changing outlooks and methods of approach. The threads of this analysis are drawn together in the concluding chapter, which offers a blueprint for the practice of criticism.

Richard Dutton is Lecturer in English Literature at the University of Lancaster.

ENGLISH GRAMMAR
LORETO TODD

This Handbook answers a specific need recognised by both students and teachers – a clear, concise description of the functioning of the English language. A well-grounded knowledge of the grammar of English is a sure way to gain confidence in its usage: yet English is an elusive subject to analyse. Traditional Latin-based grammars have proved inappropriate and confusing; many modern alternatives involve complex linguistic theory. The aim of this Handbook, however, is to provide a straightforward account of the rules governing the English language and a practical guide to the essential grammatical labels.

Loreto Todd is Senior Lecturer in English at the University of Leeds.

ENGLISH USAGE
COLIN G. HEY

The correct and precise use of English is one of the keys to success in examinations. 'Compared with' or 'compared to'? 'Imply' or 'infer'? 'Principal' or 'principle'? Such questions may be traditional areas of doubt in daily conversation, but examiners do not take such a lenient view. The author deals with many of these tricky problems individually, but also shows that confidence in writing correct English comes with an understanding of how the English language has evolved, and of the logic behind grammatical structure, spelling and punctuation. The Handbook concludes with some samples of English prose which demonstrate the effectiveness and appeal of good English usage.

Colin G. Hey is a former Inspector of Schools in Birmingham and Chief Inspector of English with the Sudanese Ministry of Education.

AN INTRODUCTORY GUIDE TO ENGLISH LITERATURE
MARTIN STEPHEN

This Handbook is the response to the demand for a book which could present, in a single volume, a basic core of information which can be generally regarded as essential for students of English literature. It has been specially tailored to meet the needs of students starting a course in English literature: it introduces the basic tools of the trade – genres, themes, literary terms – and offers guidance in the approach to study, essay writing, and practical criticism and appreciation. The author also gives a brief account of the history of English literature so that the study of set books can be seen in the wider landscape of the subject as a whole.

Martin Stephen is Second Master of Sedbergh School.

ENGLISH POETRY
CLIVE T. PROBYN

The first aim of this Handbook is to describe and explain the technical aspects of poetry – all those daunting features in poetry's armoury from metre, form and theme to the iamb, caesura, ictus and heptameter. The second aim is to show how these features have earned their place in the making of poetry and the way in which different eras have applied fresh techniques to achieve the effect desired. Thus the effectiveness of poetic expression is shown to be closely linked to the appropriateness of the technique employed, and in this way the author hopes the reader will gain not only a better understanding of the value of poetic technique, but also a better 'feel' for poetry as a whole.

Clive T. Probyn is Professor of English at Monash University, Victoria, Australia.

THE ENGLISH NOVEL
IAN MILLIGAN

This Handbook deals with the English novel from the historical, thematic and technical points of view, and discusses the various purposes of authors and the manner in which they achieve their effects, as well as the role of the reader. The aim is to bring to light the variety of options at the novelist's disposal and to enhance the reader's critical and interpretive skills – and pleasure.

Ian Milligan is Lecturer in English at the University of Stirling.

AN A·B·C OF SHAKESPEARE
His Plays, Theatre, Life and Times
P.C. BAYLEY

This is a systematic reference book to the background of Shakespeare. The aim has been to provide in one book an account of all the subjects and personalities which the student or theatre-goer is liable to encounter in the study of Shakespeare's plays and theatre. Fools, folios, theatres and music; mystery cycles and historical sources; summaries of all the plays; and details of Shakespeare's life and times – all these are presented in alphabetical order to provide easy reference, but in a form that will also reward the browser.

P. C. Bayley is Berry Professor of English at the University of St Andrews.

PREPARING FOR EXAMINATIONS IN ENGLISH LITERATURE
NEIL McEWAN

This Handbook is specifically designed for all students of English literature who are approaching those final months of revision before an examination. The purpose of the volume is to provide a sound background to the study of set books and topics, placing them within the context and perspective of their particular genres. The author also draws on his wide experience as a teacher of English both in England and abroad to give advice on approaches to study, essay writing, and examination techniques.

Neil McEwan is Lecturer in English at the University of Qatar.

The author of this Handbook

TREVOR JAMES was educated at Victoria University, New Zealand, and King's College, London. An Anglican priest, he has taught English at Waikato University, New Zealand, and is now a Senior Lecturer in English at the Darwin Institute of Technology where he lectures in Commonwealth literature. A Research Associate of Flinders University Centre for Research in the New English Literatures, and a Visiting Fellow of the Australian National University, he has written extensively on various aspects of Commonwealth literature. He is also the author of the forthcoming York Handbook on the Metaphysical Poets.